# GOWRI

# GOWRI

*A Biographical Tale about a Spirited, Resilient Malaysian Indian Woman*

V. G. KUMAR DAS

PARTRIDGE

| Library of Congress Control Number: | | 2016944115 |
|---|---|---|
| ISBN: | Hardcover | 978-1-4828-6651-3 |
| | Softcover | 978-1-4828-6650-6 |
| | eBook | 978-1-4828-6652-0 |

Print information available on the last page.

**To order additional copies of this book, contact**
Toll Free 800 101 2657 (Singapore)
Toll Free 1 800 81 7340 (Malaysia)
orders.singapore@partridgepublishing.com

www.partridgepublishing.com/singapore

# PREFACE

This book is a biographical tale based on the life of my beloved mother, Gowri – her trials and tribulations, her joys and sorrows, the events that she shared with her children and those vividly recalled by her family. It is a story that reflects the grit of an immigrant Indian woman, widowed at a young age, who brought up seven children all born in a new land, the Malay Peninsula, where her progeny now extend to three generations. Save for some individuals to whom pseudonyms have been applied, the names have been left intact.

Gowri's biography spans the history of her adopted country, from pre-independence to the late 1990s. Thus it captures significant moments of this period. Gowri was a Malayalee, originating from Kerala, a state situated on the tropical Malabar Coast of south-western India. The casual reader will find Malayalee traditions sprinkled in abundance throughout the book – the same traditions Gowri's descendants inherited and which contribute to the rich multicultural fabric of the Malaysian society they live in today. Gowri's motherly joys and woes in bringing up her brood of children in the early years add as much to her story as the challenges of single parenting that she subsequently faced.

Also woven into her biography are her travel experiences – especially in her later life – which she enjoyed sharing with her grandchildren, and interesting facets of Malay and Chinese cultures that touched her life, which she loved to share with her relatives in India and abroad. Events in her life as they happened are faithfully recorded with no malice intended to parties from any quarter. Indeed, even when disappointed or hurt, Gowri brooked no malice against anyone in her life. Her kind and forgiving nature stamped her as an exceptional individual. Her biography is written, and is to be read, in this light.

My decision to embark on this book-length work about my mother's life is intensely personal. She is the finest woman I have ever known, brimming with admirable qualities. The book depicts her gentle transformation from the daughter of a conservative aristocratic Nair household in Kerala to a more liberated woman. I want this book to convey core parts of my mother's personality. She was a strict mother of seven children with somewhat traditional core values of how individuals within a family and children in general should behave. I want to share her pride in bringing up her children, with myself being the eldest, as true citizens of the country she had come to love; her ability to love unconditionally; her boundless benevolence; and above all, her inspirational positive attitude drawn from her unflinching faith in the Divine.

"I've had a lot of obstacles in life, but God was always there with me," she would often say by way of encouraging her family and others to shed their negativity. These are the facets that made Gowri who she was. I believe they have universal relevance for all.

# ACKNOWLEDGEMENTS

I must first thank my wife, Ambika, for supporting the idea of writing this book so soon after my publication in retirement of a technical tome. I must say that I have had enthusiastic support and numerous contributions from all my family members in this undertaking, without any exception. The most difficult part was not so much in observing the chronology of events but rather in deciding how much of the story of her children could be woven into the biography of our matriarch. She was the receptacle for all our successes and disappointments, and her guiding light mattered to us even in adult life. Her presence was central to sensitising her children and grandchildren to the joys of sharing their love and being there for each other both in good times and bad times.

To my mother's lifelong friend Ponnu, I owe a vote of thanks for her vivid recollection of the Kluang years. My sisters, Valsala and Ambi, provided valuable insight and helped on a few anecdotal passages, while my niece Nisha and nephew Sharad – the literary talents in our family – unflinchingly gave critical comments on the early draft of this book that have enabled me to enhance its flavour as a novel as compared with the original narrative. My daughters, Gouri and Sathya, who were with her the most, gave me valuable personal insights on their grandmother as well as insights gleaned from their cousins, and they persuaded me to include a section for their voice in the book.

I am grateful to Sheela Nair for her assistance in the transliteration of the hymn in Appendix 2 from Malayalam into English, and to Raghavan Nambiar for his invaluable assistance in setting up the *Vishukanni* for the camera. The book has also benefitted from a critical final read by my son, Ashwin. I thank them all.

This book is dedicated to all members of Gowri's growing Malaysian *tharavad* that now includes great-grandchildren, and to all those whose lives she touched in some way or another, both in her native birthplace and in her adopted country.

# THE ARRIVAL (1939-1940)

The SS *Rajula*, the longest-serving troop and passenger ship of the
British India Steam Navigation Company Ltd. (1926-1973)
*Photo courtesy of Reuben Goossens at ssmaritime.com*

# [1]

This is a story of a woman's exceptional courage, a mother's unconditional love, and a matriarch's uncompromising will to see her family survive against insurmountable odds.

It is a story that begins in the last quarter of the tumultuous decade of the 1930s. Much of the world was still reeling from the devastating effects of the Great Depression. It was also a momentous period in the history of the Indian subcontinent, with the quest for independence from British rule led by Gandhi fuelling much enthusiasm and public unrest. The astrologers in the land may have foreseen winds of change in their charts, but they refrained from issuing strong predictions; the best among them were more drawn to the ominous global turmoil and restlessness they foresaw for the new decade that would soon dawn.

No astrology was needed, however, to predict the weather pattern in July 1939. It was monsoon month. At sea, huge waves, whipped up by gale-force winds, were lashing at the SS *Rajula*, which had set sail from Madras headed for Singapore via Nagapattinam and Penang. The passenger-cum-cargo ship was crossing the turbulent Bay of Bengal with its course set in a southerly direction to the Indian Ocean. On board the battered ship was a newly married young Keralite woman on her first-ever journey abroad. Her name was Gowri.

Fair of complexion and endowed with features that never failed to attract a second look, she seemed totally forlorn in her cabin. The tossing and turning of the ship had confined her to her bed for the most part, much to the chagrin of her spouse. He had privately hoped that the SS *Rajula* would provide a perfect romantic start to their lives in Malaya, a new enclave of the British Empire offering unrivalled job opportunities.

The young man had just turned 34. He was returning to his inventory-management job at the Johor Labis Estate[1] accompanied by his new wife, who was ten years younger than he, and his ageing mother, Sathiabhama. The estate was a rubber plantation owned by the Franco-Belgian company Socfin. He had been working there for a few years after an initial period in Singapore, where he had picked up elements of bookkeeping and shorthand at a well-known centre managed by a fellow Keralite. The decision to leave home to seek his fortunes abroad was his own, but the presence, before him, of his older cousin Unnikrishnan in Labis was enough to assuage the fears of his family.

He was well-read and very much aware of current events, including the rising crescendo of beating war drums in Nazi Germany, which had boldly adopted the swastika emblem of Hindu mythology as the national flag of the Third Reich. He fleetingly wondered about that. He was sure that Gandhi, who was bent on uniting the Hindus and Muslims, would not have opted for that as a rallying sign for independence.

Having served a brief stint in the medical corps of the British Indian Army, he had come to admire the discipline of army life, but he'd had insufficient encounters with British officers to form an opinion on them. His first encounter with a Briton had been at Labis, when he was interviewed for the job. The manager – a middle-aged, somewhat suntanned man in a smart khaki outfit – took out just one document from the file on his desk. The questions came at him thick and fast, but none had any bearing on the plantation crop or staff management; they centred in their entirety on his army training. He was hired literally on the spot. Towards the end, the manager had remarked: "Your name is too long. Can we just call you Panicker?"

And so it was that Govindan Kutty of the Velloli Panicker household from the Palakkad District in Kerala got christened as Velloli Govinda Panicker, or V. G. Panicker. He knew this meant that Gowri would henceforth be formally addressed as Mrs Gowri Panicker and that the birth certificates of any children Gowri might bear him would also carry this new paternal name. He was, however, not sure whether his children

---

[1]    "Estate" was commonly applied to the names of all plantations in the country.

would bear his Panicker clan name as their surname or, as the Keralite matrilineal custom demanded, take the clan name of his wife, who hailed from a Menon family. Either way, he felt it didn't quite matter – for after all, the Panickers and the Menons were just subdivisions of the same Nair caste. (This caste is really a group of castes in Kerala who live in large family units called *tharavads* housing descendants of one common female ancestor. They follow the matriarchal family system to this day.)

Coming out of his reminiscence on the upper deck, Govindan Kutty reached for his cigarette and tried to light it, but the wind was too strong. He retraced his steps and descended the stairs to his second-class cabin. His mother, who inexplicably took well to sea travel, was fast asleep. Gowri, on the other hand, was still in a daze, finding it difficult to lift up her head. He touched her head fondly, whispering something that brought a smile to her face. Bending down, he brought up a bottle of ginger beer and poured a small amount into a cup. He allowed her to sip slowly the invigorating drink that somehow seemed to keep nausea at bay.

On a couple of occasions, when the sea was less turbulent, Govindan Kutty had managed to bring Gowri up onto the upper deck to soak in the fresh air. Holding her close at the railings to further steady her, he would distract her by asking her to count the flying fish making their majestic leaps into the air and then gliding over the water. Gowri was fascinated by the spectacle and enjoyed the salt spray carried by the wind that landed on them both as the ship lunged into a big wave. But the nausea would return before too long.

Govindan Kutty would then urge her to fix her gaze on the horizon. It worked a couple of times, but when the rollicking became intense, he had little choice but to take her back to the cabin so she could lie down. Unfortunately, the wobbly motion of the ship was somehow more exaggerated in the cabin environment. This combined with the thick aura of chicken *kurma* that seemed to engulf the deck area only exacerbated Gowri's situation, since she was a vegetarian from birth. Porridge with a bit of salt in it and lime pickle were the mainstay of her diet.

Govindan Kutty occupied the upper berth in the four-berth cabin. He preferred to take his dinner in the ship's dining hall, but only after ensuring that Gowri and his mother had taken their meals in the cabin.

At times, Gowri, down with nausea, would resist intake of any food, but Govindan Kutty would patiently sit with her and feed her small morsels at a time interspersed with sips of ginger beer. He would then leave the ladies on their own.

Sathiabhama caught Gowri sobbing on a few occasions. The realization that she had left her loved ones behind was tearing away at Gowri's emotions. When would she see her siblings again? What would it be like living in a foreign land? Questions intermingled with acute homesickness were tossing in her mind as her body was being rocked by the ship battling the waves.

One night, the sobbing was more prolonged. Sathiabhama got up from her berth and went over to sit by Gowri's side. Gently wiping the younger woman's tears, she said in sweet Malayalam, "Don't be sad. I'm here with you. Treat me like your mother." The words had a soothing effect on Gowri, who quickly came out of her reverie. Sathiabhama then engaged her in a short prayer before returning to bed.

On another night, Govindan Kutty excitedly came down after dinner and coaxed Gowri to come to the upper deck to watch the spectacular, star-studded night sky and the shooting stars that came by. The moon was low on the horizon and the shimmering reflection of its light on the waves gave the night a romantic aura. Govindan Kutty pulled his wife close for an embrace. Instinctively, the shy Gowri tried to move away, but her husband pointed out other romantic couples at the railings and whispered into her ear, "Do we need to stand out by being the exception?" She acquiesced but was not entirely at ease with the public display of affection expected of her. Govindan Kutty was content with holding her for as long as the night allowed.

On the seventh day, the swell of the sea quieted as the ship descended into the calm waters of the Strait of Malacca. The colour returned somewhat to Gowri's ashen face, and she mustered enough energy to come to the upper deck on her own to join Govindan Kutty and her mother-in-law.

Here they had their first sight of land. Gowri closed her eyes momentarily and reopened them, engulfed by a warm beckoning feeling that she would recall time after time in the years to come. What she saw was the coastline of Malaya. The ship would anchor soon, she was told, for a day's stop at the port of Penang before proceeding further to Singapore, where they would all disembark and take the road across the causeway to the sultanate state of Johor. Singapore, Malacca, and Penang were the only provinces without a sultan as head, and they were then styled as the Straits Settlements of Peninsular Malaya.

It was a sight to behold as the ship finally docked at the Tanjong Pagar wharf at Singapore's Keppel Harbour, boasting then the just-completed largest dry dock in the world and the third largest floating dock. Although there was no British fleet in sight (there never was), one could sense a strong British presence in the strict and methodical protocols being followed for the first batch of disembarking passengers from the ship.

Gowri had her first glimpse of local residents on the wharf. Back in her village in Palakkad, one could not have imagined what a Chinese or a Malay person would look like, although her father who had served for several years in the British Indian Army in Burma had in bygone years shown her pictures of some ethnic peoples.

The harbour was bustling with activity, with cargo in wooden crates and large gunnysacks being unloaded by the ship's own derricks. The dockworkers, many of them manning handcarts, appeared to be mostly of South Indian ethnicity. They were essentially barefoot, and many were wearing tattered singlets and faded sarongs. Almost all of them carried a curled-up cloth of white cotton for wiping their sweat and using as headgear. There were also Chinese coolies among the labourers, wearing loose jackets and trousers. Some had straw hats on to shield their heads from the sun. Gowri was amused to see that they wore wooden sandals on their feet, which made such a clatter when they walked. The air was thick with the pungent smell of onions and spices – quite probably the contents of the gunnysacks that were being unloaded from the ship.

Observing the first batch of disembarking passengers from the ship's bunk and deck, Gowri was surprised to see among them a fair number of migrant Indian labourers, both men and women, who were escorted by a British official. From the noise and shouts reaching her ears from the wharf, she could distinctly make out some Tamil words, but the louder and dominant language was Chinese –the Hokkien dialect, as she later learnt. There were some uniformed personnel posted at specific exit points and also guiding the movement of passengers alighting from the ship. She spotted a

Sikh gentleman who stood out against the others with black songkoks on their heads instead of turbans. She surmised that the latter were Malays.

From her vantage point on the upper deck, Gowri was able to observe the few visitors who had come to greet the passengers. They were all assembled in one corner of the wharf, and among them were immaculately dressed European and Asian women. The European ladies, she noticed, uniformly wore light-coloured outfits but sported colourful, stylish straw bonnets or hats with their crowns variously decorated with silk, lace, velvet, and feathers. The various headgear pieces exuded an exquisite charm and individuality of their own. Gowri had not seen women wearing bonnets or hats before, let alone such handsome pieces. Women from her native country merely used their saree folds to cover their heads.

Unlike the Europeans, the Asian women seemed to prefer more loud-coloured outfits. The Chinese ladies present were all young, and they looked elegant in their body-fitting red or blue *cheongsams* (long dresses), but Gowri's attention soon fell more on the Indian ladies present. Nearly all of them wore colourful embroidered sarees. She noted with some amusement that many preferred sleeveless blouses to go with their sarees. She made a mental note of this. A new fashion, perhaps, she thought to herself.

The humidity was already getting to her when she was ushered back into her cabin to gather her belongings and ready her mother-in-law for the disembarkation. Sathiabhama was a joyful person with whom she had little difficulty in bonding. "How should I address your son?" was a question Gowri had hesitated to ask since her marriage. Since they were now for some time in close quarters, she took the opportunity.

"Not by name," Sathiabhama replied. "We women don't do that. Call him *Etta* [elder brother] or utter a verbal sound which he understands is meant for his response."

"What verbal sound?" Gowri pressed.

Sathiabhama suggested, "Try *Pinne*." (In English, "Well then ...") Both women laughed, and Gowri decided to test this out at the first opportunity.

It was a hot day, and the humidity was soaring along with the clamour as the disembarked passengers crowded the exit point after their immigration clearance. This was not a place to get lost under any circumstance. Gowri held tightly to her husband's hand and that of her mother-in-law. No sooner had they come out of the exit than a voice called out for her. In utter amazement, she turned to see her maternal cousin, Jayaram (affectionately called Jayam), waving at her. He wormed his way forward through the crowd to give Gowri a warm welcoming hug, and then he introduced himself to the rest of the party.

Gowri was over the moon at seeing Jayam, a familiar face so many miles away from home in a distant land. A captain in the British Indian Army, Jayam had been sent to Singapore for logistics training. The cousins had a high regard for one another. Gowri counted him as the brightest among all her cousins; he had topped Presidency College in his university days and also distinguished himself on the sporting field. Jayam was later to join the Indian Civil Service and distinguish himself further as an able problem-solving administrator, holding several key central government portfolios in assigned duties under the Home Ministry.

Today, he came prepared with transport, and in a typical matter-of-fact way said, "I have arranged for all of us to have lunch at Ananda Bhavan – the best vegetarian Indian restaurant in Singapore!" The restaurant, located at Selegie Road, still stands today.

"*Nyaan bakshanasalayil kazhichutilla. Oone namaldemadri ayeriko?*" asked Gowri. ("I have never eaten at a restaurant. Will the food be like ours?")

"Sure, it is South Indian cuisine. Rice, sambar, rasam, and the works!" replied a bemused Jayam

For Gowri, after the meagre porridge meal on board the SS *Rajula*, the food was simply God-sent, and it was served on the traditional banana leaf. Both Gowri and Jayam chatted away about old times. Jayam gave her an update on his married sisters – and of course, about her favourite uncle, Puduserry Kollaikal Kesava Menon, then the inspector of police of Madras State, which brought tears to her eyes.

She recalled that Kesava Menon had previously put his foot down against her marriage alliance with a Brahmin widower with some young children. The proposal was then seriously being considered by his sister, Lakshmikutty Amma (Jayam's mother), with whom Gowri had spent much of her growing-up years. Kesava Menon wanted the hand of a handsome young man for Gowri, who was the fairest and most beautiful of all his nieces. He was, after all, her maternal uncle, and he had a big say in such matters, given the matrilineal system practised by the Keralites.

The suitors for her older cousins who had come to Lakshmikutty's home – Chandravilas in Palakkad – had on one or two occasions sighted the beautiful Gowri and asked for her hand in marriage instead. But this was against tradition; the older girls had to be married off first. Gowri was often, therefore, asked to remain upstairs with her younger cousins. It was not until Govindan Kutty arrived on the scene as a suitor for Gowri that Kesava Menon finally gave his nod of approval. He even affectionately took care of the couple's travel expenses to Malaya.

Following lunch, Jayam arranged for a hired taxi to take them to Labis. It was a tearful farewell for Gowri. The taxi ride was quite uneventful, with both women dozing much of the way after the heavy meal. They passed monotonous stretches of rubber and oil palm plantations, but as they neared Labis, a tropical thunderstorm snapped them out of their slumber. It was a short-lived but vociferous unloading of one cloud's burden, and while it lasted it seemed as if the entire sky would fall down upon them. Never had Gowri experienced such long, ominous lightning streaks and deafening claps of thunder out in the open. Finally, with the downpour receding, the oppressive heat began to recede as well. Gowri welcomed the retreat of the heat, which had become unbearable.

"*Pinne*, is it always like this?" she enquired.

There was a moment's hesitation as Govindan Kutty came to understand that Gowri was addressing him. "No, I summoned it especially for your arrival!" came his reply, and everyone laughed, with the ladies exchanging understanding looks.

Moments later, they entered a bumpy dirt road which was the home stretch. In another fifteen minutes, the car came to a halt outside a staff bungalow on stilts curiously raised above ground level. Reading her mind, Govindan Kutty explained that all the houses were so constructed to ward off flood waters. As an afterthought, he added, "They keep out snakes too!" That prompted Gowri to go quickly up the stairs.

"Make sure you enter with your right foot first," whispered Sathiabhama, who was a step behind her. Gowri was aware of this traditional custom, which was followed by Hindus and Muslims alike.

The house was bright and airy, with plenty of natural light, and it seemed well furnished. A picture of Goddess Lakshmi greeted Gowri at the top of the stairs, but once she was well inside the living room, her roving eyes searched for and, indeed, found Ravi Verma's revered depiction of Lord Guruvayurappan (Lord Krishna as He is affectionately referred to in Kerala) propitiously positioned on the wall facing east. She clasped her hands to Him with a silent prayer in Sanskrit on her lips, thankful to Him for getting her safely to her new home in Malaya. She earnestly sought His divine blessings that, with her new-found family, she would finally find the happiness that had been eluding her.

As she finished her prayer, coincidentally on the hour, the grandfather clock chimed precisely seven times. Years later, she would fondly recall this chime as a lucky omen, foretelling her joy in bearing her husband seven lovely children.

# [2]

Gowri's first child, a boy, arrived in mid-1940. Govindan Kutty had seen to it that the delivery was in the safe hands of a Dr Menon at the Lily Dispensary and Maternity Clinic, located on Upper Serangoon Road, Singapore. Remarkably, the clinic still stands to this day. Govindan Kutty named his son Kumar Das, but the boy was affectionately referred to as Dasu at home.

The child quickly became the apple of his grandmother's eye, and he could do no wrong. He took to twirling her hair tightly around the fingers of his left hand while sucking his right thumb as a self-induced recipe for sleep. His grandmother, besotted with the child, muffled her groan and put up a brave front. He also had a doting uncle in Shankaran (Unnikrishnan's brother), who had just arrived from India and found immediate employment in the same plantation.

With the arrival of the baby, Govindan Kutty arranged for domestic help, which came in the form of a Chinese maid with broken English addressed by everyone as Ah Moy. She would arrive early in the morning and leave late in the evening. Gowri found Ah Moy to be a sweet person who was very gentle in handling the infant, and soon she built up the confidence to leave Dasu under Ah Moy's care once he was weaned.

Ah Moy would also oblige Sathiabhama now and again with a foot massage. Sathiabhama would point at her feet and say, "*Ah Moy, anmo, anmo*" (*anmo* being the oldest Chinese word for massage). While *anmo* was easy to remember, simple Malay words often eluded Sathiabhama – who, for example, would ask Ah Moy to make her some tea by saying "*Ah Moy, mahu tai,*" a request that always had Ah Moy in stitches, giggling away at Sathiabhama's mispronunciation of *teh*, which meant "tea" in the Malay language. *Tai*, on the other hand, meant excrement. When this was pointed out to Sathiabhama, she would laugh at her own goof, only to repeat the mistake a few days later.

One day, a well-intentioned Ah Moy brought into the house a durian.

"What on earth is that stench? Is it coming from that fruit?" Gowri demanded, pointing to the durian.

Ah Moy, who had by then prised open the thorny husk of the fruit to display its luscious seedy pulp, was soaking in the aroma. "It is delicious, mam, try it," said Ah Moy, but Gowri had already fled the kitchen, covering her nose with her saree fold.

Sathiabhama, attracted by the smell, came into the kitchen and tried one piece and then another. She seemed to enjoy the taste but later admitted that she didn't quite fancy the rotten onion smell that lingered on her breath many hours later. The fruit is regarded by many people in Southeast Asia as the king of fruits.

The durian fruit

Sathiabhama, who had no daughters, was touched by Gowri's affection for her and often confided in her. Gowri soon came up to speed with the history of the Velloli House, her husband's *tharavad*. For the Nair communities, the *tharavad* name was identified through the mother's house. Every Nair *tharavad* boasted a prominent temple for their ancestors and serpent groves. The Nair families considered the serpent to be the guardian of the clan, an old Dravidian custom that still continues to have its hold in many parts of Kerala.

## CHILDHOOD ORDEAL

Gowri, in turn, opened her heart to Sathiabhama. Gowri was a member of the Kollaikal *tharavad* at Puduserry (a village location in Palakkad), a highly respected and well-endowed family of landowners who, at one stage, owned half the territory of Pudussery, including large portions of forested land. Palakkad is the rice bowl of Kerala and derives its name from the fusion of two Malayalam words: *pala*, a tree (*Alstonia scholaris*) that is found abundantly in the district, and *kadu*, which means "forest."

Sathiabhama listened intently to Gowri's personal history, which was tinged with some sadness on account of family neglect and a lost educational opportunity that Gowri begrudged. The second of four children – the youngest the only boy – Gowri in her teens found herself, along with her elder sister, Saraswati, and younger sister, Kamalam, being placed under the care of her aunt, Lakshmikutty Amma,[2] at Chandravilas House, where

---

[2]    The suffixes *amma* and *kutty* are often appended to Malayalee feminine names, irrespective of religious differences; the suffix *kutty* is also applied to male names. The word *amma* stands for mother (as when spoken of) and *ammae* for Mum (as when spoken to). The corresponding words for father /Dad are *achan/ acha*. The grandfather is addressed as *muthacha(n)* (mother's father) *or achacha(n)* (father's father), and the grandmother as *ammama* or *muthessi*.

Honorific titles are also used by family members when addressing other elders. Thus elder male siblings are addressed as *etta(n)* or *chetta(n)* and elder female siblings as *Chechi* by their younger ones. The eldest male sibling's wife is often called *ettathiamma* by his younger siblings. A child addresses his or her father's elder and younger male siblings as *valiacha(n)* and *cheriacha(n)*, respectively, with the word *acha(n)* replaced by *amma* for their wives. The father's sisters are just addressed as *acheamma*. On the child's mother's side, male siblings are addressed as *ammaman* (or simply as *mama* following their names) and their wives as *Ammaye*; female siblings are addressed as *valiamma* (if elder) or *cheriamma* (if younger), with the word *amma* replaced by *acha (n)* for their spouses.

Gowri's education at the Moyan Girls High School in Palakkad stopped two years shy of a secondary school leaving certificate.

Lakshmikutty Amma did not resent the family decision that she should look after her nieces; she gracefully accepted the additional responsibility. However, Gowri (unlike Saraswati, who managed to continue with her pre-university studies) found herself obliged to help around the house. While grateful for the shelter, Gowri would sometimes reflect on this phase of her hapless life at Chandravilas and blame her father, T. V. Kunhiraman Nair, in particular for her predicament, although it has to be said that he did arrange for her a home tutor in Sanskrit, having heard that her formal education was being halted.

As a captain in the British Indian Army, Kunhiraman Nair served in Burma, Persia (Iran), and the Middle East, and he would only periodically return home. Gowri's mother, Kamakshi Amma, was aware that her husband had been sending regular remittances, but none of this was passed to her. Suspecting an interception of the funds, she finally summoned the courage to question her eldest maternal uncle on this matter, as well as on the lack of supervision of the labour force on their ancestral land, which she had begun to notice. This questioning was seen as an affront, and it set in motion a series of events that led to her daughters' eventual relocation to their aunt's home.

In a community steeped in the matrilineal system, the eldest maternal uncle bears sway in all major decisions, especially the management of the estate. A fiercely independent and competent woman, Kamakshi Amma decided she would regularly engage in site visits to the paddy fields and coconut and cashewnut groves, not considered then a province of womenfolk of the *tharavad*. Wagging tongues soon had it that she was involved in a romantic linkage while her husband was away. Although hurt by the aspersion and particularly by the attitude of some of her siblings who resented her "manly" actions of supervision of the estate, she was more determined than ever to ignore the distasteful rumour and fight her own cause. Her sole concern was to have her legitimate share of the annual earnings from her ancestral land in hand to take care of her children. For that, she was prepared to step into the field to oversee matters.

Her actions immediately sparked an internal feud in the family. She was seen as challenging the hegemony of the *tharavad*. Kamakshi Amma, however, refused to succumb to pressures from the family to give up her site visits. She was a true believer in women's rights. Her husband had complete faith in her, but he too could not stand the internal bickering that he found in his wife's *tharavad*. Matters came to a head one day when he overheard a snide remark from a family member that, having returned from Burma, he was now having a free ride in his wife's house. He packed up his bags the very next day and left for his own Thazhatu Veedu *tharavad* in Pattuvam, a village in the Kannur District of North Kerala.

By this time, there were already widening cracks in the once proud and large Kollaikal *tharavad* at Pudussery, especially in the lineage of Kamakshi Amma's mother, Ammalu Amma (see *tharavad* family tree). Confronted by disunity and dissatisfaction among the clan about the management of their tilled land, the aging maternal uncles agreed to partition the property.

This was hastened by the death of Ammalu Amma in 1927. Ammalu Amma had five children, two of whom were sons who had the rights to only one portion each of her landed property inheritance. The daughters had the greater share, as per the matrilineal system. The tillers of the land at the end of each harvest season would give to the *tharavad* their proportionate share of the crop yields. The teak-lined *ara* in the *tharavad* house was the traditional strongroom for storing rice grains. With the passage of time, part of the produce from the land was given in kind, and the rest in the form of cash from the proceeds of sale.

Kamakshi Amma lamented that she did not quite enjoy her share of the dues. In the absence of her husband, her brothers Kesava Menon and Parameswara Menon – backed by their maternal uncles – seized the opportunity to isolate their rebellious sister and place her three daughters under the care of Lakshmikutty Amma at Chandravilas. For all intents and purposes, Kamakshi Amma found herself ostracized by her siblings. Kesava Menon forbade any contact with her. This drastic course of action could have been motivated by their anger and embarrassment over the defamatory rumours about their sister combined with a genuine desire to ensure an unblemished future for their nieces. There was no consideration of the psychological impact of separation of the children from their mother, especially of their emotional needs. For her guardianship role, Lakshmikutty Amma received a major portion of the income derived in kind and cash from Kamakshi Amma's share of the cultivated land. In addition to this, both Kesava Menon and Parameswara Menon also generously relinquished their share of the property income to her to help manage the large household at Chandravilas.

It didn't take the siblings long to realize that Kamakshi Amma was now the sole occupant of the *tharavad* house of Ammalu Amma. Both Kesava Menon and Parameswara Menon were no longer in Pudussery, as they had joined the police force in pursuit of their careers. The siblings wanted her out, and the only way to accomplish this was to take the painful step of demolishing the house. This was, conceivably, a planned move – following partition, Kamakshi Amma and her son were reduced to holding only a marginal share of the land on which the house stood. That the demolition would yield teak wood that could fetch a lucrative price in the open market was not lost upon them either, but this was far from being their motive. Rightly or wrongly, they believed that, as a result of her overtly independent acts, aspersions had been cast on the good name of the *tharavad* and that, therefore, she was not entitled to stay in their ancestral home.

Only the detached kitchen portion of the house was spared demolition, and Kamakshi Amma resigned herself to her fate of occupying this remnant with her son, Bala Govinda Menon (Bala Menon for short). This area fortunately had a road frontage and a hundred-year-old well just beside it that had never run dry.

As the years went by, Bala Menon joined the military, and Kamakshi Amma was left alone in the house. Soon thereafter, her siblings applied to court and obtained an order to evict her from the house on the basis that she had no proprietary interest in the property. She was thus forced to vacate and live elsewhere for some time. Little did they know that Kamakshi Amma, being the fighter that she was, would challenge the eviction order with the support of her son. After a lengthy court battle, she managed to successfully set aside the eviction order on equitable grounds and move back to her house. Her alienation from her siblings further deepened as a result.

"Effectively then, the Ammalu Amma *tharavad* home ceased to exist, and the two sisters had their own homes – the one belonging to Kamakshi Amma which was the remnant part of the old common *tharavad*, and that of Lakshmikutty Amma, her own established home at Chandravilas to which her two male siblings were also connected. All of them proudly kept the initials P. K., for Pudussery Kollaikal, against their names," concluded Gowri.

"It's sad that your *tharavad* went into such disarray," commented Sathiabhama.

"I have not seen my mother or brother for some ten years," said Gowri with tears flowing down her cheeks. "I miss them very much. I pleaded many times for at least a glimpse of them, but the answer from Lakshmikutty Amma was always no."

"Why didn't Lakshmikutty allow you to go?" asked Sathiabhama.

"She was a kind soul, but I guess that on this matter, she had little choice but to acquiesce with the decision of the menfolk in her *tharavad*. I'm sure she would not have particularly fancied being burdened by her elder sister's children, and especially so given the circumstance of her marriage."

"What do you mean?"

"She was given away as a bride by the family elders in an arranged marriage that was first thrust on my mother, who had adamantly refused. Her husband, P. K. Krishna Iyer, was a Brahmin. He was a senior officer in the Salt Department of the British government (later renamed as the Salt and Customs Department). A jewel of a man, Krishna Iyer had been unlucky with his earlier two marriages. His first wife was a Brahmin lady through whom he had five children. She died in a tragic accident when she jumped from a moving train to save her son, who had fallen off it. Ironically, the son survived the fall. His second wife was my mother's elder sister, Madhavi Amma, who died after giving birth to two sons, Thangam and Chellam. After her death, my grandmother sought the return of Thangam and Chellam to their maternal Nair family household, but their father objected to this. His marriage to any of Madhavi Amma's sisters was thus proposed as a compromise. And Lakshmikutty Amma became his bride, seeing as the elder sister Kamakshi Amma had refused."

"Was Kesava Menon equally relentless on the matter of your wish to see your mother and brother once in a while?"

"He was hardly there in Chandravilas, as his job required him to be stationed in Madras. To be honest, I was frightened to communicate with him."

Lakshmikutty Amma had a son, Jayaram, and four daughters (Ramani, Chandra, Radha, and Devi), all of whom enjoyed a good university education and were married off into upper-echelon families. When it came to Gowri, however, there was no apparent rush to getting her married off, especially ahead of her cousins. There was some foot-dragging even when a couple of proposals came her way earlier, with the suitors, attracted by her looks, being prepared to overlook her lack of higher education. Her marriage ahead of her cousins was simply out of the question.

Gowri recalled that even the suggestion by both Chellam and Thangam to get her married as part of an exchange marriage proposal was not seriously entertained. This was a common enough practice in the community then, where a brother and sister of one family are matrimonially linked to a brother-sister pair of another family. Gowri's sister Saraswati, after some years, married Jayaram's older Brahmin stepbrother Krishna Iyer (same namesake as their father), who was also staying at Chandravilas. It was a love marriage.

The young Krishna Iyer had four siblings through his mother: Parameswara Iyer, Natesa Iyer, Kalyani, and Ammini. Natesa Iyer was the brother who survived the fall from the train. Parameswara Iyer's eldest son, Krishnan (nicknamed Veeramani), settled down years later in Malaya with his wife, Kamalam (affectionately known as Manni). Gowri knew him and everyone else in the patriarch Krishna Iyer's extensive family rather well, and they, in turn, very much liked their cousin who had come to live with them.

DATE : 1.5.1925

An archived photograph of P. K. Krishna Iyer (seated wearing
scarf in the middle row) with wife Lakshmikutty Amma
(on his left) and his brood of children and grandchildren.
*Photo courtesy of P. K. Devidas (2015).*

Gowri, in spite of her lack of formal higher education, picked up Sanskrit
from a regular tutor at Chandravilas that her father had arranged, and she
was self-taught in English. With her older cousins at college, the numerous
bookshelves at Chandravilas – packed with a variety of reading material –
provided Gowri with unfettered access to English books. She soon found
her command of English improving by leaps and bounds. Through sheer
force of habit, she had become a voracious reader.

She did not limit herself to just English texts but also enjoyed reading
vernacular texts in Malayalam and Sanskrit. She read the Mahabharata and
Ramayana epics inside out and would, in times to come, narrate these to
her own children. She was well versed with the Bhagavad Gita and several
of the Puranas, in particular, *Bhāgavatam* and Shiva Purana. She also began
to compose a number of *stotra* (hymns) in Sanskrit and Malayalam which
she would impart in later years to her grandchildren. She conceded to the
publication of this collection many years later. Sathiabhama admired her
daughter-in-law's courage, perseverance, and mental agility, and loudly
wished that the next child that Gowri bore would be a girl.

Gowri's second child, who was born at the same Lily Dispensary and
Maternity Clinic in Singapore in November 1941, turned out to be a boy.
He was named Venugopal but referred to affectionately as Venu. Both

mother and child returned to Labis within a couple of days, as rumours of an imminent outbreak of war in the East initiated by Japan were getting stronger by the day. Locally, there were ominous indications that could not be ignored; the Japanese were already in the country forging active links with Malay and Indian pro-independence organizations as well as with other groups, especially dwelling in some Japanese-owned plantations.

Govindan Kutty and Gowri in 1939

The proud parents with their eldest son, Dasu, and Sathiabhama
in 1940. On the extreme left is Unnikrishnan, and
on the extreme right is his brother, Shankaran.

It was certain that Japanese intelligence officers had garnered sufficient information to size up the current and potential strength of the Commonwealth forces coordinated from Singapore. If war were to come, Singapore would certainly be in the thick of it, along with the rest of Malaya. The capture of Singapore would provide Japan with a strategic military base and greatly undermine British authority in the region.

## PUDUSSERY KOLLAIKAL THARAVAD FAMILY TREE

SANGARA MENON     **DEVU AMMA**     THAPU MENON     NANJU MENON
married Karuppan Nair

THEYUNI MENON     **ETTULI AMMA**     CHAMMU MENON     CHUGU AMMA
RAMACHANDRA     married Thaya Menon                      MENON

KUNZHA KRISHNA     **MEENAKSHI AMMA**     GOPALA MENON     CHAMMU AMMA
MENON                (1846-1930)
married P.K.Nair

THAVAUNNI     **AMMALU AMMA**     DEVU AMMA    KUNJU MENON    CHAMLA
MENON @                                                MENON
KUTTA MENON     (1874-1927)     (1884-1954)     (died 1952)     (died 1953)
(died 1950, 92 yrs)    married Govindan Nair

**MADHAVI AMMA**   **KAMAKSHI AMMA**   **LAKSHMIKUTTY**    **KESAVA**    **PARAMESWARA**
                                    **AMMA**      **MENON**      **MENON**

(died 1911)     (1887-1991)     (1890-1975)     (1900-1969)     (1912-1982)
married- 2nd wife of   married T.V.Raman Nair   married - 3rd wife of    married      married
P.Krishna Iyer                      P.Krishna Iyer    Janaki Amma   Kunhilakshmi Amma

2 children:      4 children:     5 children:     2 children:    5 children:
Madhava Menon (Chellam)/            Radha/Jayaram/    Chandrasekhar/   Pushpa/Karunadas/
Krishna Menon (Thanggam)            Devi/Ramani/Chandra    Ratnam      Rema/Govindan-
                                                        Kutty/Shoba

**SARASWATI AMMA**    **GOWRI AMMA**    **KAMALAM AMMA**    **BALA GOVINDA**
(deceased 1963)     (1915-1998)     (deceased 2001)     **MENON**
married P.K.Krishna Iyer   married **Velloli Govinda**   married V.S.Panicker   (deceased 1997)
(deceased 1964)     **Panicker** (1903-1958)   (cousin of V.G.Panicker;   married twice:
6 children:      (son of Sathiabhama &    deceased 1992)     Vilasini;
**Balakrishnan (Baby)***/   Shankunni Nair)    2 children:     (deceased 1979)
**Prema/Uma*/Devidas/**    7 children:     **Prabha/Prakash (Unni)***   Jayalakshmi
**Krishna Kumar (Appan)/**   **Kumar Das/Venugopal/**                          (deceased 2000)
**Sudarshan (Babu)**    **Shivaprasad*/Ambika (Sathiabhama)/**               No off-spring
           **Valsala/Ravindran*/Kesavan Kutty (Hari)**

(*deceased)

# THE WAR YEARS (1941-1945)

Japanese troops in Fullerton Square, Singapore, February 1942
*Source: British Imperial War Museum. Reproduced with permission.*

# [3]

The much-anticipated war did, indeed, come the very next month. Startlingly, it originated in Malaya. The Japanese army, under cover of darkness in the early hours of 8 December 1941, invaded the country, landing in South Thailand (pushing into Kedah) and at Kota Bharu in Kelantan. The invasion, which took place an hour before the attack on Pearl Harbour, signalled the start of the Japanese Pacific War campaign. The Japanese knew that the western part of the Malay Peninsula was heavily fortified by the British forces operating from their base in Southern Thailand, but not so the eastern part. A two-flanked attack was thus planned under the command of Lieutenant General Yamashita.

Although the Japanese still encountered stiff resistance in their amphibious assault on the beach fronts in Kelantan, they faced no major resistance in their steady march southwards, winning battles at Slim River and at several townships in Johor. In little more than two months, they had outflanked the British forces and overrun the whole country. Their ability to move their war materials quickly was aided by their ingenious use of seized bicycles and the deployment of Type 99 Pontoon Bridges for river crossing of tanks and heavy artillery. They also had the help of a segment of the population they could count on for their on-route needs. Fear of the dreaded Japanese secret police, the Kempeitai, also played well into the hands of the Japanese. Eyewitness accounts of their extreme brutality towards dissidents were relayed daily by word of mouth. The reports also appeared in some vernacular papers.

The Japanese were particularly severe in dealing with the Chinese community, as there was spillover animosity from the ongoing Second Sino-Japanese War. Ordinary civilians whose only fault was that they had not bowed sufficiently low to the sword-bearing officers of the Japanese Imperial Army were mercilessly beheaded. There were regular bombing sprees by Japanese airplanes, and many living in towns and estates close to townships had to move to interior villages or seek shelter in trenches dug out in the jungle. Many unexploded bombs are still being discovered today.

The pet dog in Gowri's household would make a quick dash for her spot under the table even before the drone of the aircraft could be picked up by human ears. This was a bit uncanny, as she did not respond similarly to thunder. It proved to be a useful advance safety signal for the family to heed.

The garrison defending Singapore surrendered to the Japanese on 15 February 1942, only a week after the invasion of the island commenced. That Singapore's vulnerability was always a land invasion from Peninsular Malaya was a common-sense observation, but it was not seriously factored in by the overly confident British High Command at that time. Singapore's fall was a disaster that irrevocably tarnished Britain's image as a protector, but when America also declared war on Japan, hopes of its early recapture by the Allied Forces were ignited.

The period under the Japanese occupation was one of coercive rule and hardship suffered by a wide section of the population. There were daily accounts of cruelty and merciless killings. Many fell victim to psychological trauma, and many more for the first time in their lives experienced some degree of starvation. Food items became more scarce with each passing day, and particularly after America declared war on Japan and engaged them in the Pacific, supplies of rice, milk, flour, sugar, and other essential food that came by sea from Japan started to dwindle. The food shortage soon gave rise to a black market. By this time, the Japanese government-issued dollar was the official currency. It came to be called banana money because of the banana tree motif on the ten-dollar banknotes. The money became worthless at the end of the war.

The plantation's management, as part of its corporate social responsibility, organized a rice-rationing scheme to assist the workforce. Govindan Kutty was tasked to oversee distribution, and Gowri recalled the efforts of several parties to obtain favours from him to exceed their rations. Govindan Kutty would have none of that. Everyone, including his own household, received the entitled rations only.

Rationing being the order of the day, the small Malayalee community in the estate had the choicest Japanese sounding word to describe the situation: *arigato,* which means "thank you" in Japanese but when rendered in Malayalam means "guard the rice." Encouraged by the actions of others, they all started to plant tapioca (cassava) in their gardens as a starchy root-crop substitute for rice. The adults in Gowri's family found it difficult initially to adjust to the near daily intake of tapioca (*kappa* in Malayalam) in the form of *puzhukku.*

*Puzhukku* was a simple dish to prepare. First, short strips of peeled tapioca roots were boiled in a covered pan with the addition of turmeric over a firewood stove until fork-tender. The water was then decanted off, and into the boiled tapioca was stirred some turmeric, salt, and a ground paste of grated coconut, onions, garlic, cumin seeds, and green or red chillies. The preparation of the paste required a traditional grinding stone (*ammi* in Malayalam), as blenders were not then on the market. After further simmering under a covered lid, a small amount of coconut oil and a few curry leaves were finally added and the whole dish was given a thorough mix before being taken off the fire, ready to be served. It was often eaten with home-made pickles. To break the monotony, Gowri would sometimes improvise by adding green gram or yams and other tubers to the tapioca to make a hybrid *puzhukku.*

The Gowri household also managed to secure a regular supply of cow's milk from the labour lines (the common term at the time for the long rows of living quarters for the labour force). It was during this period, in early 1942, that a young destitute Malayalee girl by the name of Janaki entered their lives. They took her in as an in-house maid in charge of the two children and a few household chores; Ah Moy had by then left. Janaki had green fingers, and the garden flourished under her care, with good crops of sweet potato, tapioca, and a variety of vegetables.

Gowri soon came to hear of the plight of a few neighbours who found it difficult even to get a sufficient supply of tapioca for their daily needs, as they had large families to feed. Saddened at the thought of children going hungry, Gowri would order Janaki to send to these homes daily the extra portions of lunch she would then deliberately cook. The neighbours, on their part, were much appreciative of her generous disposition. Several decades later, one of the neighbours' children would recall this aspect of Gowri's benevolence and intimate it to Dasu when she met him at a function and learnt who he was. To Dasu's surprise, she said she would follow him home, if he didn't mind, as she simply couldn't wait to meet again her childhood Samaritan.

# INDOGEN?

Aside from the unpredictable presence each day of Japanese soldiers in military trucks plying the dirt road of the estate and an occasional search of civilians, there was no real threat posed to the employees, who went about their work as usual. The estate thus continued to operate, although admittedly not at full capacity. Over time, however, access to material supplies, in particular machinery spare parts, became a growing problem. The regular suppliers were all based in Singapore, and there was much difficulty in contacting them.

Govindan Kutty, who was in charge of inventory, was told to go to Singapore to source the critically needed supplies. Gowri was aghast that he had agreed to this. She feared for his safety. But he brushed aside any personal danger from the Japanese and left soon thereafter, promising to return within a week.

Just a couple of days after his departure, there was a knock on the door of the house towards late evening. Janaki opened the door to find a stranger standing outside with a rucksack in his hand. He asked for Gowri.

Gowri, who was in her room attending to the young Venu, stepped into the hallway, which was lit by a large kerosene lamp. Her gaze froze on the tall figure in front of her. "Guruvayurappa! It's you, Jayam! How did you find this place?" She rushed forward to embrace him.

"Finding your place was easy. Escaping from the Japs was harder."

"What?"

"Yes, when the British surrendered in Singapore a couple of months ago, the Japanese swiftly rounded up all elements of the British Indian Army stationed on the island. We were held as prisoners of war at Changi Prison."

Gowri guided him to a sofa, after sending Janaki to watch over Venu who was still half asleep. Sitting down with him, she asked the inevitable question: "How did you escape?"

"It was hard. I had made a number of unsuccessful attempts before this with others, but on each occasion there was a betrayal of our plans by those who were caught. This time I decided to go it alone, and luck was on my side."

A bout of coughing then interrupted his narration. "It's a long story, Gowri. I shall tell you all about it, but I think I need something warm to drink first and then to take a bath that is long overdue. I have been on the run for three days."

"Yes, of course," said Gowri, springing to her feet.

Sending Janaki to fetch a pot of hot tea, she went across quickly to peer into her mother-in-law's bedroom. Sathiabhama was fast asleep, with Dasu by her side firmly holding on to a long strand of her silvery hair. Not wanting to wake her up, Gowri quietly closed the door and, lighting a new kerosene lamp, ushered Jayam to the spare bedroom. Next to this was a small bathroom wherein she placed a lighted candle and a fresh towel for his use.

"I'm going down to the kitchen now to get your dinner. Do you need a pail of hot water for your bath?"

"No, that won't be necessary. A cold bath will do me fine," replied Jayam.

Following dinner, the cousins sat down for a lengthy chat into the late hours of the morning. As Jayam narrated his escapades in Singapore, Gowri felt increasingly ill at ease, her mind wandering to her husband who was somewhere on the island.

"Don't worry. No harm will come to him if he keeps the company only of local Indians," comforted Jayam.

Suddenly, Gowri became tense. "Jayam, we have to find you a hiding place in the house, in case the Japanese come looking for you!"

"I hope not. I'm here only for a few days in transit. But you are right about being vigilant."

They both then seriously explored some possibilities. It was agreed that in the event of a night-time raid, the best hiding place for Jayam was in the covered space behind the altar. To stay hidden in a daytime raid, they settled on Gowri's suggestion, which was to hide him behind the pile of splintered firewood logs that were stacked in the storeroom adjacent to the kitchen on the ground floor. The steps leading down to this area from the living room upstairs were effectively shielded from external view by the steeply sloping and wide overhangs of the roof.

The very next morning, Gowri – cautioning Janaki not to reveal the presence of Jayam in the house to anyone – started to prepare his hiding place in the storeroom. First, they placed a chair at the back of the room, parallel to the wall. In front of it, from one end of the wall to the other, they methodically stacked the rubberwood logs, leaving just a narrow passageway at one end. The passageway was deliberately blocked by a ladder that was vertically placed. Kept behind the ladder were a garden fork and an axe.

"The arrangement looks natural. No one will suspect you hiding in there," asserted Gowri, pleased with her idea.

A few days went by, with Jayam intently studying the maps in his possession. Around mid-morning one day, Janaki came rushing into the house from the garden, screaming. A group of Japanese soldiers could be seen marching menacingly towards the house. Jayam, who was then in the kitchen with Gowri, quickly dashed to his hiding place in the storeroom, while Gowri sprinted up the stairs to collect his rucksack and hide it in her room.

While other soldiers stood outside the house, three of them – one an officer – ascended the stairs and pushed open the front door, just as Gowri with Venu in her arms ventured out into the living room. Sathiabhama, who was in an easy chair, watched the scene dumbfounded. The officer looked hard at Gowri, who surprisingly stood her ground. The two soldiers who were with him went around to inspect all the rooms and returned, standing at attention. Spotting the vermillion dot on Gowri's forehead, the officer touching his own forehead enquired, "Indogen?" Seeing Gowri's blank look, he asked again, "Gandhi?"

With her heart in her mouth, Gowri quickly muttered, "Yes, yes. Gandhi. Indian."

The officer uttered some guttural sounds in Japanese to his compatriots, and turning to Gowri raised his hand and said, "Okay." They then left the house as abruptly as they had entered it. Gowri could hardly wait to rush to her mother-in-law and thank godly providence for their lives.

Just then, Janaki, carrying the elder boy, tiptoed in and asked disbelievingly in Malayalam, *"Aver poyo?"* ("Have they gone?") Oblivious to what was going on, Dasu innocently asked for raisins, his favourite snack, and this immediately broke the tense scene. But soon tears started to flow uncontrollably from Gowri's eyes, and she started to sob. Her thoughts had suddenly drifted to her husband. There had been no news of him for almost a week. Had he become a victim to the fierce Japanese force manning the causeway? She shuddered at the thought and prayed that God would in His mercy spare them all that fate.

Gowri learnt soon enough from her nearest neighbours that the Japanese had not entered their homes. She wondered whether the forced entry into her house was to ascertain the whereabouts of the escapee, Captain P. K. Jayaram, or the whereabouts of her husband, who was in charge of the plantation inventory unit and rice rationing. As the days passed and there was no news of her husband, Gowri started to panic. She demanded that the estate management make efforts to trace him.

As his absence entered a second week, she received a letter from her husband through an acquaintance he had met a day earlier at a restaurant in Singapore. The gentleman was a teacher and had kindly agreed to stop in Labis to pass the letter on to Gowri. It was with some trepidation, of course, that Gowri opened the letter, but this was followed by immense relief. The letter informed her that he was well and was planning to return within a few days. Jayam shared her relief at the news. He then informed her of his decision to leave early the next morning, as he had already strategized his escape plans to India.

Gowri's eyes welled with tears upon hearing this. "Stay on here, Jayam," she pleaded. What if you are captured again?"[3]

---

[3]  In fact, his escape plan was again foiled by untrustworthy intermediaries who betrayed him to the Japanese. He was captured and finally released from Changi Prison by the British in 1945 at the close of the war. For his bravery, he received the MBE award at the turn of the new century, when the British War Office finally managed to locate and identify the "Captain P. K. Jayaram" they were seeking in the person of P. K. Jayaram Menon, a retired senior official of the Indian Civil Service then living in New Delhi.

"No, I have to make the effort to get on board a ship. I have a name list of contacts with whom I need to touch base. Don't worry; my identity may not have been widely circulated here yet."

In the early hours of the next morning, Jayam bid goodbye to a sobbing Gowri, who placed in his palm a Guruvayurappan pendant and pointed to a hastily prepared vegetarian lunch pack that he was to take along.

Jayam hugged her warmly. "Don't cry, Gowri. God willing, we shall meet again."

The countdown for Govindan Kutty's arrival began almost immediately after Jayam's departure. He appeared finally on the fourth day, looking somewhat exhausted but laden with cookies and gifts for his family. He had a sandalwood-paste tilak boldly marked on his forehead. Anyone looking at him would have thought that he had just stepped out of a temple after offering prayers.

In the next few days, almost all the neighbours descended on the house, curious to know what was happening in Singapore. He recounted in sombre detail the harassment being meted out by the Japanese to the prisoners of war, who numbered in the thousands; of curfews being imposed in certain sectors of the colony; of merciless killing of suspects dragged out of their hideouts in shops; and of the stockpiling of food that was going on in almost every home. He recalled being frisked at several checkpoints. At one such checkpoint on his return trip, a decorated Japanese officer was standing slightly apart witnessing the scene. Turning to him, Govindan Kutty saluted smartly. The officer gave him a hard look. Immediately, he realized that his salutation would be a giveaway of his army background, and he followed it up by a very deep and lingering bow. He was allowed to pass.

Govindan Kutty stated that it was his Indian identity coupled with the tilak he carried on his forehead that perhaps saved him a closer scrutiny. His surmise was correct. The animosity the Japanese had toward the local Chinese was severe; against Indians, the reaction was mixed, with some leniency exercised toward civilians but not those serving in the British Indian Army. In fact, many Indian independence-movement activists had already found a home in Japan, and it was well known that the Indian National Army formed by Netaji Subhas Chandra Bose to oust the British through military means had Japan's full support and backing.

Not long after Govindan Kutty's safe return, his mother's health began to deteriorate. One morning late in 1942, she breathed her last. Gowri, who was by now very attached to her mother-in-law, took several months to get over the loneliness she felt. In Sathiabhama she had found not only a friend and confidant but also the mother figure she'd missed since being taken out of her Pudussery house. The woman's departure left an emotional vacuum. Dasu also missed comforting snuggles at night with his *muthessi* (granny) and especially her silvery hair that could be tugged whenever he felt like it. His father consolingly slept with him instead, but no more than a couple of days at a time, as he could not tolerate his son's hair-twirling habit.

# [4]

Govindan Kutty's cousins had often visited his home when Sathiabhama was alive, and they continued to do so. This enabled Gowri to get to know better the young Shankaran, whom she secretly hoped would be a match for her unwed sister Kamalam in India. During one of his visits, Shankaran conversationally mentioned his desire to visit his family in India at the first opportunity. Gowri suspected the purpose of the trip was to seek a bride.

One night, after dinner, she showed the young man a photograph of Kamalam from her album for consideration if he really entertained matrimonial intentions. Shankaran blushed but quickly regained his composure. He said politely that she looked great. Gowri took it to mean that he was interested and promptly gave him the necessary contact details, asking in return for his photograph and birth particulars. She hoped that the war would end soon and there would be a resumption of mail services so that she could convey the news of a prospective brother-in-law in advance to her sister.

An advantage of living in an estate was the proximity of emergency medical attention for its workforce. With two young children in the house, Gowri welcomed this amenity. The availability of a young hospital assistant who didn't mind being disturbed any time of the day for a house call was a welcome bonus. His name was Raman. He too hailed from Kerala, but he had been in service in the estate for several years. With an LMP (licentiate medical practitioner) certificate gained in India, he rose quickly to become a first-grade dresser passing all the local examinations.

Sathiabhama, when she was alive, had always summoned him when she was feeling under the weather. "The young man has the healing touch," she would often say. The children had all their follow-up vaccinations done by

33

him. The first child, in particular, tended to be a bit sickly and contracted malaria just as he turned 3 years old. It was a frightening experience for the family, but the medical attention so close at hand was a God-sent blessing.

Venu was a young terror who began walking even before he turned one. Janaki had to be assigned full-time to watch over him. He could climb onto a chair with relative ease and thence onto a table. With an intent to keep an eye on him, Janaki had the bad habit of seating him on the kitchen table while she was cutting up the vegetables, for which she was reprimanded several times.

To prise anything from Venu's hands was never an easy matter. One day, Janaki was scraping out the flesh from a halved coconut with a knife when she had to leave the table momentarily to attend to something on the stove. Dasu came on the scene and, seeing the sliced coconut pieces on the table, reached out for a piece, not realizing that Venu – who was then 3 years old – was trying to emulate Janaki in completing the scraping process with the knife in his hand. Just as Dasu was lifting up his head to walk away with the slice that he had picked, the knife in Venu's hand suddenly came down on him like a guillotine. Dasu sustained a deep cut on his nose, and in fact a piece of it was hanging.

All hell broke loose. Gowri rushed in at the scream and saw a blood-spattered face, but she had the presence of mind to hold the nose fragments together until Raman could rush to the scene to do some on-the-spot surgical stitching. Janaki, nursing a sharp slap on her face for her carelessness, had learnt a frightening lesson for life from this incident.

There were not many Chinese or Malays in the estate environment at Johor Labis; the bulk of the population was comprised of the labour force of Tamils and Telugus recruited from India. It appeared to Gowri that the living conditions provided for these workers in the so-called labour lines were pathetic.

"They are being exploited," she once observed to Govindan Kutty.

"Not really, if you consider many of them have come from slum areas back in India," he replied, adding, "Don't forget, the entire family has the potential for work here as daily wage earners, unthinkable where they came from."

The Malayalee community of immigrants who came to work in the plantations, she was given to understand, was significantly smaller in numbers, but as they were generally educated and fluent in English, they were absorbed as clerks and hospital assistants.

Curious as she was about her surroundings, Gowri found it difficult to move around in Labis, and she and Sathiabhama had only ventured out thrice to the nearest town of Chaah, some twelve miles away. There she had found more Malays and Chinese. She admired the *cheongsam* the young Chinese girls wore. The dress suited their figures. It had a high neck with a closed collar, but Gowri noticed that it was buttoned on the right side, with a loose chest. She wondered about the thigh-high slits at the sides.

"Shall I get you to try one on?" Govindan Kutty had asked in the presence of her mother-in-law, and Gowri had blushed.

The Malay women she saw in the shops were wearing the *sarong kebaya*, the traditional blouse-dress combination. The *kebaya* or blouse featured floral pattern embroidery. Most of the men around the place wore Western attire, but on one of her visits she spotted some Malay males stepping out of a house where a social function was being held. They were smartly dressed in their traditional attire of *baju melayu,* a loose tunic worn over trousers, with a sarong wrapped around their hips. They were also sporting a black *songkok* or cap on their heads. In a sense, these visits were her first introduction to the real local population since stepping into her estate house.

The years flew past, and soon it was 1943. Gowri gave birth to her third child – yet another son. The new arrival, she noticed, seemed to have features from her side of the family for a change. She named him Shivaprasad but would address him fondly as Shiva, or when enquiring of him, as Shivan.

One evening in early May, there was a knock on the door of the house. Govindan Kutty got up from his easy chair and walked to the door to open it. A group of Indians with badges bearing the photograph of Subash Chandra Bose greeted him with "*Jai Hind*" and asked for a few moments of his time. Govindan Kutty invited them in. There were a couple of females in the group, and so Gowri joined them.

The visitors explained that their beloved Netaji, who was fighting for India's freedom from British rule, would be arriving soon in Johor, and they were enlisting more civilian recruits in support of the freedom cause as well as that of the emancipation of Indian women through the establishment of a female wing of the Indian National Army. Would Madam be interested? Gowri nearly fell off her chair at the invitation.

Govindan Kutty turning to them abruptly asked, "Why is Bose flirting with the Japanese? Do you all really think Japan can liberate India without the mass support of the Indians themselves, who are behind Gandhi?"

The answer was hedgy. "Gandhi and Nehru have ousted him from the Indian Congress and branded him as renegade to please the British. Under them, independence would be a pipe dream. The British will only recognize military force. You must have heard that Netaji has already formed the nucleus of this force. He has the will and ability to win us freedom."

Govindan Kutty was not about to give up. "And you all think that the Japanese will sacrifice their lives just for our freedom without gaining any spoils of war? What guarantee is there that we will not be supplanting one imperial power with another?"

Govindan Kutty was raising legitimate questions, but the visitors had not come prepared for a debate. The guests politely took their leave, and Govindan Kutty was somewhat irate for the rest of the evening.

It was around this period too that Unnikrishnan, still a bachelor, met with a serious accident. The taxi that was bringing him from Singapore had aquaplaned and overturned somewhere en route, pinning down his left arm, which had to be amputated at the elbow. As time wore on, Unnikrishnan adapted to life with one arm and even came to see the humour in his new-found nickname: "one-armed bandit." However, although he was still a good-looking and vain man, his confidence must have been irreparably damaged, as Unnikrishnan resigned himself to bachelorhood.

His brother, Shankaran, on the other hand, felt the need for a locally domiciled spouse both as a life companion and as a practical means to continue working in Malaya. After several futile attempts, he sought out a berth on a ship towards the middle of that year and set sail for India, where he would continue his quest.

The year 1944 appeared to be relatively uneventful, save for the welcome news that Shankaran had finally married in early 1944 and had chosen Gowri's younger sister, Kamalam, as his bride. The news was made sweeter by the fact that Kamalam was also expecting.

In February 1945, Gowri and Govindan Kutty were blessed with their fourth child, a much-longed-for girl. The child was promptly named Sathiabhama, but she was also given a second name, Ambika (Ambi for short), by which she came to be more commonly known within her family and circle of friends. Govindan Kutty was so excited by the arrival of his baby daughter that he arranged for a puja (prayer ritual) at the temple and a sumptuous non-vegetarian meal at his house, prompting his neighbours to comment good-humouredly, "Looks like you're already celebrating her marriage, Govindan Kutty!"

The year 1945 also witnessed a string of defeats on the war front for Japan. By now, rumours were rife of an impending surrender by the Japanese Imperial Army and its retreat from all occupied territories. On 5 September 1945, soon after the atomic bombings of Hiroshima and Nagasaki, Japan surrendered. This brought the hostilities of World War II to a close. The formal surrender of Singapore to Lord Louis Mountbatten, Supreme Allied Commander of South East Asia Command, came about a week later.

News about the horrendous impact of the atomic-bomb explosions came in bits and pieces to the estate community. One evening some of the staff members came over to the house to discuss the recent happenings on the war front with Govindan Kutty.

"We hear the atomic bombs have destroyed the whole cities of Hiroshima and Nagasaki," said one of the visitors.

"Yes. According to what I hear, thousands of people died and many had their skin severely burnt as a result of the scorching heat and radiation released by the bombs," said Govindan Kutty.

"What is this radiation?" someone wanted to know.

"I don't know. Must be some effect associated with the bomb," opined Govindan Kutty.

"I don't know how far it's true, but I heard that the explosion created a blinding white light and a mushroom-like cloud that could be seen for miles around. Many buildings were completely gutted, and birds dropped dead from the sky," added someone in the audience.

"Oh, my God. Like it was said to have happened thousands of years ago in the Mahabharata," was Gowri's immediate reaction.

"That's nonsense," said a disbelieving Govindan Kutty. "The bomb was just invented."

Gowri just smiled and withdrew to her room, only to emerge again with a volume of the Sanskrit text of Mahabharata in her hands. "Listen to this …" said Gowri, who then went on to recite a couple of passages therein, simultaneously translating these into Malayalam.[4] Everyone was shell-shocked. They looked at Gowri with new-found respect.

The small Malayalee community in Johor Labis Estate decided to have a post-Onam celebration to mark the end of the war, and it was unanimously decided that it would be at Gowri's house. Onam in that year fell on 22 August, and Gowri observed the occasion as always with morning prayers

---

[4]   Conceivably, the passages in Sanskrit that Gowri chose to read and translate are those found in volume 7 (Drona Parva) of the eighteen volumes of the English translation of the Mahabharata written by Kisari Mohan Ganguli over the period 1883-1896. The following oft-quoted passages (see http:// veda.wikidot.com/ancient-city-found-in-india-irradiated-from-atomic-blast) have been widely attributed to Ganguli, but their veracity, it must be pointed out, has since been queried (see https://twitscope.wordpress.com/2008/07/12/ evidence-of-nuclear-explosion-in-ancient-india/):

A single projectile charged with the power of the Universe….
An incandescent column of smoke and flame,
as bright as ten thousand suns,
rose in all its splendour….
..a perpendicular explosion
with its billowing smoke clouds…
…the cloud of smoke
rising after its first explosion
formed into expanding round circles
like the opening of giant parasols…
..It was an unknown weapon,
an iron thunderbolt,
a gigantic messenger of death,
which reduced to ashes the entire race
of the Vrishnis and the Andhakas

The corpses were so burned as to be unrecognizable.
Their hair and nails fell out,
Pottery broke without apparent cause,
and the birds turned white…
…After a few hours
all foodstuffs were infected…
…to escape from this fire the soldiers
threw themselves in streams
To wash themselves and their
equipment.

and a special lunch. This time around, the celebration was an expression of relief from the trials of war.

Onam is celebrated by Malayalees of all religious persuasions in the month of Chingam in their solar calendar coinciding with the ascent of the star Thiruvonam. The festival commemorates the appearance of Vamana (the fifth incarnation or avatar of Lord Vishnu) and the subsequent homecoming of the righteous and benevolent mythical Asura King Mahabali to meet his people from Pātāla (the netherworld), where he was earlier banished to by Vamana for usurping the celestial world. The merciful Vamana had granted Mahabali this visitation or boon on account of his repentance and devotion.

The spirit of Onam resonated with the celebratory mood of the ending of the war, signifying a return to a state of peace and prosperity as prevailed when the mythical Mahabali ruled Kerala. An Onam *sadhya* (multi-course vegetarian banquet, usually lunch, served on a banana leaf) replete with the traditional twenty-four dishes, including *payasam* (dessert), was prepared – the bulk of the dishes by Gowri herself.

Lunch dragged on, and by the time the last guest had departed, the exhausted hosts could hardly wait to retire to their beds for the night. They breathed a sigh of relief and thanksgiving that with God's grace, the family had survived the war. They prayed that they would never have to endure another tense and austere period in their lives and looked forward to living their remaining years in peace and tranquility.

# MIGRATION TO SINGAPORE
## (1946-1948)

View of Pulau Sebarok, an oil storage
and refuelling port 24 kilometres off Singapore
*Source: mapletreelogisticstrust.com. Reproduced with permission.*

# [5]

With the war ended, it was evident that the restoration of Singapore as the world's maritime trade centre was going to be the British government's highest priority in the region. The rebuilding phase of Singapore would thus provide across-the-board opportunities for skilled manpower. This fact was not lost on Govindan Kutty, who started actively seeking a new job. An opportunity with the American Standard-Vacuum Oil Company (Stanvac), the supplier of Mobil products, soon presented itself. Stanvac was resuming its bunker storage services at Pulau Sebarok, a small island refuelling port accessible by a short ferry or boat ride from the Singapore mainland. The whole family, including Janaki, migrated to Singapore sometime in early 1946, staying initially at the company dwelling on Pulau Sebarok.

The house at Pulau Sebarok was a far cry from the comfort of their house in the Labis Estate. The meagre proportions of the house barely accommodated its two bedrooms, a small living room, and a kitchen-cum-dining area. Thankfully, there was also a medium-sized storeroom and an additional, albeit small, bathroom located by the side of the kitchen. Gowri placed the three boys in one room which had a large purpose-built four-poster bed sporting a large, requisite mosquito net. If there was a silver lining, it must have been the master bedroom's en suite feature. Gowri slept in the master bedroom with her spouse and her new baby girl. Janaki slept on a mat, often in the dining area and sometimes in the living room.

Gowri's three elder children in 1947, *left to
right*: Venu, Dasu, and Shivan

# A *CURTUS-Y* CALL

Sand flies proved to be a nuisance of living on an island. Hunting and
killing red centipedes, whose bites are venomous, became a daily ritual.
Gowri's fears and complaints were not taken seriously by Govindan Kutty,
who was engrossed in his new job as supervisor with a special responsibility
for inventory management.

All this changed early one morning when Gowri entered the children's
room and was greeted, much to her horror, by a snake coiled up on the
overhead mosquito net. She screamed her lungs out. Govindan Kutty,
dashing to the room, saw the cause of her scream and tried to pull her out
of the room. He must have deemed the children safe under the net, but their
mother would not budge. He beseeched her to stay out of the room lest she
agitate the serpent whilst he summoned help from night-shift workers just
outside the perimeter of the house.

Four workers came at once, armed with long poles, and helped pull the
children from one side of the bed. Then they started nudging the snake,

which looked like a medium-sized python. Govindan Kutty remembered it as a grey snake with a short tail and blotches that were brick-red in colour. The description identifies it as *Python curtus,* a non-poisonous reptile endemic to the Malay Peninsula. The workers deftly manipulated the poles so as to hold the snake's head vise-tight and slowly manoeuvre it, head first, into a large gunnysack. Other helpers had come in by now, and the captured reptilian intruder was ceremoniously taken out of the house. It was probably sold in downtown Singapore, where snake meat was valued for its medicinal properties.

This close brush with danger immediately triggered the search for a residential house in mainland Singapore, in an area proximate to Pulau Sebarok. Finally, one was found in Tanjong Rhu.

For Gowri, as much as for her growing children, Singapore provided new experiences: rides on boats and cycle trishaws, haggling over goods in covered alley bazaars, and much exposure to the Malay and Chinese languages being spoken. Gowri soon realized that the Chinese community itself was mixed. Most of the migrants were Hokkien, Teochew, Cantonese, or Hakka who arrived from Fujian, Guangzhou, and Hainan Island in China, respectively.

The chance to mingle with the local population was absent in the estate environment at Labis. But Singapore provided ample opportunity for this. Always good with languages, Gowri had little difficulty picking up words in both Hokkien and Malay that helped her to be more effective at bargaining, particularly at the Change Alley and Upper Serangoon Road shops which were her favourite haunts. In fact, her fluency in bazaar Malay surprised Govindan Kutty. She explained it by saying she found a lot of the words appeared to have a Sanskrit origin.

"Do you know why?" asked Govindan Kutty.

"I don't know," confessed Gowri.

"Before the advent of Islam in these parts in the fifteenth century, the Malay Peninsula and much of Indonesia were first under the Buddhist Srivijaya kingdom, and then under the powerful Hindu Majapahit kingdom. The kingdoms may have long disappeared, but the cultural influence remained."

The Malayalee community in Singapore was very small, but the luxury of a telephone in the house helped Gowri to maintain regular local contact as well as make occasional calls to her loved ones in India. With the telephone facility came the news that Kamalam and her 2-year-old daughter Prabha were coming to Malaya the following year, as soon as sea-travel arrangements could be finalized by Shankaran.

It was not easy for Gowri, even with the help of Janaki, to manage her four children and do all the household chores. Mobil had provided the family with a kerosene stove. Much of the cooking was done only for lunch, but Gowri sometimes would personally make an extra dish for Govindan Kutty at night during the weekdays, as he could only come home for dinner. His favourite dish was sautéed onions spiced with dried chilli, but the dish du jour often changed with his moods. Some days, he would come home and demand in Malayalam, "*Gowri, oru kozhikutan indakku.*" ("Gowri, make me some chicken curry.")

Gowri would respond, "*Eppolo?*" ("Now?")

"*Eppolthanne!*" ("Right now!") would come back the reply.

Gowri, having realized how tedious it would be to cut, scrape, and grind a coconut to make a traditional Keralan chicken curry – which needed to be simmered for some time – developed an innovative way of whipping up the dish with cut pieces of chicken and potatoes tossed with shallots, ginger, and spices. She must have drawn inspiration from the more expedient Chinese culinary methods. The tangy and piquant dish became a hit with Govindan Kutty, who often enjoyed it with a bottle of stout.

☼

## ACUPUNCTURE REMEDY

The growing family and the concomitant increase in workload started to take its toll on Gowri. One day, she felt a weakening of her left arm and noticed that the wrist was always getting inflamed. She ascribed this initially to a sting of some insect and applied copious amounts of Tiger balm, a product of the island itself, but the pain and weakness persisted. Soon she experienced intense difficulty carrying any weighty object with her left hand. The doctor examining her diagnosed it as carpal tunnel syndrome and gave her some steroidal treatment. But the pain persisted.

She was then advised by a family friend to seek out acupuncture as a possible remedial treatment. Singapore's population, then as now, was dominantly Chinese who retained many of their traditional customs and practices, including their faith in traditional Chinese medicine for many common ailments. Gowri heeded the advice and sought out a Chinese *sinseh*. After a few sittings, she found herself completely cured of her problem. But the experience, as she narrated often enough to her family, was literally nerve-racking.

"He was an elderly gentleman with a kind face," she would recall. "I had to go for three or four sittings; each was about an hour. At each sitting, he would press my hand down and insert a number of very fine heated needles at a chosen spot on the skin at the wrist. He would then twiddle each of the needles in turn, irritating the nerves. Now and then, he would swab the area with something hot and mutter some words. One day while he was at it, I thought I smelt smoke, but I knew it was not the smell of burnt skin, so I didn't panic. But the pain I felt at each sitting was severe. It was a funny kind of pain, more intense than the pain I endured at childbirth, but I managed to recover the strength in my arm after the treatment. There, you can still see for yourself the spot marks."

# SISTERS REUNITE

Towards the middle of 1946, Govindan Kutty purchased a second-hand car – a Morris Minor – having in the meantime obtained his driving licence. Driving proved easy, but not so parking in busy downtown Singapore. One weekend, he dropped his family at a shop entrance in Orchard Road and went around looking for a parking spot. He went up a somewhat steep road and towards the top found a vacant spot, where he parked after making a U-turn. He switched off the engine, put the gear in neutral, locked the car, and left to join his family.

Some hours later, he went back to fetch the car and saw the commotion that had taken place in his absence. He had forgotten to apply the handbrake, and gravity put to the test had not disappointed, causing a chain reaction of bumper damage to several cars. Because of the negligence on his part, the insurance settlement was minimal, and he had to fork out much cash, some of which he obtained by selling the car. He never entertained the idea of buying another car after that. In any case, he needed all his money, as a new child was on the way.

Gowri was admitted once again to Lily Dispensary and Maternity Clinic, where in November 1946 she gave birth to another lovely daughter. The child was named Valsala. Dr Menon, who was again in attendance, made the observation: "She is going to have more of your looks than his," which indeed proved to be true.

The eldest son, Dasu, was placed in a school in early January 1947. A trishaw was engaged to take him to and from the school. The same trishaw was used for family errands when needed.

In December 1947, Shankaran came to visit with his family. Gowri was overjoyed to see Kamalam after a lapse of eight years. Surrounded by her nephews and nieces, Kamalam too could hardly contain her excitement, for until that moment she had only seen pictures of Gowri's growing family and not yet the newborn. Kamalam and Shankaran stayed for a few days, and the sisters were inseparable. Overwhelmed by emotions, they would tearfully embrace each other now and then while talking about their childhood and of events they had no control over. They ended up chatting virtually the whole night.

They certainly had a lot to catch up on. Both sisters were pregnant – Gowri with her sixth child and Kamalam with her second, Prakash. On the second day of the visit, a trip was made to a new shopping complex that had opened up in Singapore just before the war. Dasu hung around his mother and aunt at the goldsmith counter, but his adventurous brothers, Venu and Shivan, took their sister Ambi and their newly acquainted cousin Prabha on a tour of the complex, which was generously decorated with lights. Their absence went unnoticed for quite a while, and then everyone sprang into action in all directions. The frantic search ended when the group was located near a toy counter one floor down. Needless to say, the parents had words with the brazen adventurers.

Govindan Kutty took them all to an open-air hawker centre for an early dinner. The food served at their table came from separate orders placed at several hawker stalls. The experience was new to the ladies and the children. Gowri opted for *meehoon* (rice noodles) prepared vegetarian style with a lot of exclusions, including garlic. Kamalam, much to Gowri's surprise, wanted the *meehoon* as prepared. Since coming to Malaya, she had begun to take a liking to non-vegetarian dishes, but these had to be cooked Indian style where the taste of the meat was heavily marinated with added curry powder. The children appeared to take well to the authentic fast-food Chinese cuisine. For dessert, the popular *ice kachang* was ordered and enjoyed by all. This is a traditional dessert made from shaved ice topped with red beans, corn, bits of jelly, syrups, and ice cream, and then drizzled with condensed milk.

The following day being a weekend, a visit to the zoo and some sightseeing consumed a major part of the morning. The party descended on Serangoon Road for a curry lunch and the inevitable purchase of sarees and children's clothes. The evening passed quickly, and everyone retired to bed early that evening. Kamalam and Shankaran left the next morning.

## SATURN WIELDS ITS MALEFIC INFLUENCE

The following week, trouble brewed at Govindan Kutty's workplace in Pulau Sebarok. He had entrusted his assistant with the task of issuing some specified items, giving him the keys to the store for this purpose. Over the weekend, a large number of items were found missing from the store. Govindan Kutty was sure that the assistant must have duplicated the keys before returning them. A police investigation was initiated, but any evidence of a break-in was only in the form of disarrayed items.

Govindan Kutty was suspended from his job until the police investigation was over. It was clear from the police report that he had no part in it, but while suspicion fell on the assistant, the absence of concrete evidence meant that Govindan Kutty had to take the rap for the theft. After all, he was in charge of the store and its inventory and hence, in the eyes of the company, accountable.

The loss of the job hurt Govindan Kutty badly. His morale was down, and he felt devastated. He sent Gowri and the children in late November 1947 to stay with Kamalam in Labis while he sorted things out. To make matters worse, by this stage Gowri was also due to deliver her sixth child.

Govindan Kutty stayed back in Singapore looking for another clerical job. He took on part-time jobs, but a tenured job eluded him. His sixth child, a son, was born in January 1948. He was named Ravindran, but the family simply called him by his shortened name, Ravi. Govindan Kutty who had come to Labis to witness his son's birth stayed back until the first week of February. He and Gowri were deeply distraught upon hearing the news that Mahatma Gandhi, the architect of Indian independence from Britain in 1947, had been assassinated on 30 January at the hands of a Hindu fanatic. Along with other Indians, they mourned his loss.

Returning to Singapore where he had a part-time job, Govindan Kutty spared no efforts in seeking permanent employment. He attended several job interviews in the plantation sector in Johor. But, to his dismay, the jobs available required prior experience in rubber planting, which he did not possess. His astrological chart indicated that he was experiencing the malefic influence of Saturn in transit and that it would be several months before favourable conditions returned. The crucial decision was then made to send Gowri and the children to India until he landed a firm job. The youngest child, Ravi, was then about 4 months old. Janaki was left in the custody of Kamalam. It was decided by the sisters that she would be married off to a Malayalee cook in the estate whom they both knew.

# STAY IN KERALA:
# AN UNFORGETTABLE INTERLUDE
# (1948-1949)

Kathakali Dancer

# [6]

The question of where Gowri and her children would reside in India until Govindan Kutty found a job did pose some concern. She was essentially an unknown to her husband's Velloli House. Further, what remained of her once extensive *tharavad*, the Kollaikal House at Puduserry, was now just a small plot with a little brick abode and an adjacent deep well that for over a century had never run dry. Her mother occupied the house with her brother, Bala Menon. The family home was considered hostile territory to the rest of the Puduserry Kollaikal clan, who had broken all relationship with her mother, Kamakshi Amma. And so it was that Gowri and her children ended up going to stay with her elder sister, Saraswati, whose husband was then the deputy superintendent of customs and central excise. Their house was in Mattancherry, a locality in the port town of Cochin[5] (Kochi).

Like Gowri, Saraswati had a large family to fend for. She had lost her eldest child, a son whom Gowri had seen, at an early age. Of her other five children, the two elder ones were girls (Prema and Uma) who were in their early teens, while the boys (Devidas, Krishna Kumar, and Sudarshan) were all below 10 years. Gowri felt bad imposing herself on her sister and hoped that the stay would be temporary. While in Malaya, she had instructed that her share of monies from the proceeds of the annual sales of harvested paddy and other products from her ancestral land be given to Saraswati. She had left the administration of this in the hands of her aunt, Lakshmikutty Amma. Conscious of this magnanimity on Gowri's part, and

---

5    After Indian independence on August 15, 1947, the state of Kerala was created in 1956 from the former state of Travancore-Cochin, the Malabar District of Madras State, and the Kasaragod taluk of Dakshina Kannada.

yet understandably sensing that it was not going to be easy managing the extended family for whatever short or medium term, Saraswati nevertheless welcomed Gowri and her children with genuine warmth. It was a vegetarian household, as Saraswati's husband was a Brahmin, and the spoken word was Tamil, but soon Malayalam was also heard loudly around the house.

The teaching of basic writing skills in Malayalam and arithmetic for Gowri's three elder children began in earnest with the appointment of a home tutor, a Konkani gentleman of Goan origin. Sitting cross-legged on the floor every morning for three hours, four days a week, with a slate upon which to write words with meanings they hardly understood proved too strenuous for the boys. Gowri quickly intervened to slow the pace for a more effective teaching and learning session.

The tutor proved to be a patient and understanding man. He had a pleasant personality and gave Gowri a first-hand account of the geography and history of her new surroundings. From him she learnt that Kochi has a chequered colonial heritage, beginning with the arrival of St Francis Xavier to establish a Christian mission in AD 1530, some thirty years after the historical landing of Vasco da Gama at a place called Kappad in 1498. Subsequent waves of domination by the Dutch and then by the British had left their respective footprints on Kochi, giving it a truly cosmopolitan character. Kochi, she was told, also boasted the presence of the oldest Jewish community in India, dating back to the sixteenth century.

"How far is Ernakulam from here?" Gowri wanted to know, as her favourite cousin Radha who was now married had settled there.

"It is not far – some eight miles away on the mainland across the Vembanad Lake. We can use the road-cum-rail Venduruthy Bridge to get there. The bridge is a marvellous piece of engineering. It was built by the British during the pre-independence period. The centre of the bridge can be raised to let bigger boats pass under it. Do you know that to build the bridge from here they had to first create a man-made island called Willingdon Island by extensive dredging of the lake? That very island is now the Kochi Port."

"Did we cross this bridge when I first arrived here? Or did we use some other path?"

"Most certainly, you must have used this path."

Some six months into the lessons, the tutor pronounced that 8-year-old Dasu was ready for enrolment at a local school. Dasu was promptly enrolled at a school close to the house at Mattancherry. Returning one evening from school, barely into his second week, he wanted to show his mother something new he had picked up at school. Reaching for the slate, the young Dasu quickly sketched out what was unmistakably female genitalia. Gowri gasped, hurled the slate down, and gave him a tight slap. The tutor's help was sought to get him a different seating position in class, and Dasu was warned not to mix with the wrong sort.

The stay at Mattancherry, of course, had a lot of plus points, particularly for the children. The daily open-air night market at Mattancherry had a charm of its own. Gowri's children would go there often with Saraswati's elder children in search of their favourite street sweets, especially *rasgulla*, *laddu* and *bal mithai*. On several occasions, Gowri would leave with her children for a few days' stay with her cousin Radha and Radha's engineer husband, Madhava Menon, at Ernakulam. They enjoyed each other's company, talking about old times. Their first meeting, Gowri recalled, was a tearful reunion.

"You have such lovely children, Gowri. I can see the Kollaikal features in them: the high nose, the pushed-back lower jaw, and the large rounded ear-tops."

"Ha-ha. I see the same in your girls, too, but not so much in your boy."

"He takes after his father, I guess."

Gowri's children came to like their Radha Aunty very much, as she always had mouth-watering sweetmeats and savoury snacks to hand for them.

While in Ernakulam, the children had the unique opportunity to witness the *uthsavom* (temple festival) of the famous Shiva temple there. They lined the street with other worshippers on the seventh day of the festival to witness the deity being taken on a procession with caparisoned elephants. The people mounted on the elephants held up high colourful, tinselled silk *muttukuda* (parasols), *venchamaram* (white fans) and *mayipeli* (peacock- feather fans), which they swayed to the beat of the music played by the temple orchestra ahead of them. It was a sight to behold. Getting back to their house, they would witness over the town skyline the fireworks display that marked the end of the parade. Although not on the scale of the more spectacular annual Pooram festival in Thrissur, the procession was indeed a mesmerizing one to watch.

A temple festival procession with caparisoned elephants at the Pooram festival in Thrissur.
*Photo courtesy of Maya Jayapal (2016)*

Gowri also had the opportunity one night to attend with Radha a Kathakali performance. This dance-drama featuring elaborate makeup and costumes and relying on hand gestures and well-defined body movements is very unique to Kerala. The Kathakali skit they witnessed was drawn from the Ramayana, the great Sanskrit epic poem written by the Vedic sage and scholar Valmiki.

"The character of Shurpanakha was very well acted," said Radha as they made their way back to the car.

"Yes, she acted very well. But what was cut out in the scene was her nose, not her breast!" observed Gowri with a giggle.

"I guess that was a metaphorical equivalent that was played out, and with some realism. I may go and see their Mahabharata skit as well," responded Radha.

"That should be interesting. I wonder which skit they will choose to play out?"

"I'm told that they prefer to act out Draupadi's humiliation by Dushasana and the fulfilling of her vow for vengeance by his killing at the hands of Bhima. Anyway, I'm feeling rather hungry, aren't you?"

"As a matter of fact, I am. Hope we can get some *masala dosha* ("dosha" means crispy pancake) somewhere."

"Don't worry, my cook can whip it up for us. Let's head back."

Towards the early part of 1949, the children had the unique opportunity, again at Ernakulam, to meet most of Gowri's maternal relatives. They included her aunt Lakshmikutty Amma and her uncle Parameswara Menon who, like his elder brother Kesava Menon, had risen to the high rank of assistant commissioner in the police force. Gowri also introduced her children to her other cousins who had come to Ernakulam for the occasion of Jayaram's wedding. Gowri and Saraswati, along with their children, spent the night at Radha's residence.

One pre-planned outstation visit that had a big impact on the children was their visit to the ancient temple at Guruvayur, having heard so much about it from their mother in Malaya before they set sail. Their starting point was the Ernakulam Junction railway station, where they boarded the train to Thrissur. Radha, with whom they had stayed overnight, arranged not only for their return train tickets but also prepared their lunch packs. Gowri was touched by her cousin's affection and confided that she was going to be met at the Thrissur railway station by her brother, Bala Menon, with whom she had earlier corresponded on the planned visit.

"I haven't met him since I left India. I wonder how he is," mused Gowri.

"Me too. Please give him my regards," responded Radha.

Arriving at Thrissur, Gowri looked furtively at the platform crowd trying to get a glimpse of her brother. She had no cause for worry, for there he was looking stately and tall, standing out from the crowd. He spotted Gowri at the same time and rushed forward into her compartment as soon as the train had halted.

Gowri tearfully hugged him. *"Ende Bala,"* she said, *"nende mukathe orum mattavum illa. Engene irikinnyu nee?"* ("Oh, my Bala! Your face hasn't changed one bit. How are you?") She had last seen him as a young lad, but now here he was standing in front of her, a grown man with much facial hair.

Bala Menon was smiling from ear to ear. Turning to the children, he held each one in a warm hug. His eyes welled with tears as he called each one by name. "I wouldn't have missed seeing them for the world. I'm glad you brought them all here, *Chechi*," said Bala Menon, calling her by the honorific for elder sister.

"*Makale* (children), that's your *Bala Mama* (Uncle Bala)," said Gowri. Ravi, hearing the name, cried out "Bala," much to the delight of the uncle, who held Ravi up and carried the child on his shoulders.

"I have arranged through a family friend for a car and driver, *Chechi*. It will take us to Guruvayur," said Bala Menon.

"How long will it take to get there?"

"Less than two hours. We will be there well before the evening prayers. I have also booked the *satram* (temple lodging facility) provided by the temple *Devaswom* (socio-religious trust) for our overnight stay."

"Oh, good. I hope the facilities are clean."

"They are. The two family rooms I have booked are quite spacious and come with attached bathrooms."

"Oh, that's a relief."

Brother and sister chatted away during the trip, with Gowri intent on knowing about their mother, Kamakshi Amma.

"How is her health, Bala? I wish I could see her. Does she miss us all?"

"Of course she misses you all. Not a day passes without her asking me to bring out the photo album. She is healthy for her age, but she finds it difficult to walk around because of her rheumatism. Her voice, though, is still as loud and crisp as ever."

Before long, they arrived at the grounds of the Sree Krishna temple at Guruvayur. Gowri experienced an inner thrill seeing the temple, which she had visited just once before whilst still in her teens. They grabbed a quick meal before registering themselves at the lodging facility and readying themselves to enter the temple. At around six o'clock in the evening, they joined the long queue of worshippers in a slow march to the inner sanctum. Once there, each worshipper barely had the time with folded palms to look into the sanctum sanctorum and make out the decorated idol of the Lord in the dim light of the temple lamps before having to move on, uttering the briefest of salutations.

Bala Menon, carrying Ravi, led the pack, followed by Dasu, Venu, and Shivan, who emulated their uncle in adopting the prayer attitude. Gowri managed to linger on a bit at the spot as she lifted each of her girls in turn for a view of the deity. Major temples in India, and particularly in Kerala, rarely sported electric lights in their main sanctums. Descriptions of the appearance of the deity as seen by the worshippers in the dim light have thus been varied. Gowri visualized the deity in the form of the idol she always prayed to.

Coming out of the temple grounds, they decided to have their dinner at a wayside restaurant. While brother and sister continued their chat, the children, who had moved to one side of the restaurant and huddled together, were excitedly looking out. They must have been at it for a while before their uncle, looking in their direction, noticed the object of their interest. It was a horse-drawn cart.

"Want a ride?" asked their uncle.

Their eyes lit up, and they all made a quick dash outside to get in. The children remembered the ride for a long time and came to associate it with their new-found uncle.

Main entrance to inner sanctum of Guruvayur Temple

Turning in for the night, Bala Menon shared his room with his three elder nephews. He brought them back to Gowri's room early next morning and kept vigil while she went back to the temple alone for the early morning prayers. After breakfast, Bala Menon bid a tearful goodbye to Gowri and children and left for Palakkad, clutching the new clothes Gowri had fondly insisted on buying him at one of the shops. Soon thereafter, their vehicular transport came to fetch Gowri and children back to Thrissur railway station for the return trip to Ernakulam.

In April 1949, Gowri received news that Govindan Kutty had secured a job as supervisor at Revertex Ltd., a natural and synthetic rubber processing company, located at Mengkibol Estate in Kluang, a district in central Johor. Gowri breathed a sigh of relief. Her prayers at Guruvayur had been answered. Govindan Kutty would now be in a position to send regular monthly remittances to cover living expenses, the absence of which had already begun to show tangible signals of deprivation among her children. They often fell ill and were increasingly prone to skin infections. A few more months, and it would be a year's stay away from their father. The children were becoming restless and naughty as well.

Overwhelmed by the feeling of imposing on her sister, Gowri had gone into a period of depression. She had already sensed the strain her sister felt in trying to meet the growing demands of the children of the combined families in a household that was functioning with limited resources. This worried her immensely. She recalled an incident when one night Shivan wanted an extra dosha. Gowri immediately said, "Give him my share, Saraswati." Gowri later noticed that not only had her own share been reduced but so also Saraswati's. Gowri's mind was made up. Very soon thereafter, in an emotional letter written under stress to her husband, she asked him to get her and her often sickly children, who numbered six, back to Malaya as soon as possible, "lest a difference be noted in their count."

The response to the melodramatic phrase was quick, and around July the family prepared to return to Malaya. Berths were booked on the SS *Rajula*, which had resumed its passenger service from Madras to Penang and Singapore. Gowri's uncle, Kesava Menon, with whom the family spent a few days before boarding the ship, was a tremendous help in getting their items repacked properly and upgrading their cabin class from 2B to 2A. He was then the assistant commissioner of police. He took an instant liking to Ravi, who was not yet 2 years old, and enjoyed very much the child's repartee when he playfully indulged in a name-calling game with him in Malayalam.

The family also made their first acquaintance with Kesava Menon's two grown-up children, who endeared themselves by taking Gowri's children around places of interest in the city and treating them to some mouth-watering Indian sweets. Gowri, while excited about the return trip, couldn't help wondering why God was putting her and her family through these tribulations. But her trust in her Guruvayurappan never wavered.

Gowri had her hands full minding her six children, many of whom, like her, did not take kindly to sea travel. The family was spread over two neighbouring four-berth cabins. Luckily for her, she found that the extra passenger in the second cabin was a young female doctor who was returning to Malaya. Her name was Leela Menon. Leela was a great help to Gowri during the voyage. She kept a watchful eye on the children in her cabin, particularly Valsala, who was the most seasick. Little did they realize that decades later, they would meet again by coincidence at Valsala's wedding.

Kesava Menon with wife Janaki Amma,
son Chandrasekhar (Mani) and daughter Ratnam (1949)

Family photo from 1980 of
Parameswara Menon (seated
second from right) and Family.
*Clockwise:*
Wife Kunhilakshmi Amma,
Karunadas, Rema, Govindan
Kutty, Shoba and Pushpa

Family photo from 1969
of Lakshmikutty Amma
with Radha and Madhava
Menon (*seated*).
Standing, *right to left*:
Radha's children
Deviprasad and Krishna,
and son-in-law Venu.
Krishna's son Raju
is on Lakshmikutty
Amma's lap.

# RECONNECTING WITH JOHOR: THE SCHOOL YEARS (1949-1958)

The Gunung Lambak mountain range
at the foothills of which nestles Kluang town

# [7]

Gowri took an instant liking to their new abode in the Revertex staff enclave at Mengkibol Estate, Kluang. The estate drew its name from the Mengkibol River that flows through the town. The house was the last at the end of a row of five single-storey bungalows. A beautiful flowering jacaranda tree and an overgrown cherry plant were located in its compound.

The house had a posterior extension which gave it an L-shaped layout straddling two adjacent sides of a square, cemented inner courtyard; the extension was a straight block of three rooms comprising a dining room, kitchen, and lavatory. Each had a door opening out onto the courtyard. A spacious study connected the extension and main building, which featured a living room flanked by two bedrooms, the larger one with an en suite bathroom. There was much land all around the house. Gowri quickly earmarked a large patch for a vegetable garden.

The family settled in quickly. With Gowri's green fingers, the vegetable plot soon saw the cultivation of long beans, dolichos beans, bitter gourd, ash gourd, and green chilli. Over time, the free area behind the house was fenced in to rear chickens; Govindan Kutty took charge of this, while the vegetable plot was managed by Gowri. Not long afterwards, Govindan Kutty found that despite the elaborate wire enclosure in his pen, a *musang* (weasel) managed to wring off the necks of a couple of hens one night. Infuriated, he initially patrolled the backyard, but the weasel remained elusive. After several nights of this, he decided to get a dog.

There were only two houses across the road from Gowri's house, one of which was directly opposite. This was occupied by the chief clerk, A. K. N. Nair, who along with his young wife, Seetha Devi (nicknamed Ponnu), hailed from the Palakkad District in India. The children called her Ponnu *Chechi* and him Nanu Uncle. Ponnu's *tharavad* was Thenkurshi Kolakampadath, at Koduvayur.

When Gowri and her children arrived, Ponnu and her newborn first child were staying with her parents in Renggam. She rejoined her husband in May 1951, by which time Gowri had conceived and delivered her seventh and last child, a son she named Kesavan Kutty (Kesavan Jr.) after her favourite uncle. At home, he was called Hari. Gowri recalled her elder daughter Ambi coming up to her in the kitchen and saying, "Mum, there is a blind lady who wants to see you." Intrigued, Gowri entered the living room, and there was Ponnu, a fair-looking young girl with light-coloured eyes, and her young son, who had come to say hello. Ponnu and Gowri struck up a friendship for life, enjoying each other's company and jokes and often going to town together to watch movies.

Until early 1953, there was no piped water supply. Each house had its own well water which had to be filtered before consumption. Electricity also came around that period when the company installed a DC generator. The supply was, however, restricted to fixed hours. For cooking, dried and splintered rubberwood was used in the kitchen to light up the fires, as gas stoves were not available. Almost every household had a Petromax, a pressurized kerosene lamp with a mantle, for lighting their rooms; often, these were hung low from the ceilings.

Gowri and Ponnu would wash their clothes in the clear waters of the stream that ran behind Ponnu's house, outside the perimeter fence. Ambi was their regular companion. They would head for the stream around two or three in the afternoon, after the rubber tappers of Mengkibol Estate had finished their tapping and latex collection rounds, and when the younger children were taking their afternoon nap. Once in a while, they would decide to have a cool dip in the stream at its slightly deeper end. The stream, which was a tributary of the Mengkibol River, was in quiet secluded surroundings. Its waters were free of both crocodiles and leeches, though never officially certified as such. The only noise other than the murmur of water flowing over rocks was that of woodpeckers or of monkeys swinging amongst the rubber trees in search of the rubber fruit. The friends couldn't have wished for a more serene spot. All the children would walk up to the stream now and then for a swim and to test their skill at scooping up small fish with their bare hands.

Latex collection from tapped rubber trees.
PVC shields stapled to the bark with sealant coatings at
joints serve as rain shields for the tapping panels.
*Photo courtesy of M.R.Chandran (2016)*

Within months of their arrival, Govindan Kutty had enrolled his three elder children in a private school in Kluang town, a necessity at the time as they could not directly enter the Government English School (GES) without some a priori attestation of their basic skills in English and arithmetic. After nearly a year's study, they gained admission to GES. The school had as its logo the flying fox, in line with the Malay origins of the town's name, *keluang*, given on account of the large numbers of fruit bats found in the caves of the hills surrounding the town.

Transport to and from school was provided jointly by the managements of Revertex and Mengkibol Estate in the form of a lorry service. This proved to be a great help, as Kluang town was some three miles away. The lorries had a persistent smell of rubber and ammonia, as they were also being used to transport rubber sheets and on many an occasion had been the target of Communist attacks. The schoolchildren had little choice but to endure the unhealthy odour. Also, the lorries had no canopy covers. This, of course, meant that the children had to brave the vagaries of the weather and carry raincoats with them in their schoolbags.

To help with her household chores, Gowri managed to get the assistance of a part-time housemaid for a short period. Her name was Fatimah. The interaction helped her to improve very much her spoken Malay.

Their age differences being not much, the children frequently quarrelled, even over trivial matters. Otherwise, they were in cahoots, breaking things around the house. Broken bedsteads were a regular occurrence, much to the exasperation of Jalil, the local carpenter. When things went out of control, Gowri would threaten to give them castor oil (coupled with an anti-helminthic) which they all detested but forcibly had to take every month to get rid of worms in their gut. If the threat failed to contain the squabble, she would smack their bottoms, sparing no one – except perhaps Dasu, who enjoyed keeping much to himself with his books, and Valsala, who by nature was shy and withdrawn.

Sometimes their quarrels persisted into the evening. Their father returning home would hear their voices down the road, and even if they suddenly quietened up, sensing his arrival by the parking sound of his bicycle, there would be no respite for them. Everyone would be summoned to his presence, and each one would have his or her ear twisted or on occasion receive a knuckled knock on the head instead.

More often than not, Venu would be in the thick of it. One day, the pretend "doctor" Venu tried to inject Shivan's arm with a nail. It must have hurt quite a bit when the metal pierced skin, and the victim fled crying to his mother. Gowri quickly sought an anti-tetanus jab for Shivan. Govindan Kutty, hearing of this incident upon his return from work, did not spare the rod with Venu. He was a strict father, but a softie when any one of them fell sick, pacing the floor smoking cigarette after cigarette to soothe his nerves. And with the children taking turns with measles, mumps and chicken pox, both parents had to be on constant vigil.

This had to be the case when Venu complained of severe pains on one side of his abdomen. They took him straight to the hospital, where he was operated upon the same day for appendicitis. They remembered the surgeon coming out of the theatre saying to them, "It was good that you brought him here on time." They never took any complaints of body pains by the children lightly after that.

Most nights, Gowri, after putting Hari to bed with his father, would come to the children's room and narrate to them episodes of the Ramayana and Mahabharata. She had a marvellous gift for telling stories and enjoyed very much watching the facial expressions of fear and anger in her children, who identified themselves with the heroes and heroines in the story. Govindan Kutty, on the other hand, would mostly dote on his youngest child and keep a stern exterior with his older children. He was merely following the tradition that he himself had experienced while growing up in his village in India. When requiring any errands to be performed, he would invariably call for his second son, Venu, who appeared to be the gutsiest among the children.

That was the case one evening when Venu was called upon to escort the stand-in estate dresser back home. The regular dresser (Uncle George to the children) was then away on a short leave. Govindan Kutty had noticed that this other chap had been drinking rather heavily and appeared a bit unsteady on his feet. Staggering languidly on the way back, the man stopped before the roadside Hindu temple and began to utter profanities at the deity. He had barely finished his outburst when he suddenly found his trousers around his ankles – whether by his own folly or by divine retribution, the incident was hilarious all the same. Venu, of course, couldn't wait to report this to his parents. But they quickly advised him not to speak about it to anyone else, as the stand-in dresser was not only a senior man but also belonged to a different religious faith.

Also kept under wraps by the family was another funny incident. Gowri had gone to Ponnu's house for a chat in her garden one evening just before dusk, and they noticed, much to their amusement, that their not-so-friendly neighbour (the children called him "Uncle RP" based on his initials) who was preparing himself for an oil bath had wandered out into his garden wearing nothing but his loincloth. Oblivious to their presence, he headed towards his chicken coop, which adjoined Ponnu's garden. When the two ladies came into view, the embarrassed man ran for cover towards the chicken coop. Gowri and Ponnu were mischievously content to go on chatting and laughing, confining the poor man to the coop until he was able to scurry back into his house under the cover of nightfall.

Over time, there were more ladies in the neighbourhood for Gowri and Ponnu to mingle with. They would often descend onto the road in the evenings for a chat while waiting for the bread vendor to arrive on his scooter. On one such evening, Gowri was holding Hari when she realized that she needed more money to settle the vendor. She went back to the house, opened wide the two doors of the large cupboard in her room, seated Hari on a platform inside it on one side, and bending down unlocked a drawer with the key that she always kept hidden under one of her sarees. Taking the money out from the drawer, she closed the cupboard doors and, still counting the money, walked out. The vendor took his time giving her back the change, and Gowri found herself in the meanwhile being drawn into a conversation. Suddenly, she stiffened; Hari was not with her. Screaming "Guruvayurappa!" she rushed back to the cupboard and found him sobbing, shaken with fright. Seeing her, he started to cry even more loudly. She quickly took him out and hugged and kissed him profusely till he quieted down.

Gowri had cold sweats thinking about the event over the next several nights. Years later, she blamed herself for this incident when she noticed in him a tendency towards claustrophobia. She readily understood when this condition was explained to her, as she used to suffer from sudden attacks of near choking (laryngospasm) many times when she was in Kluang. To a victim, there is no greater fear than not being able to breathe. Sometimes the spasm would quickly ebb following its onset, but there was once an unusually long spell that panicked the entire family.

It was a Saturday afternoon soon after lunch. The children were attending to their homework, some in the dining room and some in the living room seated next to Govindan Kutty, who was reading a newspaper. Suddenly, Gowri came running out into the living room from the kitchen, clutching her throat with one hand and beckoning Govindan Kutty frantically with the other. Realizing that she was choking, Govindan Kutty quickly jumped out of his seat. Going behind her, he applied pressure at the pit of her stomach and thumped her back a few times. Seeing her still struggling, he wasted no time in laying her down on the floor, tilting her head backwards, and, holding her nostrils tight, blowing into her mouth a few times.

Within moments, Gowri started coughing, and to everyone's relief, she got up into a seated position. Tears were streaming from her eyes, but in between her coughs she was moved to laughter. It must have been the terrified look on the faces of her children that brought it out. Govindan Kutty helped her onto her feet and asked Dasu to bring her some warm water to sip while he stepped outside for a smoke. The thought occurred to him that since leaving the medical corps of the British Indian Army, he hadn't until now put to test his first-aid skills.

Govindan Kutty was a man of intense faith whose piety went beyond daily prayers. He was the driving force behind the establishment of a temple in the estate for Lord Ayyappan, the offspring of Lord Shiva and Mohini (the only female avatar of Lord Vishnu). There were a lot of devotees of Lord Ayyappan among the Malayalee Hindus in the estate, some of whom had already made their pilgrimage to Sabarimala, the site of His prominent shrine in Kerala. At the opening ceremony, Govindan Kutty was honoured by the temple committee and asked to recite a short prayer. After the prayer, he followed up voluntarily with a devotional song, his frame swaying as he sang. Wondering if he might break into a trance, Gowri quickly sent two of her children to stand beside him.

Gowri instilled in her children the need to pray daily at dusk after they all had their baths. Gowri would give the younger children a traditional head-to-toe coconut-oil bath now and then, while the older ones would be required to do so on their own. (The practice is not without scientific basis, as coconut oil has been proven to be an effective skin moisturizer and hair protein loss preventer.) Following their evening bath, the children would all sit cross-legged on the floor at the altar and recite the hymns in Sanskrit and Malayalam that she had taught them.

"Do we need to pray to all Gods?" Shivan had once asked her while they were all seated at prayer. He was 12 going on 13.

The explanation that she gave (in Malayalam) resonated with the children. "Actually, there is only one Ultimate Reality, the transcendent, formless and attributeless Brahman. It is this Supreme Being that takes on many forms that we worship as gods or goddesses. All deities are thus reflections of the Brahman. The highest gods of Hinduism are Brahma, Vishnu and Shiva; together they form the *Trimurti* (Holy Trinity). Brahma is that reality in its role as the creator of the universe; Vishnu portrays its role as the preserver and upholder of the universe, while Shiva is the same reality that will one day destroy the universe. It is mentioned in our ancient scriptures that our universe is created, preserved, and destroyed in an endless cycle.

"The *Trimurti* is supplemented by each of the three gods being associated with a female energy - Saraswati, the consort of Brahma, as the goddess of knowledge, music and all the creative arts; Lakshmi, the consort of Vishnu, as the goddess of wealth and fertility; and Parvati (Durga or Mahakali), the consort of Shiva, as the goddess of power, love and spiritual fulfilment. The union of the three goddesses is the manifestation of *Shakti*, the Divine Mother. *Shakti* embodies the active energy and power of the *Trimurti;* conjoined they constitute an absolute state of oneness. Thus in our eyes God is both male and female.

"We are never far from God. It is erroneous to think that God is residing in some faraway place beyond our reach. God is actually within each one of us, in our hearts and consciousness, in our souls. We as humans can personally realize God through righteousness and spiritual practice. We believe that God incarnates on earth to destroy evil and to uphold righteousness whenever there is a decline of virtue. I have already narrated to you the story of *Narasimha* who was half-human and half-lion, and why God took that form to destroy the demon king *Hiranyakashipu*. The *Narasimha* avatar is a part-plenary portion of Lord Vishnu. The Lord Himself has also descended on earth as the supreme godhead, Krishna, whose story I have also narrated to you in the Mahabharata."

"Were there other avatars, Mum?" asked Shivan.

"Yes, indeed. According to our ancient Puranas, Lord Vishnu has appeared in different *yugas* (epochs within a four age cycle - *Satya Yuga, Treta Yuga, Dvapara Yuga, Kali Yuga*) of the earth's history, and taken various forms, both plenary and part-plenary portions of Him, to carry out certain responsibilities and to do specific things. We have only mythological descriptions of these, but a final avatar has been prophesied to appear at the end of the current *Kali Yuga* [Age of Darkness] when the world will be ridden with much evil and afflicted by cataclysmic earth changes. We are presently in the *Kali Yuga* which started with the end of the Mahabharata war. This final avatar will be the Kalki avatar. He will be the destroyer of all evil, and He will be the maker of a new *Satya Yuga* [Age of Truth]."

# [8]

Kamalam and her family – with her second child, a boy named Prakash – shifted in early 1951 to Sungai Ular Estate, near Kulim, in the northern state of Kedah. Before their departure, they came over to Kluang to see Gowri and her family.

Unnikrishnan, still a bachelor, had earlier left Labis and was employed at Lambak Elias Estate, near Kluang. He would visit Govindan Kutty and family now and then on weekends. His favourite haunt in Kluang town was the White House, where he would enjoy a quiet beer in the company of a few of his friends. The children addressed him as *valiacha* – a term of respect meaning father's elder brother. He would take the children there on many occasions in the evening and treat them to a Western meal of chicken chops or their favourite Chinese dishes – fried rice or fried *meehoon*. He had the odd habit of bringing to Revertex young job-seeking visitors from Kerala who were referred to him, and they would stay on in the house for days while awaiting calls from prospective estates for interviews.

One such visitor who came in 1954 stayed on for more than half a year. Neither Govindan Kutty nor Gowri had the heart to send him out, but with only two bedrooms in the house, the children endured cramped living conditions for some months. On one occasion following an unsuccessful interview near Skudai in South Johor, he came back bearing some social welfare lottery tickets. He presented one ticket to Dasu, who promptly gave it to his father. The draw was for the end of the month. One can imagine the exasperation that followed when it was learnt that the lottery ticket held by Govindan Kutty had missed the second prize by a variation only in the second to last digit. Govindan Kutty swore good-naturedly, but no one could prevent him from talking about the near miss to all and sundry for weeks to come.

One day an insurance agent from the Great Eastern Life Assurance Company (GELC) called to the house around the time that Govindan Kutty had received his bonus and convinced him of his need as breadwinner of a large family to take out a policy. Govindan Kutty opted for an endowment policy, and shortly thereafter decided also to take on a part-time job as an agent himself to earn some extra income from commissions. On his way home from work, he would on most evenings cycle to Kluang town and try to sell policies to business people whom he personally knew had dealings with Revertex and through them others. His diligence paid dividends, as he stood out among the top agents for two consecutive years and received commendation from GELC. It was, however, ironic that years later he suffered the misfortune of a lapsed policy, as he found it difficult to meet the steep monthly premium instalment payments that were required of him.

Gowri's children enjoyed life growing up in the estate, mingling with scores of other children of the staff of Revertex. Venu and Shivan were very adventurous in a mischievous sense and tended to play to the gallery. They would climb trees and jump off from the high branches, attempting a somersault in the process. It's a wonder they never broke their neck or bones, but scrapes and bruises were the order of the day. Gowri found herself attending to their bruises more easily than to the earful of complaints from parents whose sons wanted to imitate her sons' antics. "Why can't you all be like your Dasu *Ettan*?" she would moan in exasperation.

It was not long before Ambi also joined in their frolic. Soon she was as brown as a berry, much like them, from playing in the heat of the day. The children coined nicknames for practically everyone in the neighbourhood, often hurling these at each other when they quarrelled. While Dasu escaped a christening, Venu was nicknamed *karumandi* (Malayalam for dark complexion) because he was always in the sun and was heavily tanned. Shivan was called *pokkan* because he had somewhat protruding front teeth. Ambi was nicknamed *kaka* after her love for pappadams, the vendors of which were mostly Malayalee Muslims who were referred to as *kakas*. Everyone in Gowri's household enjoyed eating papadam, and it was often an effort for Gowri to save a few pieces for her husband when she was frying them in the kitchen. Valsala's nickname was *cheenathi* for her fair complexion and nondescript features, which to her siblings looked Chinese. Ravi was called *Gurkha* because he was then burly and short in stature.

## A CASE OF INDUCED TRAUMA

The nickname given to Valsala by her elder male siblings was also picked up by some of the boys in the neighbourhood. Valsala grew to resent it. To make matters worse, the boys would often point to an old Chinese vegetable grower who regularly used to walk past the staff homes on his way to the labour lines to collect night soil and tell Valsala, "There goes your father."

The teasing was done in bad taste, but little did they realize the trauma it was causing their sister. Valsala became insecure and somewhat of an introvert, shadowing her mother and clinging on to Gowri's saree paloo all the time. She started to distance herself from her father, refusing to sit on his lap like she used to earlier. She woke up screaming some nights. Gowri also often noticed her peering furtively into the mirror and quickly moving away when she became aware of others. Both parents failed to realize the extent and the cause of the child's aberrant behaviour.

One morning, when all the older kids were at school, Valsala – who was 5 going on 6 – came to her mother in the kitchen. Her face was ashen and her lips were trembling. Gowri immediately stopped what she was doing.

"What's the matter, *molu*?" Gowri asked, using an affectionate term for daughter. "Are you feeling sick? Did you hurt yourself?"

With tears rolling down her cheeks, Valsala asked her, almost in a whisper, "Am ... am I really a *Cheenathi*? Is ... is that *Cheenan* my father? Will he take me away?"

She was by now sobbing uncontrollably. Aghast, Gowri realized how deeply the teasing had affected her little girl. She hugged Valsala, raining kisses on the child's crumpled face. "You are *Acha*'s and my daughter. Nobody else's. Really, the boys were just teasing you, because you are fair, that's all."

Then, holding her by the hand, she took Valsala to the mirror. "Look at your face. See? You look just like me. Can't you see the resemblance? Your nose will grow higher as you get older, don't worry." Just then, a house lizard on the ceiling made a loud clicking sound. "See, even the lizard agrees!"

Gowri gathered her daughter to her bosom and kept her there for a while. It suddenly dawned on her why she had caught Valsala peering at herself in the mirror so often. It was not an early act of vanity, as she had thought, but a reflexive act by a forlorn child hoping her features would grow more Indian-like.

Gowri chided herself for not having put a stop to all the teasing. Now, she wasted no time. That same evening, she accosted her children and told them how badly they had hurt their sister. She gave them all a stern warning, and she was wielding a big ladle as she spoke. They got the message. And so it was that *Cheenathi* became a taboo word in the house and, indeed, in the neighbourhood. Simultaneously, all other nicknames were thrown out the window. Magically, Valsala drew out of her shell and seemed a happier child. She no longer resisted her father's efforts to place her on his lap.

Gowri smiled as she observed this. "One should not underestimate how a child's mind works and the conclusions he or she may draw," she would say in hindsight to her children in their adult years when they were handling their own children and nonchalantly hurling at them utterances such as "You're stupid" or "You're good-for-nothing."

The years dragged by, and soon the girls too were attending school. They joined the Canossian Convent. Ponnu, in the meanwhile, had given birth to her second son, and the estate was the venue in 1953 for the marriage of her younger sister, Pankajam. The occasion enabled Gowri and her family to get to know Ponnu's mother, Thilothamma, and the rest of her family with some intimacy.

Photo of Ambi (*left*) and Valsala (*centre*) with Prabha (*right*),
taken during Kamalam's visit to Kluang in 1950.

Photo of Gowri with her youngest two children,
Hari (*on lap*) and Ravi, taken in early 1953 at Kluang

The year 1953 carried the exciting news of the successful ascent of
Mount Everest by Edmund Hillary and Tenzing Norgay on 29 May. Gowri

immediately wanted to know whether Mount Everest and Mount Kailash, the throne of Lord Shiva and a sacred mountain also to Buddhists and Jains, were the same. She was told that they were not and she was further appeased to learn that no one has ever climbed Mount Kailash, as the climb would be considered sacrilegious.

Close on the heels of the Everest adventure came the equally exciting news of the coronation of Queen Elizabeth II on 2 June. The country celebrated with coronation parades in major towns that saw march-pasts by servicemen and Police, school children bearing the Union Jack, various cultural groups, and colourful floats decorated to represent Queen Elizabeth's crown. Gowri and Govindan Kutty witnessed the march-past by bands and the mass drill display by school children, including their elder children, at the Kluang *padang* (public open ground, often a sports field). The celebration was spread over a few days with fun-fairs and an inter-schools sports meet to boot. Gowri's daughter, Ambi, participated in the sports meet and won two prizes in the track events.

This was also the period when the Communist insurgency in the country was at its height. The Malayan Communist Party (MCP) was founded in 1930. During the Japanese occupation of Malaya – which saw the Chinese being singled out for harsh treatment at the hands of the Japanese – MCP was the backbone of the Malayan People's Anti-Japanese Army (MPAJA). In the immediate aftermath of the war, the country was beset with acute food shortage and severe unemployment problems. The widespread labour unrest was capitalized upon by the MCP, which fomented country-wide strikes by trade unions it had infiltrated, frustrating the British Military Administration (BMA).

Inheriting weapons and supplies from the then-disbanded MPAJA, the MCP, purportedly working for national independence, took an increasingly anti-British stance. With the killing of three European planters in Perak by Communist militants, the stage was set for the BMA to outlaw the party in July 1948 and declare a state of emergency. Party militants, however, regrouped in the jungle and under a new name, Malayan Peoples' Liberation Army, commenced their campaign of guerrilla warfare against the British.

☼

# LIVING THROUGH
# THE COMMUNIST INSURGENCY

There were Communist strongholds in many states of the country. In Johor, these strongholds, labelled black areas, were around Pagoh, Ayer Hitam, Yong Peng, and Kluang. The British and Commonwealth forces had their operational base, including a military hospital and an airfield, established at Kluang, given its central location. The authorities would sometimes apply a blanket curfew from dawn to dusk while they engaged upon their hunt for the Communists who would come down from their jungle hideouts at Gunung Lambak to the plantations to get their food supplies.

The area around Mengkibol Estate appeared to be one such supply source. The families in the estate, keeping themselves indoors, would often witness the Commonwealth soldiers alighting from armoured trucks clad in jungle uniform and in quick formation fan out deep into the plantation. Besides the British soldiers, there were regiments of Gurkhas, Australians, New Zealanders, and Fijians. In stealth they would move forward, wary of the unseen enemy who might have set booby traps and ambushes.

There were days when the overnight curfew would be lifted in the early hours of the morning, permitting the children to go to school. Loudspeakers were employed by the authorities to announce this in English, Malay, Tamil, and Chinese. It became nothing unusual for Gowri's children to see bodies of slain Communists openly displayed on a mound in the compound of the Kluang police station, which they had to pass on their way to school.

Radical measures had to be taken by the BMA to cut off food supplies to the Communists. These included large-scale relocation of squatters and peasants in sensitive areas into new villages and banning cafes and restaurants to operate or be set up in food-restricted areas. Around Mengkibol Estate itself were some of these new villages. The security of the villagers was safeguarded by regular patrols by the newly formed Home Guards and Auxiliary Police. Collectively, such steps helped weaken the Communist resistance.

British soldiers in jungle patrol led by Malayan
guide hunting Communist guerrillas.
*Source: British Imperial War Museum. Reproduced with permission.*

In July 1955, Malaya held its first general elections, with Tunku Abdul
Rahman becoming the chief minister. Tunku offered an olive branch of
amnesty to Chin Peng, the Communist leader, to lay down arms, but
in talks at Baling in Northern Perak, Chin Peng insisted on MCP being
legalized. The talks broke down, and it was to be another five years before
the emergency was completely lifted.

The Commonwealth forces continued to stay on, and many of them,
especially Fijian soldiers, soon became household names on account of
their sporting prowess displayed at the Malayan National Athletics
Championships. Gowri's children idolized some of them.

Sporting facilities in the estate were meagre for both staff and their children. Save for a football field and several outdoor badminton courts, there were no amenities, but this did not deter the bigger children of the staff of both Mengkibol Estate and Revertex from organizing their own athletics meets and introducing such net games as quoits and volleyball in which even staff would participate. A tug-of-war between the staff of Mengkibol Estate and Revertex would be held at the close of every annual athletic meet, which would be fun to watch. Govindan Kutty would sportingly participate in it.

He and his children would on most evenings descend onto the badminton courts near the house and there, joined by other junior staff of Revertex, engage in some hard-fought doubles matches. The intensity of the matches was such that sometimes the senior players would lose their cool when they perceived a younger player was consistently engaging in body-line smashes. Govindan Kutty excelled in the subtle drop of the shuttlecock at the net from the baseline of the court, but his raised left foot before delivering a smash was always a giveaway. The country's own prowess at winning the Thomas Cup consecutively in 1952 and 1955 provided both young and old with much impetus to play the game.

# [9]

In 1956, not feeling the need to inform others, Govindan Kutty took the bold step of registering himself as a citizen of the State of Johor. "Why did you do that?" was the question on everyone's lips when they finally found out.

"Simple. I wish to finally settle down here and not in India. The future of my family is in Malaya. My children are all born here."

In one bold stroke, he had changed the fate of his children and descendants for generations to come. He was chided for this hasty act by some of his colleagues, but he was not bothered. He was confident that there would be no purge of immigrants when the country secured independence, noting that the Alliance Party headed by Tunku Abdul Rahman was already a composite of the main political parties of the Malays, Chinese, and Indians. It was unlikely, he further argued with his sceptical colleagues, that Britain would permit here a repeat of the bloodshed that came with partition in the grant of Indian independence.

In early 1957, Gowri had her umbilical hernia surgery performed at the British Military Hospital in Kluang. Not allowed for some months to carry heavy things, Gowri to her surprise found her husband and children rallying around to lessen her housework. Dasu would sweep and clean the house, and Ambi would help in the washing of clothes, as piped water supply to the house was then already available.

At his workplace, Govindan Kutty's dedication at his job came to be recognized when Coleman, his former boss, on a visit to Revertex from the company's head office in the UK, openly complimented him at a meeting with the staff and rewarded him with three months' bonus. The occasion was also used to introduce a new executive staff recruit from

India. Radhakrishnan was his name, and he had a chemical engineering background. The company had employed him to oversee the production of new elastomeric products for the local and export markets.

Upon hearing this, Dasu – who had just entered the school certificate year – became curious about the field of chemical engineering. He had an opportunity to meet up with Radhakrishnan shortly thereafter and gain some insights into the subject, which excited him. He told his father that he too wanted to be a chemical engineer one day.

On the eve of Coleman's departure for the UK, Govindan Kutty sought a brief meeting with him. He enquired as to whether some form of financial assistance could be obtained from the company to further his son's education in chemical engineering in return for which he could serve the company following graduation. Coleman promised he would look into it and asked that the son's particulars be sent to him, including his examination results when they came to hand. The news was well-received by Gowri, who had been nursing some worries about the furtherance of her son's education.

# EUPHORIA OF INDEPENDENCE

For the country as a whole, there was a mood of great expectancy. The independence talks in London had not faltered and had successfully entered the final stage. The euphoric news soon broke out that independence would be granted to Malaya at the end of August 1957 and that it would uniquely have an elective monarchy system. Singapore, which had a mostly Chinese population, would remain outside the federation as a British Crown Colony.

Before the midnight hour on 30 August, a large crowd gathered on the grounds at the Royal Selangor Club (now renamed Merdeka Square) in Kuala Lumpur to witness the handover of power from the British. Prime Minister-designate Tunku Abdul Rahman arrived at 11.58 p.m. and almost instantly, as had been planned, the square fell into darkness. On the stroke of midnight, the lights were switched back on, and the Union flag was lowered. The new flag of Malaya was raised as the national anthem "Negaraku" was played. Led by the Tunku, the crowd then joined in the chanting of "Merdeka!" (the rallying cry of the independence struggle) seven times, chants which were reciprocated in households across the country listening to the broadcast. It was announced that the ruler of the State of Negeri Sembilan, Tunku Abdul Rahman, having been duly elected by the Council of Rulers, would be installed later in the day as the first *Yang di-Pertuan Agong* (monarch).

On the morning of 31 August 1957, the festivities moved to the newly completed Merdeka Stadium. A huge crowd witnessed the ceremony, which began at half past nine. The queen's representative, the Duke of Gloucester, presented Tunku with the instrument of independence. Tunku then delivered his address to the nation. It was a heart-warming speech. Noting that the country's colonial status had now given way to full equality, he exuded confidence that ties with Britain would enter a new chapter of collaboration and assistance in overcoming the many problems independence would present. There was much sincerity and pragmatism in his words. The newspapers carried the full text of his speech the next day. In part, it read:

> We look forward in faith and hope to the future; from henceforth we are masters of our destiny, and the welfare of this beloved land is our responsibility. Let no one think we have reached the end of the road: Independence is indeed a milestone, but it is only the threshold to [a] high[er] endeavour[;] the creation of a new and sovereign State. At this solemn moment, therefore, I call upon you all to dedicate yourself to the service of the new Malaya: to work and strive with hand and brain to create a new nation, inspired by the ideals of justice and liberty ...

Following the address, Tunku proceeded to read the Proclamation of Independence, which culminated once again in the chanting of "Merdeka!" seven times, with the crowd joining in. The national flag of Malaya was then raised to the accompaniment of the national anthem played by a military band. A twenty-one-gun salute followed. The ceremony ended by an azan call and a thanksgiving prayer to mark the historical occasion.

Iconic picture of Tunku Abdul Rahman raising his hand and crying out
"Merdeka!" after reading the proclamation of the nation's independence
on the morning of 31 August 1957 at Merdeka Stadium. Seated behind
him are His Majesty the *Yang di-Pertuan Agong*; the Duke of Gloucester
(representative of Queen Elizabeth II); the Malay rulers; and foreign dignitaries.
*Photo courtesy of National Archives of Malaysia. Reproduced with permission.*

Gowri had the intuitive feeling that the prince-turned-politician would
live up to his speech and peacefully build a united multi-ethnic nation.
She counted herself now as a domiciled citizen of a newly independent
country. Reaching for an aerogram from her desk, she wrote to her elder
sister, Saraswati, about the historic event that had taken place. "There is
much excitement everywhere," she began, and then the words flowed from
her pen:

> Malaya has now been declared an independent sovereign
> country comprising of all its original states and settlements,
> except Singapore. Three main parties are making up the
> Government, representing the three main races here. The

name of this ruling party is the Alliance Party, and it is the same party that was running the country under self-rule prior to this. The component Indian Party is called the Malayan Indian Congress. It is led by V.T. Sambanthan who holds the post of Minister of Labour. His young wife, I'm told, is a Brahmin girl, Umasundari, who is active in women's organisations. She appears to have visited some estates in Johor recently, urging the Indians, in particular the womenfolk, to take up citizenship. Govindan Kutty has already made up his mind to become a citizen, but not some of his colleagues who are still undecided. My neighbour, A. K. N. Nair, and his wife, Ponnu, whom I had written to you about earlier, are among those planning to return to India. They have already identified a land to purchase in Palakkad. I have not spoken to Kamalam yet to find out what she and Shankaran are planning to do. I hope they decide to stay on as well as citizens.

The letter then drifted to touch on family matters.

A positive answer to Gowri's query came from Kamalam. She was too well entrenched in Kulim to think of ever getting back to an Indian environment. She was the proud owner of a car that she could drive around and had already come to be well known around town. Her circle of contacts extended to most estates in Southern Kedah and Penang, including Bedong, where she learned of the presence of an eligible bachelor, P. Sethumadhavan Nair (Sethu for short), working at the rubber processing plant at Harvard Estate. The processing plant and the surrounding plantation belonged to the Uniroyal Group, an American-based concern. Sethu was appointed as an Asian Assistant, which in those days represented an executive status immediately below the senior management posts reserved for European or American personnel. His initials, P. S., sufficed to identify him in Bedong.

Kamalam confided in Gowri and got the green light to approach him for a hand in marriage to Saraswati's second daughter, Uma, a beautiful girl whose sporting and musical talents matched her scholastic achievements at college. Sethu was interested, and when it was revealed to him that their horoscopes had matched well, he agreed to call on Uma during his planned visit to India in early November 1956. He liked her at first sight, and Saraswati agreed to conduct the marriage before he left Kerala at the completion of his leave. They were married towards the end of November, and Sethu brought his bride back with him to Bedong the following month.

Kamalam and her family brought Uma to visit Gowri around July 1957. Sethu could not join them. The visit, although short, was a reunion of sorts. The families made a joint trip to Singapore to do some shopping and shared together many hours of joy. Gowri's older children, in particular, just could not get enough of their cousin from India. She had to be with them all the time.

They were thrilled one evening when Uma decided to join them to watch the monthly open-air cinema organised in the large public space outside the Mengkibol Estate Office. They had to go early to gain access to the front row of plastic chairs that were reserved for staff and their children. It was mostly Tamil films that were shown, reflective of the estate demographic. The one they sat through was about Ali Baba and the forty thieves – a familiar storyline in any language. It was a swashbuckling adventure film starring M. G. Ramachandran and P. Bhanumathi. Luckily, it was a clear night, and the time lapse between the changing of the film reels was sufficient for the audience, the children included, to purchase stick ice-creams, roasted peanuts, and steamed corn from vendors on the road fringe. This turned out to be a unique, although somewhat deafening, experience for Uma, who had a seat close to a loudspeaker.

# THE PROPHECY

As the year finally drew to a close, Govindan Kutty one night complained of some gastric discomfort, with occasional pains radiating upwards to his chest. This was soon after his dinner. He took some omum (ajwain) water, and after several moments the pain subsided. The episode recurred a few days later. Gowri was worried and asked him to see a doctor the next day.

There was some basis for her worries. A week earlier, a fellow worker in the estate, deaf in one ear, who was also a Panicker (no relation), had come to meet them late one evening to convey news of the events in Kerala following independence. Govindan Kutty was then readying himself for his bath in his customary fashion. Wearing just the traditional Kerala *thorthamundu* (thin white cotton towel) around his waist, he was pacing the floor in the walled back courtyard as he normally did after massaging copious amounts of gingelly oil onto his scalp and the rest of his body. This would take the best part of a half hour and proved no hindrance to the flow of conversation.

The subject of astrology came up, and Govindan Kutty mentioned that no horoscope had yet been cast for his children. The visitor mentioned that he could arrange for it in India, given their correct birth times and dates. Govindan Kutty hoped that it would be written on paper rather than scripted on palm leaf, as was his.

Suddenly, he asked Gowri to bring out his *jathagam*, an astrological forecast based on one's date of birth. The visitor sifted through the palm-leaf manuscript until he neared the end and started reading the contents. The entire script was in high-flown Malayalam. He read several lines, including one that he paused several moments to read. Somewhat disbelievingly, he read out loud the line, and in more colloquial language, said, "According to what is written here, you have only a few months left!"

The words were uttered with a finality that shocked both Govindan Kutty and Gowri.

"Nothing written in my *jathagam* has so far really materialized. No astrologer can predict death; that power remains only with God," countered Gowri.

Nonetheless, the visitor said he would perform some *apagaram* (sacrificial offering to God) at the temple, and then he left. Gowri and Govindan Kutty retired to bed, but it was a troubled sleep for both of them. In the other bedroom across the hall, their eldest son, still awake, was busy preparing himself for the all-important forthcoming senior Cambridge examinations.

# [10]

Govindan Kutty somewhat reluctantly submitted himself to a medical examination in early January 1958, where it was revealed that he had high blood pressure and was mildly diabetic. He was asked to cut down severely on his smoking, but he found it difficult to break that habit. Ponnu, who was near full term carrying her third child, was a regular visitor in the house in those days. She hoped the child to be born would be a girl, and she asked Govindan Kutty to suggest some names. He gave her three names to choose from: Sarala, Shoba, and Sharada. In doing so, he made a prophetic wish: If the child were to be a girl, she should be married to one of his sons when she grew up.

Ponnu got herself admitted to the maternity ward in the third week of February and delivered a baby girl on the 18th; she named the girl Shoba. It was whilst she was in hospital on the 23rd that she heard that Govindan Kutty had been hospitalized with a heart attack.

Gowri recalled him complaining on the night of 22 February about severe heartburn which was becoming more intense. Dasu rushed to inform the estate dresser – who, suspecting a heart attack, promptly arrived. Having no morphine to hand, he administered aspirin orally to help control the pain, placed a GTN pill under Govindan Kutty's tongue, and stayed at his side until the ambulance came to take him to the Kluang District Hospital.

At the hospital, Govindan Kutty was monitored intensely by the doctors attending to him, as his pressure had hit the roof. They managed to stabilize him. He experienced slight anginal pains on and off over the next few days, and the doctors, realizing that he needed further management of the coronary problem, had him transferred to the larger General Hospital at Johor Bahru towards the end of February.

Gowri and Dasu visited him in Johor Bahru the day after his transfer. He was in an isolation ward, and the doctors were planning further tests on him, as they suspected coronary thrombosis. His pain had subsided, and the doctors told him that he had to give up smoking for good. Even so, the hospitalization did not appear to have curbed his jovial nature. Heartened by this, Gowri and Dasu left him after a while to head back to Kluang. Yet they both knew in their heart of hearts that he was not yet out of the woods.

At home and alone with her children, there were many moments when Gowri would wipe her tears with the end of her saree to hide her distress. She shuddered to think what would happen if Govindan Kutty succumbed to his coronary ailment. Minding her children and doing the household chores was also taxing on her. The presence of her eldest son, who was out of school awaiting his examination results, was a comfort, as he would help out in some ways around the house. He took over housecleaning and the ironing of clothes, sometimes calling upon his siblings to lend a hand. The girls would help wash the dishes.

But Gowri's mind was not at ease. She recalled her husband's wish to see all his other children, and on the following Sunday, the whole family visited him in the hospital. Upon seeing the children, Govindan Kutty wept uncontrollably, hugging and kissing each one of them as if he might not see them again. Gowri chided him for being so emotional, saying *"Deiva sahayam, ningkalke onnum varilla. Kadekette ah panikere!"* ("With God's grace, nothing untoward will happen to you. Ignore that Panicker!")

After returning to Kluang, Gowri was updated daily on her husband's condition by concerned neighbours who had called up the hospital. The news was that he was on the mend and was on medication to help dissolve the blood clot and prevent further clots. On 7 March, Gowri suddenly felt the urge to visit him again with Dasu. They saw him seated on the bed at the far end of the ward, chatting away with fellow patients. He appeared to have had a haircut which took ages off his face. He was initially a bit emotional at seeing them but soon regained his composure. After a while, he got up from his bed to go outside the ward. Gowri followed him, while Dasu sat on the bed, flipping through a magazine.

Once out in the open corridor, Gowri – to her utter amazement – saw him bring out a half-cigarette that he had hidden in his hospital pyjamas.

Putting it in his mouth, he lit it quickly. Gowri became furious. "What on earth are you doing? Are you trying to kill yourself and leave us all destitute?"

He just smiled back. "I'm not taking the smoke in," he said nonchalantly. Throwing away the cigarette stub after a few puffs, he held her close. They returned after a while to his bed and saw that the lunch trolley was by then already in the ward. He appeared to be on a special diet, which looked very bland. Gowri, sitting by his side, fed him. Gowri and Dasu were the only visitors in the ward that late morning, having gained permission for the visit on the grounds that they had come from out of town. An hour or so after lunch, and after buying him a few magazines to read from the hospital bookshop, both of them took their leave.

"Promise me you won't touch cigarettes again," pleaded Gowri, tearfully holding his right hand and bringing it to her chest.

He smiled and, kissing her forehead, replied, "Don't worry. I won't. Give my love to all at home."

Mother and son were in a happy frame of mind when they left the ward. Gowri turned and gave him a lingering look again just before she stepped out of the exit. He waved at her, smiling.

## GOVINDAN KUTTY'S DEMISE

The return trip by taxi to Kluang was short. Passing by the town cinema hall, they noticed that a Malayalam movie titled *Sneha Seema* was being screened. Tamil and Hindi movies were the norm in theatres; a Malayalam movie was a rarity. Along with an intriguing premise and a usually complex plot, they assured a good dose of familiar and welcome humour. With time on their hands, mother and son decided to catch the matinee before heading back to Revertex.

After the movie, Gowri bought for Dasu a new pair of shoes that he had wanted for some time, and also some savouries for the kids at home. It must have been half past seven in the evening when they finally arrived home. They were welcomed at the front gate by their pet dog, wagging his tail and barking at first. The dog's bark quickly gave way to an eerie wailing sound, which ceased when Gowri rebuked him sharply. That night she woke up several times to the dog's wailing and an uneasy feeling took hold, one that she could not easily brush off.

The next morning, Dasu, as he would ruefully recall time and again in the years to come, was awakened by one of his siblings to the sight of his new pair of shoes, which had been bitten by their dog overnight. As if to ratify the prior omen, a couple of hours later, Ponnu's husband, accompanied by a group of other males that included his estranged neighbour, approached the house. Seeing them, Ambi ran into the kitchen to inform Gowri that "Mum, Uncle RP is coming to the house with others." With utter innocence, she added, "I think he wants to be our friend."

Hearing this, Gowri, who was making *dosha* for breakfast, instantly threw the ladle down screaming and dashed to the living room. The sight of the group was enough to confirm her worst fears, and she collapsed to the floor in a heap. Her loving husband, her Govindan Kutty, had left her and all of them. With tears uncontrollable, she repeatedly beat her head in agony, crying out to her children that they had lost their *acha* and would never see him again.

Ponnu, also crying, came around to hold Gowri and console her. Dasu, after an initial burst of intense crying, realized, almost intuitively, that he had to put up a brave front. He gathered his sobbing siblings, bringing them all together to embrace their mother, whose head he held tenderly against his own bosom. It was a poignant sight that Ponnu's husband would later recount to them, each time with tears welling in his eyes. He left the scene almost immediately to make arrangements for the body to be brought back from Johor Bahru and to inform Unnikrishnan and Kamalam about the tragic news. He asked his Brahmin colleague, Hariharan, to be on standby to conduct the funeral rites.

Wreaths began to arrive as the news spread. It must have been three in the afternoon when the coffin arrived at the house, and the preparation for the cremation ritual commenced. The Revertex manager came to offer his condolences. He went out of his way to assure Gowri that she could continue staying in the house until she had fully sorted out her matters.

The hearse left the house at around half past five that evening for the cremation grounds, where the final rites were performed under the guidance of Hariharan. Dasu, accompanied by his four brothers, set the funeral pyre alight. The next day, Dasu was led to the crematorium to collect his father's ashes. His momentary elation on account of news received earlier that day – that he had passed his senior Cambridge examination with first grade – was washed away by the reality of his father's absence. He tried to quell the turbulent emotions and imagine the pride on his father's face to no avail.

Guided by a priest, he gathered the ashes into a ritually purified urn, which he then carried in his hands for immersion in the sea at Mersing. He was accompanied there by Ponnu's husband and a fellow staff member. A tombstone was subsequently erected at the site of the cremation by well-wishers in Kluang as a mark of remembrance.

The days following Govindan Kutty's demise were pure agony for Gowri. The floodgates of her memory immediately opened, recalling the pangs of separation from her parents as a teenager, but this was a more traumatic experience that she was going through now. Waves of grief and fear gripped her as she huddled with her children at night on the one bed, wondering how she was going to face the future.

It was easy to blame a merciless God, but she couldn't bring herself to do that. It was perhaps her past karma or the collective karma of all of them that had led to this, but she decided that rather than question the inscrutable will of God or ascribe a pitiless indifference to Him, she would instead have complete faith in Him to show her the way forward. This thought process helped settle somewhat her anguish and kindled her resolve to face life anew, whatever the handicap.

Their pet dog, who was much attached to Govindan Kutty, refused to eat anything for several days, until one morning the children noticed that he too had breathed his last. Kamalam and Shankaran arrived a week later along with their family friend, V. K. Menon from Slim River. Unnikrishnan had brought along a nephew of his from Kuala Lumpur, who was introduced to the children as Mani *Ettan*. The usual practice of *adiyantharam* (death commemoration prayers and attendant feast) was not observed in the house on the sixteenth day. Instead, Gowri arranged for prayers for the departed soul of her husband to be conducted at a nearby temple and an *annadanam* (sacred tradition of offering food to the masses) by the temple authorities on that date.

Govindan Kutty (1905-1958) (*left*)
and Gowri, the young widow (*right*)

Along with her beloved husband and life companion, a large part of Gowri had died too. But widowed at the age of 42 with seven children under her care, she also knew that she had to summon the courage to soldier on. She braced herself for what was to come.

# AN UNPLEASANT SOJOURN
## (1958-1959)

# [11]

The weeks immediately following the demise of her husband were emotionally charged and filled with much introspection for Gowri. She knew that whatever decision she took would irrevocably affect her children. She had to transcend her grief and weigh the options carefully.

Her husband's insurance and provident fund dues would barely suffice to support their livelihood for much more than a few years. Her children were still of school-going age, and she flinched at the prospect of any of them turning into early breadwinners. She hailed from a *tharavad* of land-owning farmers dating back several generations, whose offspring had become English-educated graduates and professionals. She felt confident and believed whole-heartedly that, endowed with good genes and innate intelligence, her children would thrive anywhere. But if destiny were to play a cruel hand to deny this for her children, she felt intuitively that a new country like Malaya would be a better haven than her motherland.

Given the strained relationship between her kinsfolk and her own mother, returning to Puduserry was out of the question. Beyond being a transient shelter, there would be nothing else awaiting them or to build upon there. She might be ready to acquiesce for the sake of her children, but she was sure that none of them would take kindly to subjugation from her family elders. Govindan Kutty had never entertained the idea of settling down in India, even in retirement; he had made up his mind that Malaya was his new home and the only home for his children. She reflected on this, and in her mind's eye she quickly recalled the warm feeling that had first engulfed her at the sight of land from the deck of the SS *Rajula* on that fateful day at sea in 1939. And there grew in her now a new-found resolve to not only realize her late husband's dream but also to share in it.

While her husband's provident fund dues were being arranged for, the Revertex management gave Gowri in hand the full March salary and some ex gratia payment to cover the funeral expenses. She had never operated an account of her own, but now there appeared the need to open one.

Kamalam, in a letter to her, wrote to say that there was no need for her beloved *chechi* to contemplate a stay in Kluang, and that she would be coming over to take them all to Kulim within a week. Upon receiving the letter, heeding also the opinion of her close neighbours, Gowri phoned Kamalam from the estate office to say that she was inclined to stay on in Kluang. She pointed out the possibility of securing a rented house in town in close proximity to the schools. But Kamalam would not hear of it; she threatened to cut off ties if Gowri turned down her invitation to stay at Kulim.

True to her word, Kamalam arrived around the first week of April by car and started making arrangements for the shift. In order to get the children admitted to schools that would reopen soon for the second term of studies, she suggested that the shift be in two stages. She would take the three older children back with her first, leaving the others to come by train the following week with Gowri. She personally supervised the packing and audaciously told Gowri to forsake all her cooking utensils and tableware, which seemed to her unnecessary items to cart to her well-equipped home in Kulim. The unpacked items that Kamalam insisted be given away included the youngest child's bicycle, to which he was much attached – the last gift from his father. All this seemed a bit surreal for Gowri, who was still in a confused and helpless state, and Kamalam easily prevailed upon her. Gowri had by then also received Govindan Kutty's provident fund money in the form of a cheque, but Kamalam said that it was best to cash it in Kulim and loaned her the money she required to settle sundry debts.

A week after Kamalam's departure, Gowri with the rest of her children boarded the train to Slim River, where they were to stay overnight at the residence of V. K. Menon, as per the arrangements made by Kamalam. Gowri took an instant liking to her hosts for the warmth of their welcome and hospitality. The next day, Gowri and her children boarded the train again, with V. K. Menon insisting on buying the tickets, to Bukit Mertajam where they alighted. They were met at the railway station by Kamalam (the children addressed her as "Kamala Aunty") and driven straight to her home in Sungai Ular Estate, Kulim.

Kamalam's home was a rambling double-storey wooden house surrounded by a large manicured garden, at the back of which flowed a small pebbled stream. Flowering plants, ferns, and shrubs of all types grew in the garden. There were also lots of potted flowering plants which were tended personally by Kamalam, who took much pride in her cultivated garden. The children were told at the very start not to pluck any of her flowers. Given that restriction, their entry into the garden was more often an excuse to wade in the stream. They were impervious to the rubber scum and other effluents that would sometimes be seen floating in the stream, which were the run-off from the factory. On some days, there would be the inevitable smell of bacterial degradation of the rubber wafting into the house. There was no strict enforcement of environmental control in those days in most estates.

The ground floor of the house had a large kitchen with a dining table set at one end, should one wish to dine there. A little away from the kitchen were two rooms that served as quarters for the household staff. The cook stayed in one of these, while the other was used as a storeroom. The housemaid did not live in; she came in the mornings and left in the evenings. There was a washroom for the domestic workers and a laundry room. The ground floor also featured a small seated reception area directly overlooking the garden.

The main staircase led up into a spacious, well-appointed, cosy living room with plush carpets, which in turn opened out to a dining area and was linked to an adjoining study. The many windows on this floor had mosquito-proof nettings on them, but these did not in any way affect the brightness and airiness of the place. At the far end of the dining room, on either side of it, were located the two bedrooms, each fitted with an en suite bathroom and modern flushing toilet. Gowri and her four youngest children occupied the smaller of the two bedrooms. There was another staircase at the rear wall of the dining area, between the two bedrooms, which led to the ground floor. Against a side wall, before the entrance to the other bedroom, the master bedroom, was a folding bed on which Venu and Shivan slept at night. Dasu rarely stayed in the house, as he was boarding in Penang doing his sixth form (higher school certificate) at the Methodist Boys' School.

Kamalam had arranged for Venu and Shivan to be enrolled at the Bukit Mertajam High School; Ambi and Valsala at the St Anne's Convent in Kulim along with her daughter, Prabha; and Ravi and Hari at St Patrick's School in Kulim along with her son, Prakash. Kamalam took the children to the Kulim schools herself in her car, a Morris Minor, while for the schools at Bukit Mertajam, transport was via a prearranged van.

Her initiative knew no bounds. Her good command of English combined with her outgoing personality was recognized by the Kedah Women's Institute, which had admitted her as a member. This gave her the forum to venture into the sale of Pyrex dishes, in which she excelled. The boot of her car carried at all times sufficient supplies for any chance sales that might occur.

She was also a good organizer, and her home was the venue of a number of parties. Her husband was content to be a wage-earner; she ruled the roost. Her entrepreneurial spirit was in evidence when she embarked on a money-lending business. Kamalam had impressed on Gowri to place the money that she had received from the late Govindan Kutty's provident fund into her money-lending business, as the returns would be more lucrative than if it was merely kept in the banks. Naively, Gowri agreed.

# [12]

The Malayalee community from neighbouring estates, having learnt of the compassion and magnanimity that she had shown towards her elder sister, came to visit Kamalam at Sungai Ular and praised her endlessly. Over time, Gowri came to know a few of the visitors quite well, among them Dr Bhaskaran Pillai, who had a practice in Kulim town; Mrs Pillai, Dr Nambiar, and Mrs (Dr) Meenakshi Nambiar from Parit Buntar; the Poduvals, who ran a textile shop in Penang; and ASP Pillai and his good lady, who were based in Kulim. Gowri's niece Uma and her husband, Sethu, made regular visits from Bedong with their daughter, who was born in the very same month that Govindan Kutty was stricken. On such visits, the children found themselves regularly being taken out for treats by Sethu. He endeared himself readily to them with his arsenal of jokes. The children called him Sethu *Ettan*. He had a Volkswagen, and it intrigued the children much to learn that a car could have an engine at its rear.

Through Sethu, Gowri got to know of a relative of her father, one T. V. Kunjappan Nair, who was settled in Bedong, running a grocery business. He had a large family of nine children, some of whom in their later years became close to Gowri's children. One of his daughters, whom Dasu got to know well, was Mrs Sharada Balan, who rose to prominence as the head of the women's wing of the Malayan Indian Congress in the state of Kedah.

# DARKENING CLOUDS

It took some time for Gowri and her children to settle into their new environment, with its dos and don'ts imposed on them by a domineering Kamalam. The school-day mornings were rushed, as she had to drive so many of the younger children to their primary schools in Kulim and also had to ensure that the two older boys, Venu and Shivan, were on time to take the van from Kulim town to Bukit Mertajam High School. Gowri understood the stress Kamalam was under to make all this possible. Time management was crucial. Gowri was always up early, hurrying the children through their morning routine.

As Kamalam raised poultry in her ample backyard, the children were expected to eat a half-boiled egg for breakfast quite often. Everyone complied except Valsala, who had been a vegetarian since birth. It was a matter of taste, as she had Gowri's taste buds. Gowri had grown up a vegetarian for the very same reason, and so she understood her daughter's predicament. Kamalam's opinion differed: "Children have to be disciplined, taught to obey, eat what is served!"

In tears, Valsala would try to eat the half-boiled egg, but she convulsed, throwing up each time. In her determination to teach Valsala a lesson, Kamalam very often would refuse to take her to school until she ate the egg. "I will turn her into a non-vegetarian if it is the last thing I do!" Kamalam would swear as she took off in her car with the rest of the brood. Gowri had to console a sobbing child who loved school. When Gowri tried reasoning with Kamalam, she was bluntly told to keep out of it. "You should have done a better job of raising them, not given in too much to their whims and fancies!"

Finally, however, after months of trying, Kamalam had to concede defeat. The Reverend Mother of the Convent had asked to speak with her regarding Valsala's absenteeism from school. Kamalam had little choice but to explain the situation. Gowri concluded that the Reverend Mother had objected to the force-feeding of the child, especially food items that her taste buds naturally rejected. The very next day, Kamalam dropped her harassment of Valsala on the egg issue. Neither Valsala's siblings nor her cousins, Prabha and Prakash, liked to witness the morning drama that had been dragging on for months. Gowri heaved a big sigh of relief. It had been a torment to watch. Her prayers had been heard.

Kamalam also kept a tight rein on Gowri's sons. They soon grew wise to the fact that their carefree days had ended with the move from Revertex. No horsing around, teasing, and chasing. No one could be up to mischief. There was a set pattern for studies and homework. Gowri did not frown upon this form of discipline initially. In the months that followed, however, Gowri observed that Kamalam's demeanour towards her and her children was fast changing. It was as if Kamalam was beginning to resent their presence in her home. It was obvious that when inviting them to stay with her, she had not considered how the presence of her sister's family in her house would rob her and her family of their space, their privacy, and the opportunity to enjoy small family outings without the horde of her sister's children.

Gowri was wise enough to understand the situation that was unfolding, and she accepted the reasons behind it. But there was little she could do, as any step she took would interrupt her children's education. She made excuses for her sister. "She meant well. I should be patient and not fault her. It is the added stress of our presence that is causing her to behave like this," she consoled herself.

Kamalam had mood swings, too. She could go from being extremely pleasant at one moment to being downright nasty at the very next. Needless to say, Gowri bore the brunt of her sharp and caustic remarks. She started with making snide remarks about Gowri's weight. "*Chechi*, do you realize how fat you have grown through the years of child-bearing? You should have stopped with two or three, like I did. Did Govind *Ettan* and you give any thought as to how you are going to educate them past high school?"

Gowri's face burned at such harsh criticism aimed at her now dead husband. In defence, she replied, "My children are intelligent, and they have all fared well in their studies. *Ettan* always believed that there would be a lot of opportunities in this newly independent nation. With their good grades, they may obtain scholarships or government bursaries and—"

Gowri never got to finish the sentence, for Kamalam would break in and scoff, "Huh? Fat hopes! One must be realistic."

Soon, Kamalam dispensed with her maid, which served as a direct hint to Gowri to engage more actively in household chores. Gowri was by then nursing a recurrence of her umbilical hernia, but she never mentioned this to her sister. More abuse was to follow in the coming months. On a number of such occasions, after shouting at Gowri, Kamalam would suddenly leave the house in a tantrum and go to Penang to meet up with Dasu and spend some time with him. She liked him immensely, but she never revealed to him anything of the souring of relations with his mother. This enigmatic behaviour was difficult to fathom. Alone at home with her chores while the children were away at school, Gowri would weep in privacy whilst reflecting on her fate.

With the passage of time, Gowri's children also became the target of Kamalam's indiscriminate scoldings. They could not understand why their Kamala Aunty was always finding fault with their mother and with them. Venu and Shivan kept saying to Gowri, "You always said one should show respect to those older, but why is Kamala Aunty being so rude to you? You are the *chechi*, so why don't you tell her to stop bullying you?"

"I can't very well do that without openly quarrelling with her. We are living under her roof, remember. We have to be thankful. Don't show her any disrespect. Sometimes she is tired and stressed. That's why she raises her voice." One thing she had to concede was the fact that Kamalam, for all her faults, had never raised her hands to the children, even when in a rage.

"*Amme*, can't we go and live in another house? Our own house?" asked Ambi.

"We will, at the end of this school year. I promise. For the time being, study hard and be on your best behaviour at all times. Be patient and don't do anything to anger Kamala Aunty."

Of course, Venu, at 17, knew that his mother was underplaying the tense situation at home. Even as a child, he was given to expressing his opinion against what seemed unjust. She had many a time caught his eye, pleading with him to remain silent, knowing his explosive nature. His speaking up in defense of his mother or siblings would only aggravate matters.

☼

# THE SPLIT

As the months wore on, the atmosphere in the house became increasingly tense and supercharged. Gowri knew they were fast approaching breaking point. Things came to a head one day when Kamalam was shouting rudely at Gowri to shut up and Venu descended on the scene. "How dare you tell your elder sister to shut up? You shut up," he yelled at her.

Kamalam pounced back: "So, you dare to shout back at me? Wait till I tell Shankara Uncle about this."

"What is there to tell him? He is always hiding behind your skirt," countered Venu.

For Kamalam, Venu's reply was the straw that broke the camel's back. She fumed out of the place to the privacy of her own room. That night, she cooked a meal only for her family, and immediately quenched the kitchen fires by pouring water onto the burning wood. Gowri had to gather fresh splinters of wood in order to rustle up a meal for her children. Her patience and forbearance had been tested to the very limits by the emotional abuse that she had received at the hands of her sister, and she knew that the time had come for final reckoning.

The very next day, she summoned Uma and confided in her the critical state of affairs at Sungai Ular. "She must want us to leave just as much as we want to. But she won't come out and say it, because she feels it will reflect badly on her, since she invited us here in the first place. Please ask Sethu to find us a house to rent in Bukit Mertajam as quickly as possible."

Kamalam came to hear about it, and anger shook her whole frame as she pounced on Gowri. "What is this I hear? You asked Sethu to look for a house to rent in Bukit Mertajam? Why in God's name did you do that? I brought you here when your husband died for good reasons. You are ungrateful, *Chechi*! Really! Have I not fed and clothed your children?"

"Look here, Kamalam. Don't ever think I have not appreciated all you have done for us. Remember, I was all for sourcing a house to rent and staying on in Kluang town so my kids could continue their education in the same schools they were in. Losing their father was bad enough, and I always felt changing schools would be more of an upheaval. It was you who insisted, overriding my decision. I know that was an offer made out of compassion. But you never really weighed the enormity of the undertaking and consequences of that offer – how our continued presence in your home would rob you and your family of your privacy, and how burdensome it might turn out to be."

"*Chechi*, I never said you were a burden, did I?"

"No, you didn't say it per se, but I have sensed this in your demeanour, well before a year was up. It is written all over your face. Don't try to deny it. You are forever in a foul mood. You have been harsh in your criticisms of me, making unwarranted comments and shouting at me at every turn, overlooking the fact I am your *chechi*. You have shown no respect for me at all. I have now become your regular punching bag. I bore it all only because I thought you were under tremendous stress and were releasing your pent-up frustrations upon me. I know you regret having brought us over. We have done nothing to warrant such anger in you. It is our continued presence here in your home that is the root cause, not what I or my children do. You have to accept that fact. Being older, I kept forgiving you, making allowances for your stress-related outbursts and rudeness. It has been affecting my children. It is such a tense atmosphere here in your home now. Not healthy for my children or yours. I would have moved out earlier, but I did not want to interrupt the studies of my older children, especially Venu. He is sitting for his Cambridge school certificate exams."

"And how do you think you will manage?" Kamalam snapped. "You are not capable of managing your finances. All you did when Govind *Ettan* was alive was just cook and wash. I shudder to think what would have happened had I left you to manage on your own in Kluang. You probably would have had to ask me to come to rescue you all!"

"I may not have a college education like you, Kamalam, but I am not a fool. You don't give me much credit for anything, not even parenting skills! There is a saying: 'You never know how strong you are until being strong is the only option you have left.' I am capable of bringing up my children. Two will soon be adults. I will manage, Kamalam. Have no doubts about that. I will make sure they achieve the dreams my husband had for them."

"Well then, if you are so confident, why wait at all? Just leave!"

"Don't be mad, Kamalam. It is for the best. You are my sister, and I have watched you turn into someone I don't recognize anymore. You and your family need your own space and privacy in your own home. I understand that, I truly do. Let us not part ways with misunderstanding. Let us be happy, each in our space, our own home." The only response Gowri got was a loud slam of Kamalam's bedroom door as she walked away in a huff. Speechless, perhaps, as the analytical truth of her *chechi*'s words sunk deep.

The very next day, Gowri summoned Uma and Sethu to come at once and liberate them from their misery and to find immediately a house for rental in Bukit Mertajam. And, importantly also, to secure the return of the adjusted balance from the sum of money she had entrusted to Kamalam.

Sethu, who had been hearing of the turn of events at Sungai Ular, arrived very early the next morning. The children had not left for school. He went straight up the stairs to Gowri's room – ignoring Kamalam, who was standing at the door. Working herself into a frenzy, Kamalam charged into Gowri's room after a few moments and shouted at Sethu, asking him to leave. "Who are you to interfere?" she asked, but Sethu cut her short and ticked her off for the cruelty she was meting out to her widowed sister. She tried to interrupt him many times: "You have heard only one side. Don't forget, I brought you into the family."

Sethu stood his ground. "She also happens to be my aunt through marriage. I have come to take them all to Bedong. They don't need to suffer here any longer." Shankaran, who was getting ready to go to work and hearing the commotion had also arrived on the scene, was but a silent witness to what was being said. Sethu continued, "I want to see the accounts, the money that belongs to her."

Kamalam was caught by surprise, as she had utilized part of the money as start-up capital for her new business venture, a kindergarten. Shankaran, reading Kamalam's face, knew something was amiss. He told Sethu he would look into it and contact them soon. Sethu then led Gowri and her two bewildered youngest children down the stairs. The sisters were parting with emotional bitterness in their hearts.

Just before the descent on the stairs, Gowri turned her gaze towards Shankaran, her husband's own cousin and the person she had handpicked to be her brother-in-law. Their moist eyes met, but the supine look that he wore conveyed his helplessness. Sethu told the other children he would be back soon and asked them to assemble their belongings quickly. The children did not mind missing school, as the annual December school holidays were just around the corner – except for Venu, who was in the fifth form preparing for the imminent, all-important, senior Cambridge examination. In Penang, Dasu, who was shielded from news about this disturbing turn of events at Kulim, was also about to sit for his higher school certificate examination. But the news got to him soon enough through Sethu's relatives in Penang, Mr and Mrs T. Shankaran. He liked his aunt Kamalam very much, but he was both shattered and embittered upon learning of this side of her character. He knew in his heart he would find it difficult to forgive her even if the sisters one day reconcile.

# BUILDING LIFE ANEW
# (1960-1969)

Sprouting broad bean
*Source: https://www.flickr.com/photos/wheatfields/sets/72157605205902240/*
*photo by Christian Guthler in My Vegpatch, page 2,*
*and is licensed under CC BY 2.0*

# [13]

Sethu was, in every sense, a man of action. Bukit Mertajam High School was a boarding school, and he quickly arranged a place there for Venu so that his studies would not be interrupted. From his enquiries for residential houses in Bukit Mertajam, he gathered that a new housing estate was coming up at the foot of Berapit Hill. With Gowri's consent, he made an instant booking for a terraced, single-storey house. As an interim measure, he managed to find them another single-storey terraced house for rental in the same vicinity. The rental was 55 Malaysian dollars per month.

Gowri and the children moved into the rented house at 1475 Berapit Road after a couple of weeks with Uma and Sethu at Bedong, during which time Sethu and Shankaran sorted out the financials with Unnikrishnan, who had been summoned from his nephew's place in Kuala Lumpur, as mediator. Unnikrishnan had never taken to Kamalam from day one because of her acid tongue, and he was content to stay away from his brother. He decided to stay with Gowri and her children at the rented premises for a while before he returned to Kuala Lumpur.

Dasu joined them as soon as his examinations were over. While awaiting his results, he decided to seek a temporary job as a teacher. He found one at St Mark's Afternoon School in Butterworth in January 1960, where he taught until May before finding a teaching position at the Jit Sin High School in Bukit Mertajam itself. This was a Chinese medium school, but he was tasked to teach general science, mathematics, and history. The classes were in English. Seeking a more permanent job as a breadwinner for his family, he applied to join the police force as an assistant superintendent of police (ASP) cadet officer on the strength of his HSC qualification. The application was lodged though their family friend, ASP Pillai.

The youngest two boys, Ravi and Hari, were emplaced in Stowell School in Bukit Mertajam, while Shivan remained at the Bukit Mertajam High School, having entered the fifth form. The girls, Ambi and Valsala, who were in the third and first form, respectively, shifted their schooling from Kulim to St Margaret's Convent in Bukit Mertajam.

All the children had to walk to their schools for almost a year until Gowri arranged trishaw transport for them. The closest bus stop was some four hundred yards away at the Tanah Liat junction. Here, the public transport buses plying between Alma and Bukit Mertajam town centre could, in principle, be availed of, but they would hardly stop when hailed, being full of passengers. The journey to school of just over a mile from Tanah Liat was a long, arduous walk for the children, carrying their heavy books in rattan school bags which were de rigueur purely on account of being the only variety then available.

On stormy mornings, they ventured out wearing raincoats and covering their school bags with a wrap-around plastic. It was difficult to keep an umbrella unfurled under those conditions because of the strong gusts of wind. They would thus often arrive at school with squelchy canvas shoes and also partially wet clothes. In the afternoons, they often had to brave the scorching sun as they returned home. Gowri's heart would melt upon seeing them wearily trudging in. Some of Gowri's neighbours were teachers whom she subsequently came to know. They would, during heavy downpours, go out of their way to offer the children lifts to school in their cars. This gesture was very much appreciated by Gowri.

Towards the middle of the year, Dasu bought himself a bicycle on hire purchase. Most times, he would let Shivan use it. Soon Ravi and Hari enthusiastically learned to ride the bicycle and won the confidence of Gowri to let them ride to school for their physical education classes in the afternoons.

# IT TAKES FAITH ... AND WILLPOWER

Sitting on the bed alone in her room while the children were all away, Gowri would often gaze at the portrait of her late husband and roll out her anguish.

"Why did you have to leave me all alone? How am I going to manage? How will I educate our children? How could you leave me so helpless like this?"

Her sadness was particularly intense one afternoon. She could sense no answers to the questions she had been hurling at her late husband. She was inwardly exposing her real fears. The bravado with Kamalam didn't mean anything. None of her husband's relatives in India had even bothered to write to her after his death. She had no emotional pillar whatsoever to lean on, save her Guruvayurappan. Reaching for her locket, she snapped it open to reveal the image of her beloved Krishna. A teardrop fell on Him, which she quickly wiped. She pressed the locket to her forehead and cried.

After a while, the window curtain in her room fluttered. She felt a strong gust of wind in the room. A green leaf floated in and landed on her. She picked it up and saw it as a sign from the Almighty. "Yes, my Krishna has heard me. I know that. He will show me the way," she muttered to herself. Her confidence partially restored, she wiped her face with the edge of her saree and went to place the leaf at the lotus feet of Lord Krishna at the altar. Bowing to Him, she then took a pinch of *bhasmam* (holy ash) from the altar and applied it to her forehead.

Later in the evening, she mentioned this incident to her children, adding, "We have nothing much now, my dear children. But with Guruvayurappan's blessings, we shall work towards our dreams and achieve them. I know that we will." Her lips curved into an irresistible smile. The children smiled back at her, happy to see their mother in a positive frame of mind.

## EDUCATE THEM, I WILL

Among Gowri's closest neighbours were the Kumarans, who were regular visitors to her house, and Mrs Thiagarajan, from whom Gowri learnt to read Tamil. She subsequently became an avid reader of subscribed Tamil magazines that came from India. She also read English novels by the score, including some classics, which Ambi and Valsala borrowed for her from their school library.

The Kumarans had three children, two girls and a boy. Their eldest daughter, a teacher, was married to Balan, who himself was a teacher while still enrolled as an external student for the Part 1 of his Bachelor of Laws degree from the United Kingdom. At his prompting, Gowri's eldest son, Dasu, enrolled for an external Bachelor of Science degree from the University of London. One day around the middle of 1960, Balan rushed into the house excitedly to point out an advertisement in the newspaper calling for applications to the Colombo Plan scholarship for undergraduate studies in science, engineering and medicine. He helped Dasu draft the application to the Ministry of Education.

Meanwhile, Venu was already pursuing his higher school certificate at the Penang Free School and had expressed an interest in a medical career. Gowri was seriously contemplating sending him to India. She sought the assistance of her cousin Jayam to find Venu a place in a suitable college to do his pre-university and pre-medical studies. A place at Madras Christian College was found, and around April 1960 Venu set sail for India, with all hopes riding on him to do well and later become the financial anchor for the family as a doctor.

Venu carried a letter from Gowri to Thanggan, the loyal head of the family of tillers of her ancestral land. Thanggan and his family had become the new landowners as a result of the Kerala Land Reform Acts that were set in motion in 1950 by the Communist government of the state. Thanggan, she recalled, had been generous in paying her *tharavad* a fair rental or *kanapattam*, both in kind and cash, although Gowri never took her share which she assigned entirely to her elder sister Saraswati. In her letter, she enquired whether Thanggan could help provide some subsistence allowance to Venu for at least a year. As this meant Venu seeking the intermediacy of Bala Menon at Pudussery, she asked Venu to be discreet about the visit and not to create a storm. Venu's reply was predictable. "No one can prevent me seeing my *muthessi* and my *ammaman* (maternal uncle). It is my right. If any of your relatives question me on the visit, I know how to handle that!"

A couple of months into college, Venu visited Pudussery. Kamakshi Amma was bowled over with joy seeing her grandson. And so was his uncle Bala Menon and his aunt, Vilasini. Venu spent three days at Pudussery. On the second day, hearing from Kamakshi Amma that she had on a couple of occasions tasted *matthi meen* (sardine fish) curry and enjoyed it, Venu quietly arranged for a fish curry meal with her in the kitchen when Bala

Menon was out of the house. Grandmother and grandson thoroughly enjoyed their togetherness.

While in Pudussery, Venu met up with Thanggan. Reading Gowri's letter and sensing her desperation, his eyes welled up with tears. He told Venu, "Please convey my respects to *thamburatti* (honorific title conveying respect and esteem for a lady) and tell her it shall be done." Then, withdrawing momentarily into his room, he came back with a bundle of cash. Giving it to Venu, he said, "Please let me know when you need more. I shall send you by money order." Venu thanked him profusely, and promptly conveyed the news to his mother by letter. Gowri was very much touched by Thanggan's generosity.

Around June 1960, Dasu was called for an interview in Kuala Lumpur at the Public Services Commission with regard to his application for the Colombo Plan scholarship. The panel of interviewers quizzed him on the financial status of his family, his decision to enrol for the external degree, and his aptitude for teaching based on his work experience. He felt that the interview went well.

# GRIHA PRAVESH

Towards the end of 1960, Gowri's house at Lot 1663, Jalan (Road) Chow Boon Khye off Jalan Berapit was completed. The excitement was irrepressible – not only for Gowri but for all her children. They finally had a house they could call their very own.

At a prescribed hour one auspicious morning – chosen as per the almanac – before any house items were moved in, Gowri performed the traditional *Griha Pravesh* or housewarming ceremony. This involved a simple ritual of milk being boiled-over in a new saucepan, symbolically meant to usher abundance into the new home. A new coal stove was brought in for the purpose. As soon as the milk boiled over, a coconut was broken outside the front door, symbolically to keep at bay all obstacles. The milk was then sweetened and offered first to God (in the form of various deities, with Lord Vishnu and Goddess Lakshmi being prominent among them) in a puja set up in an east-facing direction to honour the sunrise. Following the puja, portions of the milk were given as *prasadam* (food sanctified by the Lord) to all the family members, including Uma, Sethu, and Unnikrishnan, who were present. The *Griha Pravesh* has its origins in the Atharva Veda[6] (3.13.7-9; 5000 BC).

The family moved into the house in mid-January 1961. Unnikrishnan had by then left for Kuala Lumpur. The front door of the semi-detached house led into a rectangular living/dining room, to the right of which were two bedrooms. The living area was partitioned by a wooden screen behind which was a dining table with chairs, which also doubled up as a study area.

An archway at the rear wall of the dining room led to a modest kitchen which barely accommodated the addition of a small round table with stools at which the family usually dined. The kitchen stepped down to a utility area, where the bathroom and lavatory were. This section featured a small, open-air well which was covered by means of a pulley-driven awning on rainy days.

Gowri's Berapit house fronted by the neem tree

---

6   One of four Vedas which represent the religious tradition of the Hindu religion, the philosophy of which is derived from the Upanishads. The Vedas are a treasure-house of knowledge extending beyond metaphysics, spirituality, or philosophy into the depths and subtleties of the supraphysical world. They form, along with other auxiliary branches, the corpus of ancient India's view of the universe and of life.

The rear garden featured a vegetable patch. The front lawn also straddled the right side of the house. Here the children planted allamanda, shrub roses, and the inevitable *thulasi* (holy basil) and curry leaf shrubs favoured by most Indian households. Several potted ferns and flowering plants also adorned the garden. On the street, just before the driveway to one side, there would in time stand a tall, shady tree, which had as its humble beginning a neem sapling the children had planted.

# [14]

No sooner had they moved into the house than word was received that Dasu had been successful at his interview. He was offered the Colombo Plan scholarship to read for an honours degree in chemistry followed by a diploma in education in Australia, subject to his passing the medical examination.

Although initially elated, Dasu was suddenly gripped with the fear of leaving his mother and the rest of the family alone, as Venu was also not there. Acceptance of the scholarship award further meant that he would have to be away for at least five years from his family, albeit with the provision for a visit home at the end of three years. Both his mother and Sethu counselled that this was a once-in-a-lifetime, God-sent opportunity that he shouldn't pass up. Shivan, who had just completed his Cambridge school certificate, could work as a temporary teacher for a while.

This sentiment was echoed by other well-wishers, including the Kumarans and the Nambiars from Parit Buntar, who happened to be visiting their *chechi*, as they did from time to time. Sethu and his relative in Penang, Mr T. Shankaran, generously agreed to stand as guarantors for the scholarship contract that Dasu duly signed. Finally, in February of 1961, Dasu bid a tearful adieu to his family and boarded the long flight to Australia from Kuala Lumpur.

This was Dasu's first-ever flight. The aircraft was a Qantas Super Constellation bound for Perth via Jakarta. There were other Colombo Plan scholars on that flight; for some, Perth was the study destination, as they had already secured a priori admission on their own at the University of Western Australia. Following an overnight stay at Perth, Dasu and others yet awaiting placements at university boarded another plane for Sydney, where an orientation programme was conducted at a hotel close to Bondi

Beach. For Dasu and his fellow travelling scholars, Bondi furnished a first-ever glimpse of bikini-clad women. He was to write home about this, and also about the relatively warmer weather that greeted him a week later when he was sent to the University of Queensland at Brisbane for his studies.

## CULTURAL POTPOURRI

Gowri found the absence of her elder two boys unnerving at first, but the demands of establishing a new home began to occupy her attention. Her next-door neighbours were a Chinese couple with a child who kept much to themselves. In fact, the majority of residents in the new housing area were Chinese who spoke the Hokkien and Teochew dialects. Living amongst the largely Chinese community, Gowri was interested to observe their customs, particularly their noisy festivals. All of their festivals were based on the lunar calendar, with the first lunar month standing out as prominent: Chinese New Year (first day), the Jade Emperor's Birthday (ninth day), Chap Goh Meh (fifteenth evening). The entire seventh lunar month would be devoted to the Hungry Ghost Festival. The eighth lunar month (fifteenth day) would see the start of the Lantern Festival, a sort of harvest festival. This was also called the Mooncake Festival because of the popular tradition of eating mooncakes during this occasion.

Fireworks and dragon dances were a common sight during the Chinese New Year, and most shops which were Chinese-owned closed for two weeks. The family had to make sure they stocked enough provisions for the period from the nearby sundry shops. Gowri managed to arrange for credit with one such shop, with full settlement of bills at month's end. This was a help, as it allowed the family to manage carefully their finances. The shop was in her previous rented house, which had been converted into a grocery store by its new tenant, Ah Hock. He was an extremely nice and understanding person and got on well with Gowri's family. He would give the younger boys, Ravi and Hari, *angpow* (monetary gift in a red envelope) during Chinese New Year, a tradition practiced by the Chinese diaspora the world over. Often the amount of money in the envelope ends with an even digit.

As his business grew, Ah Hock bought the rented premises, as he considered it "a lucky house" that Gowri had vacated for him. He soon bought himself a car. Over time, Gowri prevailed upon him to use it as a hired taxi to transport her children to and from school.

For the Chinese community at large, the New Year's Eve reunion dinner is a must, as it represents the first big family gathering of the season. Custom demands that they wear red clothes and fling open the doors and windows of the house at midnight to let the old year out. The more traditional among them would also honour the departed by placing food and burning incense at their home altars. The celebrations go on for fifteen days, but much of the focus is on the first three days; the last day (Chap Goh Mei) is celebrated with much enthusiasm and thunderous fireworks.

Gowri would visit her immediate neighbour to extend greetings and partake of the snacks offered, which invariably included luscious mandarin oranges sourced from China and home-grown peanuts from the Menglembu district in Perak. Most hotels would have their Chinese restaurants fully packed. A favourite dish served before other dishes was the *yee sang*, which is a sort of fish salad, although a vegetarian version of this has also come into vogue and become very popular in the country. The salad contains shredded radish, carrots, cucumber, turnip, green apples, unripe mangoes, and jackfruit mixed together with pomelo wedges, crackers, toasted groundnuts, and toasted sesame seeds. The whole is then emptied into a large bowl and combined with the *yee sang* sauce – a combination of plum sauce, honey, and lime juice into which a bit of pepper and some spices are sprinkled. All the diners stand up and, using their chopsticks, twirl the ingredients of the *yee sang* and lift portions of it high in the air with a shout of "*loh hey*" ("toss high"), and them release them to fall back into the bowl. This act symbolizes the prosperity toss and is repeated several times before the *yee sang* is eaten.

Gowri had just one Malay neighbour several houses away down the road. Muhammad Rashid was his name, and he was a physical education instructor at Bukit Mertajam High School. His wife, Hanum, was a homemaker who took a special liking to Gowri. They would both come over for a vegetarian meal whenever invited by Gowri, often together with her other close neighbours when celebrating the birthday of one of her children.

She was also close to the Nathans, an elderly couple who lived in the town. They were aware of Gowri's struggle to make ends meet and would generously loan her money whenever she needed it in a crisis. Gowri would pay them back with interest at the first opportunity, but they often waived the interest, especially for smaller sums. Gowri's only source of income until Shivan landed a temporary job in 1962 was the biweekly remittance she received from Dasu in Australia, who dutifully sent a portion of his unspent scholarship stipend towards her household expenses. The Australian environment had not dented his filial sensitivities.

Through the introduction of the Nathans, Gowri cultivated the friendship of Dr Siva, who ran a successful general practice in the town. He was to be their family doctor for many years to come.

Gowri, like most other Hindus of Kerala origin, rarely observed Deepavali, the lunar festival of lights, although she would use the occasion to make *murukku* (a savoury crunchy snack), vegetable fritters, and loads of *mithais* (sweets) – prominent among them *boondi* and *rava ladoos*, *mysore pak*, ribbon *pakoda* and coconut burfis, which the children simply loved. They would all visit the Thiagarajans on Deepavali day to partake of their festive board. And so would the other neighbours, invited or otherwise. This open house concept of participating in each other's cultural celebrations was soon recognized and applauded as a vital element in fostering tolerance among the major races in the country.

An important festival that is celebrated by the majority of the population in the country is the Muslim festival of Eid al-Fitr, referred to locally as Hari Raya Aidilfitri. It is the festival of the breaking of the fast at the end of Ramadan, the Islamic holy month of dawn-to-dusk fasting. The Islamic calendar is a lunar calendar, with each month beginning with the sighting of the new moon. Because the lunar calendar is about eleven days shorter than the solar calendar used elsewhere, Hari Raya Aidilfitri moves each year. There is less such movement with Deepavali, which is based on the Hindu lunar/solar calendar; the festival normally falls in either October or November.

Except for Valsala, who disliked meat, the children would unfailingly attend the open-house party that the Rashids would throw on the first day of Hari Raya. They would dig into the sumptuous dishes of *ketupat*, *rendang, lontong,* and satay, and thereafter into the *dodol, kueh lapis,* and *wajik* desserts. The most anticipated festival dishes are the *ketupat* and the *rendang.* The *ketupat* is a glutinous rice dumpling wrapped in a woven palm-leaf pouch and steamed. It is often served with chicken satay and sauced with a crunchy peanut dressing and chunked cucumber. The *rendang* is an aromatic caramelized meat (normally beef) curry made with a variety of herbs and spices that is slow-cooked in coconut milk. Before Gowri's children left the house, Hanum would pack some sweetmeats for their vegetarian mother and sister.

Malaysian Festival dishes: *yee sang* ingredients (*left*)
and *ketupat* with chicken satay and peanut sauce (*right*)

Gowri had no regrets in choosing Berapit as a location for her house, as she really was blessed with some wonderful neighbours. She would always have company, and it was not lost on her that she could also count on them for immediate help if she ever needed it. Thrust into widowhood barely four years earlier, she needed the companionship of an understanding community around her. Berapit seemed to her to be that place. She knew that she had made the right choice. Indeed, some of her neighbours, sensing her financial plight, asked her if she minded giving their young children tuition in English. Gowri appreciated their gesture and actually enjoyed her tutoring role.

# [15]

With Dasu and Venu yet to enter working life, the breadwinner's role fell squarely on the shoulders of Shivan. Lodging with Uma and Sethu, he got a position as a temporary teacher at the Bedong English School, a private school, in early 1962. Ambi, who was studying at St Margaret's Convent in Bukit Mertajam, had by then entered the fifth form. She was an extrovert, unlike her sister, Valsala, and had a good mix of friends of all races, some of whom she would bring home for a social get-together.

One day, Ambi told Gowri that she wanted to be a Christian. Gowri gently took her aside, sat her down, and said, "Look here, *molu*. If God had wanted you to be a Christian, you would have been born into a Christian family. You are born a Hindu. Besides, all religions are the same. They teach you to pray to God, be good, and not do wrong things or sin in any way. They teach you to lead a righteous life. As a Hindu, you are not barred from going to church or praying to Christ. Hinduism is a beautiful religion that gives you freedom to pray in whichever way you want to because, after all, there is but one Almighty God, whose divinity is in all of us and can be sensed if we are capable of setting our minds to the state of pure consciousness."

Upon reflection, Ambi felt that her mother was right: she could go to church with her Christian friends to pray to Lord Jesus and Mary and still be a Hindu.

There was another occasion when Ambi told Gowri that she wanted to become a nun. Realizing that this was nothing more than the whimsical fancy of a teenager, and knowing only too well her fashion-conscious daughter, Gowri's reply was deliberately curt. "Seeing as you won't be needing your lovely dresses anymore as a nun, shall we give them away?" The subject never came up again.

# GOWRI'S DREAM

One evening well after dinner, Ambi was at her study table when she heard Gowri gasping for breath with a sudden attack of laryngospasm. She dashed to her mother's aid, thumping the back of Gowri's chest repeatedly. It was truly alarming, as Gowri didn't seem to recover and continued gasping for breath. She was turning blue and staggered as if she was going to collapse. Ambi screamed, and Valsala and Ravi rushed from the bedroom. Three hands went *thump, thump, thump* vigorously on Gowri's back. Their faces mirrored their fear and anguish. *"Amme! Amme! Amme!"* they cried.

Finally, a breath escaped into Gowri's throat and her body shuddered. The children's tear-stained faces broke into smiles of relief. Gowri flung her arms around them, enveloping them. Hari was fast asleep in his bed, completely oblivious to what had transpired.

The following morning at breakfast, Gowri said to her children, "I had a dream last night. I saw your *acha*."

"Really?" cried Ambi. She had always considered herself her father's favourite child – for after all, she, more than the others, carried his features. *"Acha* never comes to me in my dreams. He hasn't so far," she said wistfully. "I miss him so much. What did he say?"

"He said he misses us too. He also told me that he is still looking out for us from up above. He said that in the world where he is now, with those others who had come there after death, they have a way of knowing who is going to cross over – that is, who is about to die. It seems the face of that person appears in a flash of light. He said he saw my face and so knew I was going to die. He said he pleaded with God to spare me, not take me just yet. 'My children are too young to be parentless. Please don't bring her in.' He said that that is why I was spared. I was supposed to have breathed my last when I had my laryngospasm last night."

Ambi burst into tears hearing the narration of her mother's dream, and looking upwards to the heavens said, "Thank you, *Acha*, thank you."

# A SAILOR WENT TO SEA

Shivan continued his teaching tenure at his school for some two years while privately studying sixth form in the arts stream. It was then that he heard of a recruitment drive by the Malaysian Navy for officer-level training in England. Gowri had reservations when Shivan mentioned his interest in applying for this, as being in the navy meant to her a prolonged absence of her son from home. Venu, who was then back home on vacation, assuaged her fears and said a naval career would suit Shivan's physical stature and temperament. Furthermore, the career prospects were better than in the army. An application was duly made, and success came quickly. In early 1963, Shivan left for the Brittania Royal Naval College in Dartmouth, England, with the blessings of the family.

Meanwhile, Ambi, having finished her Cambridge school certificate at the end of 1962, had landed a temporary teacher's post at the Bedong Government Primary School. She was now the sole breadwinner, as her brother, while on naval training, would only be receiving a subsistence allowance. She too stayed with Uma and Sethu, and worked for two years helping to support the family until fate decided for her the next course of action.

In early October, Sethu received news that Uma's mother had passed away. Sethu immediately sent his car to fetch Gowri to Bedong before breaking the news to Uma. Uma flew to India to meet up with her father and found him to be emotionally distraught. He was dependent on Saraswati, and she was all to him. Little did Uma realize that he too would be laid to eternal rest within a period of four months. Uma and her four siblings took consolation in the fact that their parents were a truly loving couple, inseparable in death as in life.

Valsala, who was two years behind Ambi in age, completed her Cambridge school certificate in 1964. She was selected the following year to read for the sixth form at St Xavier's Institution in Penang, as there were no such courses in schools in and around Bukit Mertajam. This meant boarding in Penang for two years, which immediately presented a financial problem. The family not only couldn't afford it, but they also badly needed extra income. Her mother, Gowri, had started giving tuition to preschool children in the evenings at their home. But the earnings were marginal.

Valsala was also mindful that Ravi would be finishing school a mere year later and that her mother was planning to send him to India. She recalled her mother saying somewhat apologetically that the boys ought to be given preference for pursuing their higher education. She reasoned that they would one day, as menfolk, have to become the principal breadwinners in their own families, while the girls as wives would be spared this obligatory onus in the eyes of society. It was a sacrifice Valsala was willing to make. She decided to forego the sixth form opportunity and applied instead for a temporary teacher's post at her alma mater, St Margaret's Convent in Bukit Mertajam.

Whatever ambitions the girls had entertained for university education, they were forced to place them on the back burner, given the circumstances at the time. They decided to join the teaching profession, and both submitted their applications to the Malayan Teachers' Training College (MTTC) in 1966. This would normally have meant leaving home, but luckily for them there was an acute shortage of teachers in the country then, and the MTTC being unable to cope, the education ministry had decided to introduce regional training centres (RTC).

Under the RTC scheme, trainee teachers would teach students four days at school, attend lectures on Fridays and Saturdays at the centres, and on Sundays attend to assignments as well as prepare their school lessons. The centre which Valsala attended was at Penang, while Ambi was assigned to the centre at Sungai Petani in Kedah. Both girls could not avail themselves of school holidays for two years, so intensive was their programme. They endured it, as this was a case of survival. They were, however, gratified by receipt of a salary instead of the subsistence allowance they would have otherwise got had they enrolled as full-time trainees at MTTC. For the training, Ambi was posted to Bedong Secondary School, while Valsala continued at St Margaret's Convent. Both graduated as teachers after two years in the strenuous programme.

Dasu, who was studying at the University of Queensland, came home on vacation in early December 1963. The country had by then become a larger geographical unit: Malaysia. Formally established on 16 September 1963, the Federation of Malaysia incorporated the British protectorates of North Borneo (now Sabah), Sarawak, and Singapore. These territories, which were granted independence on 31 August 1963, had earlier given their assent to join the Malaysian union and duly signed the Cobbold Report of the Commission of Enquiry established to ascertain their stand on the proposed union. Peninsular Malaya came to be called West Malaysia, and the territories of Sabah and Sarawak, East Malaysia.

There was opposition to the formation of Malaysia from both the Philippines and Indonesia, even when the idea was first mooted by Tunku Abdul Rahman in 1961, but when the union became a reality, Indonesia embarked upon a confrontation (essentially an undeclared war). This was largely confined to skirmishes along the border of East Malaysia with Indonesia on the island of Borneo (Kalimantan). The confrontation was to last three years. It ended when President Sukarno lost power to the Indonesian military led by General Suharto in 1966, after a failed attempt by the Communist Party of Indonesia to stage a coup d'état.

In the aftermath of the confrontation, which economically affected both Malaysia and Indonesia, it was recognized that there was a need for an organization of nations of South East Asia that could deal with reducing intra-regional tensions and promoting stability through domestic socio-economic development, whilst also limiting competition among them. The Association of Southeast Asian Nations (ASEAN) was thus born on August 8, 1967; its five founding members were Indonesia, Thailand, Malaysia, Singapore, and the Philippines.[7]

## UNMITIGATED TENACITY

Dasu arrived home in the first week of December. He was overjoyed to be reunited with his mother for the duration of his university vacation. He was somewhat surprised to learn that the assassination of John F. Kennedy

---

[7]     ASEAN has since expanded to include Brunei Darussalam, Laos, Cambodia, Vietnam, and Burma, and emerged as an influential regional grouping. One of its major projects in the making is the establishment of the ASEAN Economic Community, which aims to integrate South East Asia's diverse economies, a region with 600 million people, and a combined gross domestic product of USD 2.4 trillion.

on 22 November had evoked much sympathy and emotion in the country. It was still the centrepiece of conversation between Gowri and her friends. He attributed this to the wide international coverage that the event had sparked. Nevertheless, he was curious to know why Gowri was so moved by the tragedy.

"Haven't you been reading the news in Australia? The family has been facing one tragedy after another. He had lost two children at birth, and now with his death, his wife and two children face another round of tragedy. The world is poorer for his loss."

"How so?", Dasu wanted to know.

"He was in my eyes a world statesman. Look at his efforts in wanting to end racial segregation in his country. He understood the aspirations of the developing world and reached out for world peace through his Peace Corps initiative. I actually had the chance to meet one of the Peace Corps volunteers at the Government Rest House the other day. I was impressed by her desire to serve our community. I have read that he was also fighting for a fair immigration policy for his own country which he had categorically described as 'a nation of immigrants'. More great things were expected of him. He should not have lost his life."

Dasu had momentarily forgotten that his mother was a voracious reader, and she certainly seemed up to speed with current affairs.

Reflecting on family matters, Dasu appreciated the sacrifice that Shivan, Ambi, and Valsala were making and promised his mother that it would be his duty to get his sisters married to well-placed spouses upon his return. He was amazed to learn how his mother had managed to earn for his brother, Venu, not only a place in the medical school in India following clearance of his pre-university course but also subsequently a scholarship to complete his medical programme. Listening to her, he couldn't help but admire her for her initiative and tenacity in writing personal notes on both occasions to Shrimati Lakshmi Menon, who was the minister of external affairs in India over the period 1962–1967.

In her first letter to Shrimati Lakshmi Menon in 1962, she explained her plight as a widow with seven children to rear. In search of a future, she had sent one of her sons to her motherland to study, and she hoped that he could be granted an opportunity to do medicine, as only limited medical seats were available for foreign students at universities in India. Lakshmi Menon obliged by securing Venu a nominated seat under the quota for foreign domiciled students of Indian origin at Bangalore Medical College. Venu lived up to his end of the bargain by passing his premedical examination with distinction. In her second letter, a year later, she beseeched Lakshmi Menon's help again for some financial assistance for Venu by way of a bursary or scholarship to enable him to complete his medical studies. She was immensely gratified that Lakshmi Menon arranged for this as well, with Venu receiving the application forms for an Indian Government Cultural Scholarship direct from New Delhi.

Dasu left for Australia in late January 1964 to resume his studies. He sensed Gowri's sadness a few days before his departure and was relieved when Sethu and Uma decided to send their daughter Priyadarshini (Priya for short) to live with her *ammama* (grandmother or grand-aunt; alternative to *muthessi*) while attending to her kindergarten studies at St Margaret's Convent. Priya's presence, he knew, would be a soothing remedy for his mother. And, indeed, it was. Doting on her grand-niece, Gowri felt the time seemed to fly. She would accompany the child to the convent and back on the cycle trishaw. As the years went by, Priya proved to be her constant companion when visiting her neighbours or shopping in the town. Priya went on to stay with Gowri until she completed her standard five in 1968.

Uma and Sethu would regularly visit Priya on weekends. As Gowri refused to entertain monetary aid for Priya's stay with her, Uma and Sethu resorted to assistance in kind through stocking up Gowri's larder on a biweekly basis.

# [16]

In July 1964 came news of ethnic clashes between the predominantly Chinese and the minority Malay segments of the population of Singapore. This occurred during a processional march marking the birthday of Prophet Muhammad. It was alleged that this clash was instigated by Indonesian provocateurs and that its origins lay at the heart of the confrontation. However, it was widely acknowledged that the Malays in Singapore unequivocally wished to have a similar privileged status as enjoyed by the Bumiputras (native peoples) in Peninsular Malaysia.

The racial tensions eased after a few days, but the clash erupted again in September. This, combined with the strained relations between Singapore's ruling People's Action Party (PAP) and Peninsular Malaysia's ruling Alliance Party and, in particular its major component, the United Malays National Organization, led to Singapore's expulsion from the Federation of Malaysia in August 1965. Many on both sides of the Causeway rallied behind the news of the separation, which was simultaneously announced in Kuala Lumpur and Singapore, with relief. But the announcement was tinged with some anguish for Singapore's Prime Minister, the astute and dynamic Lee Kuan Yew, who had long been an advocate of the union of the two territories built on a vision of "Malaysian Malaysia" with political equality for all its citizens. As it transpired, the ethnically-sensitive political mindset of the day was vehemently opposed to upsetting the apple cart on the matter of special rights granted in the Constitution of Malaysia for indigeneous peoples. Given the economically privileged position of the Chinese in Malaya, and with strong hints of PAP wanting to expand its base into Malaya, the call for political equality for all citizens was viewed with considerable alarm by Malay politicians. They saw it as a threat to the assured Malay political control over the state and, therefore, dismissed it as an untenable proposition. Racial tensions in Singapore, however, did not ease with the separation, but continued to simmer, and, not unexpectedly, spilled over to Peninsular Malaysia whose dark chapter was yet to be written.

## VENU'S BOMBSHELL

Gowri followed these political events somewhat keenly on her new television set, but not for long as she was thrown completely out of her complacency by news she received from the dean of the medical faculty at Bangalore Medical College. Venu had withdrawn from his course to commit himself fully to the Moral Re-Armament (MRA) Movement. The MRA's projected moral and spiritual ideals appeared to be a panacea for uniting the peoples of the world of different faiths. Developed by the American minister Dr Frank Buchman, the phrase caught the zeitgeist of the time and the movement spread to many countries, including India, where it was led by Shri Rajmohan Gandhi, the grandson of Mahatma Gandhi and also of Shri Rajagopalachari, a veteran statesman of Indian politics and the last governor-general of India. MRA centres were set up in most cities, and Bangalore was one of them.

One day, on his own accord, Venu made the decision to discontinue his studies and devote himself to working full time for the MRA, delivering oratory and actively engaging in field activities. The family was both shocked and angered by the aberrant behaviour of shunning his studies and his filial obligations for some new-found global cause. Valsala, who was constantly in the house with Gowri, was witness to her anguish. Gowri shed many a tear and spent many a sleepless night looking for a solution. Finally, she put pen to paper and wrote an appeal letter to Shri Rajagopalachari. She beseeched him to use his good offices and talk to his grandson Rajmohan Gandhi about reorienting Venu back to his studies, as he could be more useful to the world as a qualified doctor than as a dropout.

Gowri received a prompt reply in an aerogram from the grand old man of Indian politics, addressing her as "Dear Sister." He stated in his letter that he would contact Rajmohan Gandhi on the matter and advised her to be patient and not to lose heart. Shri Rajagopalachari also wrote to Rajmohan Gandhi a short letter explaining the plight faced by Venu's widowed mother and asked him to release Venu to complete his medical programme before involving him more deeply in the spiritual movement. This letter was copied to the dean of the medical school with a note to give sympathetic consideration to Venu should he decide to rejoin the programme.

A year and a half went by before an incident took place that was to convince her hard-headed son that his mother was right. At a medical camp in a village in Karnataka, Venu noticed that the doctor attending to the patient had in haste made an incorrect diagnosis. He pointed this out, only to be sharply rebuked. He realized there and then that he was not qualified to express a medical opinion, and he decided to resume his studies. Rajmohan Gandhi enticed him to stay back and work for MRA with a promised trip to the United Kingdom to meet up with Peter Howard, the head of the spiritual movement there. But Venu declined. He went to see his dean, who accepted him back, as he had been a good student – but more so on the grounds of the strong support letter from Shri Rajagopalachari for Venu's readmission. Venu sought a few months' leave before rejoining, as he wanted to return home and set things right. Breathing a sigh of relief at the turn of events, Gowri went immediately to the altar to light God's lamp and thank the Almighty for the divine providence.

## FULFILLING HOPE AND DREAM IN EDUCATION

Dasu telegrammed his mother in the first week of January 1965 to convey the news that he had passed his honours degree with first class. He followed it up with a letter indicating considerable encouragement from his lecturers to enrol for a PhD degree. His enquiries revealed that the Colombo Plan scholarship could be extended by another three years for completion of the postgraduate degree if the Malaysian Ministry of Education gave its consent.

Gowri discussed this development with Sethu and her daughters. They all felt that with Shivan's impending return, Dasu should stay back to complete his PhD. Sethu said he would personally broach the subject with his member of parliament in the Gurun constituency, who was then the education minister. Sethu wasted no time on the matter and duly received an official response from the Ministry of Education stating that it would have no objections to approving the extended study, provided Dasu completed first the programme for his diploma in education. Sethu was further informed that Dasu would be required to put in a longer period of compulsory service upon his return, which no one really minded.

Ravi entered the fifth form in January 1965. He had expressed an interest in medicine. He was a talented boy, gifted with good vocals. Gowri was reminded of her husband whenever he burst into a song at home. Both he and Hari enjoyed sports and represented their school at cricket. For Gowri, it was gratifying that they were on top of their studies as well.

Ambi would often engage Ravi in a vocal duet whenever she came down on her school weekend from Bedong. This fell on Friday and Saturday in the state of Kedah. On one such visit, not long after her arrival, she complained of stomach pains. The pain became acute the next morning, and Gowri was instantly reminded of Venu's appendicitis pains. She took Ambi straight to hospital in Muhammad Rashid's car. The surgeon on call confirmed it was appendicitis, and the girl was operated upon the same day. Sethu and Uma were informed, and they promptly came that evening and stayed over the weekend to comfort a worried Gowri.

Shivan returned from Dartmouth towards the latter half of 1965. The Royal Malaysian Navy (RMN) then was still very much a brown-water navy and was based at Woodlands in Singapore. Shivan would come home to Bukit Mertajam whenever the ship he was on or commanded berthed at Penang (the Lumut Naval Base to which RMN finally shifted from its historical base at Woodlands still being in its conceptual stage then). While the RMN, in the wake of Malaysianization, was diversifying and modernizing its vessels, Shivan set about modernizing his mother's house – adding a refrigerator, a washing machine, and a television set. The TV was particularly welcome, as it took the boredom off long dragged-out dreary days for Gowri, who got hooked on some interesting programs of the period, among them *Peyton Place*, *The Big Valley*, *The Fugitive*, and *The High Chaparral*. In later years, Tamil films were also televised.

It was around this time that Gowri began to be troubled again by her umbilical hernia. Dr Siva would quickly respond to her call and manipulate the hernia back into her abdomen. She was told to wear a corset and cautioned against performing any heavy lifting or pulling. Valsala and Ambi decided to employ an elderly woman as a washer-maid. She was bow-legged and had lost the sight in one eye early in life. The younger boys, Ravi and Hari, mischievously nicknamed her Jacqueline, connecting her agility with the character in the film *One-Eyed Jacks*. She worked for them for three years.

With the results of his senior Cambridge examination to hand, Ravi set sail for India as planned in early 1966, where he joined St Joseph's College at Trichy for his pre-university studies. Before he left, his mother extracted a promise from him that he would focus only on his studies. While he was at Trichy, Gowri asked her cousin, Dr Devi, who was running a lucrative medical practice in Chandigarh, to assist in securing Ravi a place in a government college anywhere in the country to do his premedical. Devi used her influence to gain him admission to the government medical college in Chandigarh itself, where he pursued a one-year pre-professional programme.

Gowri coaxed Ravi to apply for the Indian Cultural Scholarship when he was in his final term and sent him the application forms procured from the Indian High Commission in Kuala Lumpur. He obtained good grades, which secured him the scholarship and a medical seat at the University of Kerala, Trivandrum.

# [17]

With most of her children away from home save for Hari and Valsala, Gowri preoccupied herself by trying her hand at cooking new dishes following the recipes she read in magazines. She applied some innovation to a few such dishes, and her Portuguese chicken curry soon became a hit. Some afternoons, in the company of Priya or Mrs Thiagarajan, Gowri would take in a movie at the Cheok Sah Theatre in town to get over her boredom. She had a favourite trishaw driver whom she would summon for this and other downtown trips.

In early 1967, there arrived a new neighbour, an industry expert on hides and leather from India who was on secondment to Malaya. His name was M. P. Singh. He was later joined by his wife and child; they had a second child born in Bukit Mertajam within a couple of years, and they named her Aruna Malaysia. All of them addressed Gowri as *Mataji*. From them, Gowri learnt to cook some North Indian dishes – and she taught them, in turn, some of her dishes which they particularly liked.

M. P. Singh was a sociable person and endeared himself to Gowri's family. He was knowledgeable on a number of subjects, and his discourse on Indian politics was both truly fascinating to hear and hilarious. He knew the names of all Gowri's children and what they were doing, even though he hadn't met all of them, and he embarrassed Gowri on a few occasions in front of new acquaintances by praising her role in bringing them up as a widowed parent. In late 1967, he had a chance to meet Shivan, who came down for a couple of weeks on vacation. He quietly enjoyed a beer with the young man on some evenings, both of them heading to the pub in Bukit Mertajam town for this purpose.

☼

# GOWRI'S DILEMMA

One morning while Gowri was down the road at Ah Hock's grocery shop, she got a hint from M. P. Singh that Shivan had some exciting news to tell her. Bewildered, she closely watched her son when she got back to the house. He certainly looked a bit edgy, as if he was hesitating to tell her something sensitive. He appeared to be engaged in soft conversation for long periods in the morning on the house phone. Gowri, holding back her maternal inquisitiveness, busied herself in the kitchen.

After lunch, Shivan approached her. Seating himself opposite her, he took both her hands in his and, in a quiet tone, broke the suspense. "Mum," he said, "I have something to confess to you."

Gowri braced herself as Shivan continued. "I have met a girl, Mum, and we both love each other very much. She is Eurasian and is a nurse in Tampoi Hospital, near Johor Bahru. Her name is Stella Read. Her great-grandfather is the famous Singapore British pioneer W. H. M. Read. I would like to marry her with your permission."

Disbelieving, Gowri delivered a barrage of questions: "What am I hearing? When did all this start? Have you forgotten that you have two unmarried sisters? Have you thought about their future?"

Unfazed, he replied, "One doesn't plan to fall in love, Mum. It just happens. She is a nice and sincere girl. She has gone through a lot in life, and I respect her very much. Her father died just before she was born. Her mother is of Portuguese-Indian mix and remarried when Stella's father died. Stella grew up with her grandmother in Penang. She is a very sweet person, and I know you will like her."

"Respecting is different from getting married," Gowri countered. "Marriage is a lifetime responsibility. Mixed marriages can bring problems. Are you ready for this? What will our community think? I don't want you to make a hasty decision of going into a marriage that you might regret in the future."

"I am not blinded by emotions, Mum. I know her very well. She will fit well into our family."

"Are you sure about that? Surely she will experience cultural and religious differences."

"You have not met her yet, Mum. She is not at all how you imagine. And I don't care about what our community might think. I care about you, and I want to include you in every happy occasion of my life. That's why I'm asking for your consent."

Not in her wildest dreams had Gowri imagined herself put in the position of discussing an interracial marriage for her own children. She knew how her community would react to such a marriage. Although she was a liberal-minded person and had no qualms about going to St Anne's Church in Bukit Mertajam along with the worshippers every year on 26 July for the St Anne's Carnival and Feast, this was different. It had real-life implications of coming to terms with racial and religious differences. She was too steeped in her own culture to give in to her son's idea of bringing in a life partner who might pose a family dilemma with her culturally alien attributes. She felt the need to point out to him a few things.

But he quickly read her mind: "I will not change my religion at all. I promise you that. She can keep hers, and if we have children, we will expose them to both religions."

"What are her views on this?" Gowri countered.

"She is agreeable. In fact, she even came with me to temple one day in Singapore," he replied.

"Well, let me meet her," said Gowri, trying to hold on.

Her son continued with his surprises: "Actually, Mum, she has come down to Penang to meet her aunt. I can bring her down to see you."

Valsala, who had been a silent witness to this conversation, barged in finally, saying, "We need to talk to her woman to woman. Why don't you bring her down for lunch tomorrow? I can come with you."

Gowri then got up and withdrew to her room. She knew that if she objected strongly, he might still go ahead with his wishes. She wanted to preserve the oneness of the family at whatever cost.

☼

# GOWRI RELENTS

Gowri got her first glimpse of Stella the next day. The girl was everything that her son had described. Except for the Western dress and the make-up that she wore, she appeared distinctly Asian in her mannerisms. Both Gowri and Valsala spent some time with her. Gowri found her to be simple and courteous, and very natural and spontaneous in her conversations.

She talked about her childhood with her grandmother and aunts, her large family of stepbrothers and a stepsister she subsequently came to know, her early independent struggles to build a career in nursing, and how she met Shivan through a mutual friend, Chit Kuttan, in Singapore. She seemed somewhat knowledgeable about Gowri's background. Although she did not elaborate, this was clear at one point in the conversation when she said, "Your son, Shiv, admires you a lot. I wish, Aunty, that I could like you develop inner strength and fortitude in my life."

Gowri was touched. Towards evening, Shivan took Stella back to the ferry terminal at Butterworth to catch the ferry boat to Penang Island. When they had left the house, Gowri confided in Valsala, "She seems a decent girl. I was worried that she was just someone who had charmed him. Something tells me they will get married soon."

"I think so too. He is going to follow in the footsteps of Devidas *Ettan*."

"Hmm," muttered Gowri, recalling Uma's brother's marriage to Aggie in February 1965 and how she had to appease a distraught Uma, who had sympathized with her late parents' reservation about their proposed union. Venu, who was then in India, had attended their church wedding. Gowri asked Valsala to bring out the photo album and found therein the photograph that she was seeking of their wedding reception. They looked a happy couple.

A few days later, Stella came over to the house for a visit before she left to resume her duty. She and Shivan jointly sought Gowri's approval and blessings for marriage early in the following year. Gowri, who had reconciled herself to the inevitable, said simply, "If you are going to be happy in marriage, that's what matters. My blessings will always be there. But bear in mind that a marriage is a lifetime commitment to live a joint life with shared responsibilities to your family, and loving each other always, whatever be life's circumstance. Divorce is certainly not an option, and especially in our community. Do you both understand this?"

Both of them nodded vigorously. Then Gowri pulled Stella to her room. Pausing to collect herself, Gowri said, "I want you to promise me one thing, which is, you will not try to convert my son. I gave him Lord Shiva's name for a reason. Hinduism is no less a religion than Christianity; all major religions have acknowledged its antiquity and resonate many of the values and tenets that it preaches. I strictly have no say where your children are concerned, but over mine I have. As a matter of fact, once you get married and come into my family, I will call you Shanti, not Stella." (*Shanti* is an Indian word meaning "peace.")

Stella's eyes welled up. "I promise you, Mum. You don't have to worry. Shivan will always remain who he is."

Family photo of Uma and her siblings taken on her visit to India in late 1968.
*Left to right, seated*: Prema, Uma, Aggie, Shanta (Sudarshan's wife);
*standing*: Aggie's relative, Krishna Kumar, Sethu, Devidas,
Sudarshan, Priyadarshini.

Saraswati and Krishna Iyer (Uma's parents)

St Anne's Church, Bukit Mertajam

Before Shivan left, he and Gowri discussed briefly the subject of his marriage. She was told that they were planning a traditional naval wedding at the military chapel in Johor Bahru. A simple temple wedding would subsequently be held. He promised to keep her updated on the plans.

# [18]

In January 1968, Ambi, having received earlier notification, found herself attached to a new school in Padang Serai, near Bukit Mertajam. By this time, Priya had gone back to stay with her parents in Bedong. Sethu had Priya enrolled at Father Barres Convent, Sungai Petani. Soon thereafter, around March, Venu returned after completing his MBBS examination for a housemanship posting, but it was pointed out to him by the Ministry of Health that he was six months short of fulfilling the mandatory six-year period of the programme, which included compulsory housemanship in India.

Gowri and Venu attended Shivan and Stella's naval wedding ceremony on Sunday, 6 April. Ambi and Valsala could not accompany them to the wedding, as it was not the school vacation. It was an impressive function and included the traditional arch of swords under which the bride and groom had to pass. Venu returned to Bangalore the same month to complete the regulatory Indian portion of his housemanship.

The newly married Shivan and Stella (Shanti) pass under the arch of swords.

Not long after Venu left, Gowri had a surprise visit from her sister Kamalam. She came in unapologetic, with no hint of remorse on her face. She had a hurried look about her and came straight to the point.

"I have come here because a proposal had come to my house in my absence from some Nair family in Kuala Lumpur seeking a hand in marriage with Mrs Panicker's daughter. The name Ambika was mentioned by the third party, who only left a contact number with the maid. Do you know anything about this?" Kamalam was still standing as she spoke, declining an invitation to sit.

Gowri genuinely replied that she was in the dark about the proposal, although she couldn't help wondering about the unknown Nair family who knew about her marriageable daughter.

Kamalam then continued: "In that case, do you have any objections if I treat it as a mistaken identity and explore the proposal for Prabha? She is also of eligible age for marriage."

Gowri thought for a moment. Kamalam obviously must have found out something about the Kuala Lumpur party that interested her; otherwise, there would have been no special reason for her to come. But then, Prabha, after all, was her niece, and older than Ambi.

"Go ahead. You know very well that I cannot think of marriage for Ambi until Dasu returns from his studies," was Gowri's response.

A wry smile crossed Kamalam's face. These were the words she'd hoped to hear from Gowri.

"All right then, I'm leaving," said Kamalam, who left as abruptly as she came. For the rest of the day, Gowri found that she could not take her mind off her sister. That Kamalam still had an attitude was clear. But deep down, she sensed her sister was an unhappy woman nursing some bitterness that she was hiding.

Shivan and Shanti paid their first visit to Gowri as a married couple over the Christmas period. Gowri found it awkward and downright embarrassing to see Shanti walk about the house in short pants, openly hugging Shivan when they were seated together in front of the television. All this was alien to her eyes and did not fit in with her Indian standards of modesty. She remarked quietly to Valsala, *"Ivereke lajja ille? Nalakalam ende valia aankuttikel evide illa. Ende umurthe vachha ithoke avisham indoe?"* ("Don't they feel any embarrassment? Just as well my elder boys are not around. Do they have to do all this in front of me?")

Valsala appeased her. "It is not abnormal Mum. We are just not used to seeing this. That's all."

Gowri continued, *"Enthe ayalum parenjevekke, porthe poghumbol shorts iddan paadila. Aallugal enthe parayum?"* ("Anyway, say to her, shorts should not be worn when going out. What will people say?")

"Okay, Mum," replied Valsala. "I shall give them both a hint of your discomfort."

Later, recollecting this episode, Gowri told Shanti about her feelings at that time. Her daughter-in-law replied, "Yeah, Mum, Valsala gave me a sarong to wear and smilingly said something to Shiv in Malayalam. I suspected you found my wearing the shorts indecent." They had come a long way since then, and Gowri found in her daughter-in-law a truly loving girl who never wore a grumpy face.

Towards the end of 1968, the family decided to sell the house in Bukit Mertajam and shift to Butterworth, which was nearer to Penang Island where Hari would need to go to pursue his sixth form studies at St Xavier's Institution. They managed to find a double-storey linked house at Peninsular Park in Butterworth which would be available for rental at the end of August 1969. The Bukit Mertajam house was put up for sale at double the original purchase price. Gowri planned to use the down payment money she would receive to settle her outstanding housing loan, which she had been meeting in monthly instalments of M$59. The house was finally sold in June and formally vacated as per agreement with the new owner in early August.

# HAND OF GOD

Ambi got a chance during the April school holidays in 1969 to visit Shivan and Shanti at their home in Century Gardens, Johor Bahru. She took Gowri with her. It was the weekend, and after an early lunch they drove up the causeway to Singapore to indulge in some shopping. Ambi bought for herself a red saree. On their way back, Shanti drove them to Woodlands, as Shivan had wanted his mother to see the ship he was commanding.

It was dark when they reached the naval base, but the lights at the wharf shed enough light on the scene. They had to walk up a narrow pontoon bridge to reach the gangway to ascend to the starboard side of the ship. As it was high tide, the roll of the ship intermittently widened the gap between the pontoon bridge and the gangway. Shivan, in full naval uniform, was on board the ship holding out his hand to his mother, who was followed by Shanti, with Ambi bringing up the rear.

Nearing the end of the pontoon bridge, Gowri took a few paces forward holding the ropes gingerly on both sides of the pontoon bridge. She then stretched out her right hand before her right foot had landed on the gangway. The gangway swayed badly, and Gowri lost her balance, falling into the sea between the pontoon bridge and the gangway. The girls screamed. Shivan sprang into action. Quickly removing his hat and boots, he ran to the other side of the ship and dived into the sea. There was just the flicker of light on the water's surface, but he went into the dark waters and made his way toward the area beneath the pontoon bridge and the gangway where she would conceivably be.

Gowri, upon hitting the water, instinctively held her breath and closed her eyes. It was amazing that she did not panic. She could not recollect how long it took, but her feet struck sand, and in the consequent steadying effort so also her right palm, which she then clenched. She remembered the thought rushing through her head: "Krishna, is this my end?"

She was about to resign herself to her fate when she felt strong hands on her back and buttocks giving her an upward thrust. Her son, she knew, had located her. After surfacing, Shivan guided her close to the wharf's edge. By then, others had gathered on the wharf. Noticing that she was still clutching her handbag in her left hand, Shivan pulled it away and raised her to the waiting hands of his fellow naval officers, who had rushed to the scene. They gently placed Gowri, whose head was partially covered by her saree folds, onto the ground. They were very relieved to know that she needed no resuscitation. Everyone started clapping as soon as Shivan joined her.

"I managed to locate her because of her floating saree. But I guess it was her pale behind that made it certain!" he said jokingly. Everyone laughed. All realized, of course, that they had witnessed a miracle. Gowri then unclenched her hitherto closed right fist, and she was as surprised as everyone else to see that she was holding amidst some sand a small seashell. It could only have been by God's grace that Gowri survived that misadventure.

Ambi quickly brought out the red saree from the car. Gowri wore it reluctantly, as being a widow she did not fancy wearing bright colours. Ambi recalled that her mother looked exceptionally beautiful and elegant in the saree that night with her grey hair and fair complexion.

Speculating on the incident later, Gowri felt that her childhood experience of bathing in her private village pond had come to her rescue. As a child, she would play the breath-holding game in the water and consistently emerge the winner. The wet saree folds covering her head could also have trapped life-giving air at some stage during the descent or ascent. The quick response of her son and his spotting of the loosened bit of her off-white saree in the sea depth were undeniably also crucial. Perhaps it was a combination of all these factors that saved the day for Gowri.

The seashell she had picked up on the sea floor was placed at the altar when she got home. The miracle of God's presence was clear to all members of the family, as it was to be for a generation or more of their offspring.

# [19]

On the local political scene, the ending of the Indonesian Confrontation in August 1966 was welcomed by the country at large. But the expulsion of Singapore from Malaysia based on racial strife between the Malays and Chinese continued to strike a discordant note among these two segments of the population in the country. Opposition political parties started to emerge. One of these was the Malaysian People's Movement Party (Gerakan Party), which was formed in March 1968 with its base in Penang. In a membership drive, some party leaders approached Gowri, but she politely declined, saying that she was indebted to the ruling government for the opportunities her children had derived and would not want that in any way jeopardized.

The general elections were called on 10 May 1969 amidst growing Sino-Malay sectarian tensions. The ruling Alliance Party won the national ballot but with a reduced majority in Parliament. At the state level, it lost the state of Kelantan to the Pan Malayan Islamic Party (PAS) and Penang to the new Gerakan Party, and in two states no party commanded an absolute majority.

## THE 13 MAY INCIDENT

Bolstered by the unexpected gain of votes at the general election, the Gerakan Party and the Democratic Action Party (DAP), which had reconstituted itself from the Singapore People's Action Party, organized a victory rally in Kuala Lumpur on Monday, 12 May. The rally turned rowdy, with party members shouting racial epithets at Malay bystanders.

It was widely expected that Gerakan would form a coalition with DAP to form the government in Selangor, but on the afternoon of 13 May, Gerakan announced that it would remain neutral in the Selangor State Assembly, thus allowing Alliance to form a minority government. The same afternoon, the Malaysian Chinese Association (MCA), a component of the Alliance Party which had suffered a heavy defeat, decided it would not participate in the Alliance government, although it would support it in Parliament. This proved to be an irrational decision, as it served to inflame the Chinese community, which saw itself being marginalized.

A retaliatory rally that had previously been called for on the evening of 13 May by the United Malays National Organization (UMNO), the major partner in the Alliance Party, set the scene for a racial clash that had been percolating for some time. A full-scale bloody riot erupted and spread quickly through the city. Many lives were lost, and scores of innocent civilians on the streets were badly injured. There was considerable damage to vehicles and property.

Although the imposition of a curfew throughout the state of Selangor and the strong presence of the Royal Malay Regiment and the police force contained the crisis, minor isolated skirmishes occurred also in other states. The marketplace at Bukit Mertajam saw some violent slashing of individuals, but the security forces were quick at hand to quell the unrest and seal off the market. A state of emergency and accompanying curfew were declared on 14 and 16 May throughout the country.

Berapit was abuzz with rumours that it could be a scene for racial clashes, as the largely Chinese community was surrounded by Malay kampongs (villages). In the wake of the nationwide curfew, almost everyone preferred to stay indoors, and they were all stocking up on food items. Gowri was worried. She too stocked up on provisions supplied by Ah Hock on credit terms and forbade Ambi, Valsala, and Hari from venturing out of the house. She reminisced about the Japanese occupation and the emergency period she had endured. Compared to those periods, the present tense situation in the country seemed to her to be less overpowering, and she felt that the passions, which were politically fanned, would soon die down to contain the conflict. She was, therefore, not as distraught as her neighbours were.

Sethu and Uma, who were in Bedong, felt much reassured after listening to her. So did Dasu, who was waiting to come home, and whose departure was being held back by the Australian authorities on security grounds. He contacted Sethu to find out about the extent of the racial clash and was relieved to know that no family member was caught in the skirmish.

Nonetheless, everyone – Gowri included – was quick to recognize that the 13 May incident would remain in the psyche of the nation for years to come. Indeed, for the remaining months of the year, the public continued to be wary of further racial clashes. Even the global excitement attending the first manned landing on the moon by the United States' Apollo 11 spaceflight on 20 July 1969 did little to distract public focus away from the incident. The date 13 May stood out as a black-letter day in the history of the nation. It would serve as a constant reminder to aspiring politicians that the path of moderation should be pursued in managing the affairs of a multiracial country.

Dasu finally arrived from Australia in the third week of May. The curfew in Kuala Lumpur was still on, but it was lifted for certain hours in the day. He had to wait for a month before he received a letter from the Ministry of Education asking him to report for duty at Sultan Abdul Hamid College in Alor Star, Kedah.

As was widely expected, the Parliament was suspended and a National Operations Council (NOC) was established by royal assent on 16 May. Headed by the deputy premier, Tun Abdul Razak, the NOC ran the country for eighteen months. Tunku Abdul Rahman was forced to resign from his premiership post in the process. The NOC implemented security measures to restore law and order in the country, including the establishment of an unarmed Vigilante Corps, a territorial army, and police force battalions. It suspended the press and actively enforced the Internal Security Act (preventive detention law) of 1960. Normalcy, with restoration of parliamentary rule, only returned in February 1971. Tun Razak assumed the premiership of the country. To enhance national unity, he set up the National Front (Barisan Nasional) in 1973, a coalition party to replace the ruling Alliance Party. He went on to serve the nation until his death in 1976.

The 13 May incident served notice to the nation at large that the subject of social integration could not be taken lightly. While tolerance was essentially there, racial sensitivities remained. It was clear to the thinking public that real understanding and appreciation of each other's culture could only come with close interaction, and this needed to be actively forged. It had to remain a top priority of the government, and concrete measures to achieve this – particularly among the youth – needed to be strategized while ensuring a democratic way of life.

The first step in this direction was the introduction of the national ideology (Rukun Negara). The five principles of the national ideology were spelt out at the end of August 1970, these being belief in God, loyalty to king and country, nobleness of the Constitution, sovereignty of the law, and courtesy and decency. In the same year, the Razak government introduced the New Economic Policy (NEP), an ambitious twenty-year policy, to address the widening imbalance of wealth distribution between the races, the origins of which traced back to the division of labour that was practised by the country's colonial masters. Although done for economic reasons, this unfortunately led to the segregation of the races, breaking bonds of close interaction that once existed among them. The Malays stayed in their kampongs as farmers, while the Indians cultivated rubber and the Chinese, initially brought in for tin mining, went on to become merchants and businessmen and hence to gain a monopoly on the economy.

The heightened focus on the NEP was understandable, as it was aimed at reducing the economic disparity among the races, thereby removing socio-economic reasons as a strong cause to start any interethnic discord. Although not politically savvy, Gowri sensed that a stronger reinforcement of Malay hegemony was on the cards, but she saw no reason to share the fear of some of her neighbours that the country was headed for a bleak future.

(Since 1990, the country has, in a welcome move, established the Ministry of National Unity and Social Development, explicitly to encourage unity of the multiracial society and to promote national integration. That cultural diversity must constitute a strength rather than a weakness in forging a national identity was one of the clear lessons of the 13 May incident.)

Years later, Gowri – reflecting on this incident – recalled how true it was that she hardly had any friends among other racial groups when she was in the Indian-dominated estate environment. The same could be said of the Malays, who in vast majority were in the villages and in government and armed services. The Chinese remained largely content in their predominantly urban business environment. Only when she started living near townships did the opportunity arise for intermingling. "Without intermingling, racial prejudices and barriers cannot be transcended," she would openly say in conversations with the academics that Dasu sometimes would entertain in the home. No one disagreed.

"The only place where I have found real intermixing is in the hospital environment!" she once quipped. "The schools present us, of course, with the best opportunity to instil this cohesion. I know we all can unite as one people, looking beyond our differences. I have faith in the nicety of our people. I hope one day we can do away with racial politics."

# [20]

Dasu reported for duty at Sultan Abdul Hamid College on 1 July 1969. He found a room to rent in a house close by to the college. It was at a new housing colony built around paddy fields. Most Thursday afternoons, he would take a taxi to Butterworth, sharing it with three other passengers. The school observed a Friday–Saturday weekend in common with the rest of the state. He was put in charge of a fourth form class and assigned to teach chemistry.

The principal of the college then was Joginder Singh Jessy, and the senior chemistry teacher was K. B. Menon; Dasu got on well with both of them. They understood his aspiration to teach and undertake research at the university level and were also aware that he had applied to the University of Malaya (UM) for an academic post prior to his arrival from Australia. Dasu was called for an interview in early December, and in January 1970 he received news of his appointment as lecturer in the Department of Chemistry, Faculty of Science. On 7 February 1970, soon after the Chinese New Year holidays, he formally reported for duty at UM in Kuala Lumpur.

Venu had returned home from India in June 1969. He was posted to do a one-year housemanship at the Penang General Hospital. While still in India, he had, unknown to Gowri, made some overtures to Kamalam. His previous MRA leanings not forgotten, he was thinking seriously of a reunion between his mother and his aunt. He knew that without a forgiving Gowri and a repentant Kamalam, a reunion would not materialize. He knew his mother too well to worry about any objections from her on the matter. He had, therefore, to tackle Kamalam using the most persuasive language that appealed to her emotions and sensibility. It had to be underscored that "life is too short to carry a grudge to the grave" and that "the power of love transcends everything else in the universe."

He wrote her a long letter. Kamalam was not used to such sentiments eloquently presented by anyone, let alone her nephew. She responded to him and said that on her return from her conference in Sweden with other delegation members of the National Council of Women's Organisations Malaysia, she would be in transit briefly at Bombay Airport. She wondered whether he could meet up with her at the airport. Venu managed an entry, and the aunt and nephew were reunited. She said to him that she would go to meet her *chechi* the moment Venu returned home.

# RECONCILIATION

One weekend in late August 1969, Kamalam arrived unannounced at Gowri's new home in Butterworth. Dasu, who was at the front door, deliberately turned his face away upon seeing her. Kamalam, noticing this, said loudly that she had come because Venu had asked her. At this, Venu, who was in the living room, quickly got up from his chair. Brushing past Dasu, he went out to greet Kamalam and ushered her into the house.

"There's no rhyme or reason for her to be here. We have had enough of her insults," said Dasu, who appeared visibly irritated.

"I didn't ask to come here …" Kamalam began, and then, looking at Venu, began what appeared to be a tirade against the whole family. But she didn't get far and found herself thick in a multiple exchange of heated words.

Gowri then broke her silence. She asked all of them to control their temper and bury the past. In measured tones, in a mixture of Malayalam and English, she said, "We should not continue to hurt each other with hateful words. *"Erinja kallum paranja vaakum thiruchedukkan avilla."* ("You can't take back the words that you speak or the stones that you throw.") We must drive out the hate in us and replace it with love. Families are made in the heart. However chaotic and messy a family turns out to be, it is the only unconditional relationship its members have. Hate cannot drive out hate, only love can. There should be no place for hate in our hearts, only love. Where there is injury, let us sow pardon. All said and done, she is my sister and your aunt."

The sisters embraced each other. Ambi and Valsala, although initially wary, finally gave in respectfully. Dasu remained aloof and cold in his response, and after a few moments he went up the stairs to his room. The betrayal of the trust that he had in his aunt was still raw in his memory, and he could not help feeling that what he had witnessed was merely an empty embrace with no remorse or regret over wrongdoings on the part of his aunt.

# WEDDING BELLS

Whether it was a case of relief at being let off the hook or not, Kamalam started visiting Gowri and the girls weekly in Butterworth. She helped Ambi get a car on hire-purchase – a mustard-coloured Toyota Corolla. It was like welcoming a new member into the family, such was the excitement. The arrival of the car coincided with Ambi getting her driving license. She simply couldn't wait to take Gowri and Valsala on a spin round the block.

The jubilation was understandable. It was their first family car. Even Gowri, who had some reservations on account of the financial commitment her daughter was getting into, agreed that it was a worthy investment. The car would enable Ambi to drive to work and also provide a lift to two colleagues who were prepared to pay for the ride.

While in Butterworth, Gowri received news sometime in December that her uncle Kesava Menon, who had retired to live with his wife in Calicut, had passed way. She remained distraught for a few days, her mind flooded with memories of the past. He had been like a father figure to her. Whether he was in his police uniform or in the traditional dhoti attire, he had a charisma about him that had long remained embedded in her mind. He brooked no nonsense or disobedience, but behind the stern exterior was a man who had a caring and generous heart.

Her Palakkad *tharavad* might now no longer exist in physical terms, but of the members of that *tharavad* none, she was sure, would scale the heights and respect her uncle had enjoyed while serving the police force in Madras State, which then included the present-day Indian state of Tamil Nadu and the Malabar District of North Kerala. She recalled the oft-mentioned incident, when she was at Chandravilas, of her uncle abruptly diverting Nehru's motorcade while the prime minister was visiting the Malabar District to another route on the grounds of security. Only he would have the temerity to do that. When he personally conveyed the message to Prime Minister Nehru, the astute politician took a hard look at him and, with an understanding expression on his face, asked, "Are you a Malayalee?"

Gowri felt a deep sense of loss at her uncle's passing away, and she messaged Ravi in Trivandrum to go to Calicut, pay his respects to the bereaved family, and, if possible, attend the *adiyantharam* at their home for her departed uncle.

Kamalam, on one of her trips to Butterworth, took Gowri to meet up with Mrs Pillai who, on the demise of her husband, Dr Bhaskaran Pillai, had shifted from Kulim to their second home in Butterworth. Mrs Pillai was happy to see Gowri, whom she had last met at her daughter Vimala's wedding in Kulim. Later it was Mrs Pillai who coaxed Gowri into looking into a marriage proposal for her eldest daughter. She hosted a tea party in her house for the two families to meet sometime in late 1970. The boy, Ravindran by name, came with his father, P. K. A. K. Menon, and a younger brother, Balram, as his mother was in Kuala Lumpur with the rest of his siblings. He was a Perlis State scholar who had graduated with a degree in pharmacy from the University of Singapore and was serving at the Taiping General Hospital. The girl's side of the family was represented by Gowri and Venu.

Gowri found Ravindran's father to be a humorous person. He had a large family like her own, with five boys and three girls. His long initials served as an initial talking point. He explained that his full name was Achuthan Krishnan, represented by the abbreviations A. K. The first two initials stood for Pullipura Kuttikad, which was his *tharavad*. His wife's *tharavad*, he pointed out, was the Kanyanpath Puthen Veedu at Edappal.

"I have heard of Puthen Veedu. Is it in Thrissur District?" Gowri promptly asked.

"More like at the centre of Thrissur, Palakkad, and Malappuram districts, if you ask me," replied Menon.

As their conversation continued in Malayalam, Gowri noticed that Ravindran had not said a word yet. Turning to him, she asked, "*Ravi, epol joli thodungi?*" ("Ravi, when did you start in your job?")

Smiling, Ravindran replied, "*Moonnu kolam ayi, Aunty.*" ("Three years ago, Aunty.")

Turning to Balram, Gowri next enquired, "*Mon padikkyanne?*" ("Are you studying, son?")

Menon replied on his behalf, "*Athe, avan Form Six'l anne.*" ("Yes. He is in sixth form.")

Menon then went on to talk about his two daughters, both of whom had followed their husbands to India. He appeared genuinely happy that his son's horoscope had matched with Ambi's. Both parties agreed that it was merely a matter of the two young people in question meeting to see if they fancied each other. Ambi had by then transferred to the Bukit Kuda Girls' School in Klang, and she was staying with Dasu at his assigned residence at University Quarters in Petaling Jaya, then a residential suburb of Kuala Lumpur.

Ravindran met Ambi several times in Kuala Lumpur and introduced her to his mother, Karthiyayini, and his siblings. All of them liked her immensely for her conviviality and straightforwardness. Ravindran found her to be an affectionate and effervescent person, and a live wire at any function he took her to. She was the perfect balance he was looking for, as he was more of an introvert. He also sensed in her a strong independent streak and a very confident personality.

On her part, Ambi found Ravindran to be a gem at heart, gentle and correct in his behaviour, and passionate about his work. He was not prone to easy irritations and was cool about most things. She found that to be quite an admirable quality. His principal social circle centred around Rotary and golf, and although he indulged in a few drinks at such functions, she noted with much personal gratification that this was not a daily need. Nor was he a smoker. Her only initial complaint was that she was taller than him, but her attention was drawn by her friends to many celebrity couples, including royalty, who did not have any height hang-ups. The pair gave their nod to marriage in December 1970, which was enthusiastically welcomed by the older folks, who then arranged for their formal engagement in the same month.

Earlier in the year, in March, Shanti and Shivan were blessed with a son. They named him Suraj Gerard Prasad. Gowri just couldn't wait to get to Johor Bahru to hold her first grandson in her arms. He was so cute, and holding him, Gowri couldn't help thinking how wonderful it would be if her husband was alive to share this moment with her. Ponnu had also come to see Shivan's son along with her husband and her daughter, Shoba. They were planning to return to India shortly to take up permanent residence in Palakkad. The occasion was thus a warm reunion for both Gowri and Ponnu.

# INTO A NEW DAWN
# (1970-1997)

Gowri's great-granddaughter Rhea in 2015

# [21]

Dasu, upon confirmation of his post six months into service, became eligible for a car loan. He settled for a Peugeot 404, costing around 9,000 Malaysian dollars, which he was to drive around for several years. With a bench seat in front, the car could comfortably accommodate six or seven persons, thus suiting the family. Most weekends he would drive up to Butterworth and bring back items to be placed in his quarters while a larger house for rental was being found. With the help of Krishnan, a cousin of Uma from her father's side who was then a lecturer at the Kuala Lumpur Technical College, he managed to find a double-storey, back-to-back linked house at University Gardens, Kampong Tunku. This was in the Petaling Jaya suburb of Kuala Lumpur.

Krishnan's wife, Kamalam (the family called her Manni), helped Dasu and his sister Ambi perform the housewarming ceremony. The shift from Butterworth took place around the end of the second week in December 1970. Valsala had by this time received her letter of transfer to the National Secondary School at Jalan Temerloh, Kuala Lumpur. Towards the early part of 1971, Gowri's cousin-in-law, Unnikrishnan, came to stay with the family, shifting his base from his nephew's house. It did not dawn on the man that his permanent presence in their new home could be a source of embarrassment to Gowri as his late cousin's widow, but neither she nor her children had the heart to send him away.

Hari, following release of his higher school certificate examinations, applied to study at the University of Malaya and was granted a place in the science faculty with a second choice to do pre-engineering. A casual meeting with his new neighbour, who was a journalist at the *New Straits Times* national daily, led him instead to opt for a professional course in accountancy in the UK. He felt that such a course would be more remunerative. He was up to the challenge, although his background was essentially science-based.

He was particularly attracted by the possibility that articleship-cum-study at a professional accounting practice would enable him to be self-supporting. He enrolled himself at the Stamford Education Centre in Petaling Jaya for the Association of Chartered Certified Accountants (ACCA) course in June whilst awaiting a response from the UK. Within a month, he applied for and won the National Electricity Board scholarship for accountancy, electing to pursue the ACCA course in the country rather than a degree programme at Brighton. This was a relief to the family, who were now endeavouring to re-establish themselves at their new residence in Petaling Jaya.

There was a large and established Malayalee community in the nation's capital, and Gowri came to know them over time. Dasu would willingly take her to some of their homes on weekend visits. Some of them were her old friends from Johor and Kedah who had also shifted to Kuala Lumpur/Petaling Jaya. They included Mrs K. C. A. Menon (Thangam), Mrs Savithri Viswanathan, Mrs V. K. Menon, and Mrs Sukumari Ramakrishnan. Through them and Gowri's new neighbours at Kampong Tunku – notably Mrs K. B. Nair (Madhavi), Mrs. T. S. Nair, and Mrs Balakrishna Pillai – Gowri became well acquainted with several others. Counted among them were Mrs K. P. B. Menon (Narayani Kutty) and Mrs Padmini Ramachandran, whom she learnt were distant relatives; Mrs Y. B. Menon (Shanta); Puan Sri Sukumari Sekhar; Mrs K. R. Pillai; Mrs V. D. Nair; Mrs Govindan Kutty Nair (Rajalakshmy); Mrs R. K. Paniker; Mrs P. K. Nair; Mrs Ammujakshi Govindan; Mrs C. C. Menon; Mrs M. G. Nair; and Mrs A. V. G. Menon (Padmini). This list expanded as she began to attend more social functions, including theatrical performances by the Kairali Arts Club, which was actively led by Raghavan Pillai and his talented team of Bosco D'Cruz, G. O. Kennet, A. J. Stellus, and Rajan Nair. Gowri enjoyed such outings very much.

☼

# A SPATE OF WEDDINGS

Gowri had previously met Sukumari Ramakrishnan at her parents' home in Kluang. Her husband, Ramakrishnan, was very knowledgeable about Kerala Hindu matrimonial ceremonies, and his help was sought by Gowri in conducting the marriage of Ambi with Ravindran on 28 March 1971 at the *kalamandapam* (wedding ceremony hall) at the Sri Thandayuthapani Temple in Ipoh Road, Kuala Lumpur.

Ambi and Ravindran posing after their temple wedding

Two wedding receptions were subsequently arranged for the newly-weds, one in Kuala Lumpur by Gowri and the other in Alor Star by Ravindran's father, P. K. A. K. Menon, who was holding a hospital assistant's post at the Government Health Clinic at Pokok Sena. Gracing the wedding reception in Kuala Lumpur were Sethu's relatives, who Gowri was meeting for the first time. They included Sethu's widowed sister and family; uncle and aunt, Mr and Mrs K. K. M. Nair; and cousin P. P. Narayanan and his wife. Narayanan was a household name in the country by then as a trade union activist. He was the founder president of the Malaysian Trade Union Congress and the first Asian to be elected to the post of president of the International Confederation of Free Trade Unions.

Another luminary of Keralan descent who graced the function was Tan Sri B. C. Sekhar, a polymer chemist of exceptional calibre who put the Malaysian natural rubber industry on the world map as director of the Rubber Research Institute of Malaysia. He went on later to become the chairman of the International Rubber Research and Development Board. Not one to rest on his laurels, he established many years later the Palm Oil Research Institute of Malaysia. Dasu very much looked upon him as a role model.

Following marriage, Ambi left on transfer to Taiping within a few months to join Ravindran. Soon, she had to leave Taiping for Ipoh following Ravindran's transfer there in October. It was in Ipoh that Ambi delivered her first child in February 1972, a baby girl whom Gowri named Bindu. It is a Sanskrit word meaning "dot" and represents the sacred symbol of the cosmos in its unmanifest state. She was the first darling granddaughter (of many yet to follow) for Gowri, who would carry her maternal lineage.

Shivan, in the meanwhile, had left the Navy in 1971 and joined the plantations sector. He went on to serve in a number of estates under the management of Plantation Agencies Pvt. Ltd. in various states that included Kedah, Kelantan, and Negeri Sembilan. He also had a short stint in Indonesia.

One of Gowri's close neighbours at University Gardens was Dr Ganesan and his wife Sarojini. In mid-1972, Sarojini invited Gowri and family to the marriage of her brother Ramachandran with Bhanu. It was here that Sarojini introduced Valsala to the bride's brother, Dr Aravindakshan, who was called Aravind for short. He was preparing to leave for the UK within a couple of weeks to do his primary FRCS (Fellow of the Royal College of Surgeons) examinations. Aravind took a liking to Valsala at their first meeting and, with the intention of marriage, made it a point to meet her again a few more times. He told her that his elder brother Vijayan's wife also carried the name Valsala.

Aravind's mother, Bhargavi Amma, and Gowri favoured the alliance, and it was jointly decided that the marriage would be held after a year. Bhargavi Amma hailed from a well-known *tharavad*, the Kunneth House, at Chittalancheri, a village in the Palakkad district of Kerala.

Later that year, Gowri was admitted to the University Hospital for surgical treatment of her umbilical hernia. In the meanwhile, Gowri's cousin-in-law, Unnikrishnan, also underwent surgery for intestinal tuberculosis. Venu, who was completing his military service in Malacca, came home one weekend and felt that Unnikrishnan required special caring. It was not possible for Gowri to look after him. It was then decided it would be best to send Unnikrishnan to be with his younger brother Shankaran. But the reception that they received from Shankaran upon arrival at his house in Kulim was beyond belief.

"It would be a tragedy if he stays with us. He is an evil man!" declared Shankaran.

A saddened Unnikrishnan turned to Ambi – who he fondly called Ambili, which in Malayalam means "moon" – and said to her, "*Ambili, makale, yenne pooghunna vazhiyil yevedeyingilum valiche eriyu. Yenne konde aarukum ubathrovam venda.*" ("Ambili dear, please throw me out somewhere along the way. I don't want to be a burden to anyone.")

"No, *Valiacha*, don't say that. We will take care of you. Let us go from this forsaken place," replied Ambi, tearfully hugging him

A month or two later, Unnikrishnan himself suggested that he would go to India and stay with his unmarried sister in Palakkad. The family duly sent him and promised him regular bimonthly remittances to cover medical and living expenses.

Valsala's fiancé, Aravind, having passed his primary, decided to stay on in the UK for a while longer to gain experience. He worked at Southend Hospital in Essex and also at Llandough Hospital in Cardiff. He returned home towards the beginning of December 1973 and married Valsala some ten days later on 12 December. Ramakrishnan helped conduct the marriage ceremony.

All of Aravind's family, including his sister-in-law Valsala and her cousin, Dr Leela Menon, came for the wedding. Gowri was thrilled to see Dr Leela Menon, who had been a great help to her on the 1949 return voyage to

Malaya on the SS *Rajula*. She came in the company of her husband, Datuk Dr K. A. Menon, a prominent general surgeon at the General Hospital in Kuala Lumpur, under whom Aravind had worked for a period prior to leaving for the United Kingdom.

Following her marriage, Valsala left to stay with Aravind at his house in the SEA Park locality of Petaling Jaya. In January 1974, Aravind left for Edinburgh to complete the second part of his FRCS examinations.

Valsala's marriage with Aravind. Also in
the photograph (*left to right*):
Ramakrishnan (*second*), Aravind's married sisters (*third* and *sixth*),
Meenakshi Nambiar (*fourth*), Kamalam, Bhargavi Amma
(Aravind's mother, *partially hidden*), and Gowri.

Venu, upon completing his housemanship at Penang General Hospital in June 1970, found himself posted for two months each at hospitals in Kepala Batas and Bukit Mertajam as a medical officer. Thereafter, he opted for a two-year army posting. Upon leaving the army, he joined a private practice as a medical officer working with Dr Tan Chee Khoon at his Sentosa Clinic in Kuala Lumpur. Dr Tan had been a well-known opposition leader in the Malaysian Parliament from 1964–1978. Originally the leader of the Labour Party of Malaya, he was the co-founder of the Gerakan Party. Venu worked for two years at Sentosa Clinic before entering into private practice in the new town centre at Petaling Jaya.

It was while working at Sentosa Clinic that Venu got married to Ponnu's sister Presenna on 30 March 1973. Presenna was many years younger than Ponnu, though just as beautiful. From Palakkad, Ponnu had written to Gowri seeking her consent on behalf of her mother, Thilothamma, to consider matching Presenna with Venu. Gowri was pleased, but when she broached the subject with Venu, his first reaction was, "She would need a ladder to climb up to kiss me!" He was, of course, referring to the gross mismatch in their heights, him being six foot three and she being of rather short stature. But following a stint of initial army posting in Kluang, that perception was turned on its heels. Venu went to see her and went out with her on a few dates. He decided to marry her, but made it known to Gowri only when he had secured the consent of Thilothamma.

Gowri chided Venu for keeping her in the dark about his intentions. "Haven't you to get my permission as well?"

He hugged her and said simply, "I thought since you already know her and the family, I would save you a formal approach. Your blessing is what matters to me the most."

Gowri smiled at the response. She hid her hurt at being bypasssed. Her unuttered thoughts could conceivably have been, "So now you don't need a ladder!" As the two families had known each other for over two decades, this marriage was seen as cementing the alliance between them.

Both Venu and Presenna stayed at the University Garden House. There were moments Gowri viewed Presenna in the same light as Shanti – a daughter-in-law thrust on her by her son. There was no resentment, really, only a sense of lost pride in not being the one to have chosen brides for her sons as tradition would have demanded. However, her capacity for love knew no bounds, and soon those feelings evaporated away with her proximity and regular interactions with them.

Venu ties the *thalimala* around the neck of Presenna assisted
by his sisters, while Gowri and Kamalam look on. Standing behind
the bride are the bride's sisters-in-law, Indira (Mema) and Komalam.

A month after Venu's wedding, Dasu left on his first sabbatical leave
for six months at the University of Western Ontario in London, Canada.
He was happy that there was a resident doctor in the house in Venu to care
for Gowri while he was away.

# THE REUNION

In late July, Gowri felt a strong inner calling to see her mother, Kamakshi
Amma, in Puduserry. She had been dreaming about her mother for over a
fortnight and began to wonder at this independent stage in her life what
was really holding her back from breaking the ice and seeing the woman.
She didn't care about the sensitivities of her clan anymore.

It was the first of many trips she was to make. She flew to Madras
(now Chennai), where she was met by her niece Prema, who arranged for
the overnight train ride to Kerala. Arriving at the Olavakkode junction in
Palakkad, she was met by her brother Bala Menon. It was a tearful reunion
for them, and they chatted all the way to Puduserry.

Kamakshi Amma was on cloud nine seeing Gowri, repeatedly saying, "My Gowri has come! My Gowri has come!" It was an emotional homecoming for both of them. Gowri tearfully hugged her mother, apologising for not coming to see her earlier.

Kamakshi Amma, looking at her lovingly in the face, said, "No, don't apologize. My poor darling, you have suffered so much. I blame myself for the fate you found yourself in."

Mother and daughter continued to hug each other for several moments, hurt by the separation but relieved to have a new start. Kamakshi Amma wanted to hear all about Gowri's years in Malaysia bringing up her children. She knew them all by name. Sitting with her and aided by a photo album, Gowri patiently satisfied her mother's curiosity on each one of them. Gowri had also the photographs of Priya, Suraj, and Bindu to show Kamakshi Amma, who kissed the photographs, pining to see them all in person.

Gowri told her about Valsala's marriage and about Dasu being away in Canada for a few months. "I have asked him to come and see you, if possible, on the way back," added Gowri, which gave rise to another wave of excitement.

While in Puduserry, Gowri took the opportunity to go to Guruvayur temple and also to visit her cousin Radha in Ernakulam. She introduced Ponnu, who had settled with her husband in the Chandranagar locality in Palakkad, to Kamakshi Amma. Gowri returned home to Malaysia in early September just ahead of Dasu, but not before installing a couple of much-needed ceiling fans in her mother's house and buying some new cutlery. She promised Bala Menon that she would send some money as soon as she got back to initiate repair works to the house that had long been pending. Gowri felt good that for the first time in her life, she was in a position to cater to the needs of her mother.

# SHANTI VENTURES INTO THE
# BOUTIQUE BUSINESS

With Dasu's return from his sabbatical leave, the family decided to shift their residence to a bungalow house in Section 12, very close to the University of Malaya. This was a spacious single-storey house with several bedrooms. There was a well-manicured garden to the front of the house containing a champaca plant (magnolia family) in full bloom with orange flowers. Gowri was mesmerized by its floral scent. Quietly, she was planning for her eldest son to get married, and she sensed that this house just fitted the bill.

Shanti and her son Suraj also came to stay in the new premises, following Shivan's brief posting to Indonesia by the estate agency to resolve some matters at one of its plantations in that country. Shanti had just ventured into the boutique and modelling business and hoped that the city of Kuala Lumpur would provide an opportunity to exhibit her creative design talents at fashion wear. Indeed, within months of her arrival, her resourcefulness began to yield results. Interacting with well-known boutiques and modelling schools, she participated in several haute couture weeks at leading hotels, delivering her majestic clothes on the catwalk. Among those in the audience were socialites and fashionistas who enjoyed her designs of classic looks enhanced by edgy and contemporary elements. The attendant good publicity in the local dailies won her some laurels and, more significantly, boosted her confidence in seriously starting her own boutique-cum-modelling school in the near future. The only hitch, the family noted, was that the business demanded that she remain in a city area, and this, at least for the moment, appeared difficult with Shivan's rotational estate posting.

# [22]

Dasu, although a very liberal-minded individual, had conservative views when it came to marriage. He wanted a girl with a matched horoscope and one who would not be so ultra-modern as to demand independent family living. His family ties were too precious to him. He considered that it was his personal responsibility, more than that of his siblings, to care for his mother. He also said that he would meet up with a girl only after his mother, along with any others in the family, had the chance to meet her and found her suitable for the next stage of a mutual exchange of horoscopes. Any meeting that did not end on a positive note would be distasteful for both parties, and he didn't want to be involved with that. A few proposals had come to Gowri with photographs, but Dasu was in no rush. Working on his research, he seldom came home early and tended to shy away from discussing marriage proposals.

One day, at his mother's insistence, he went to see her friend, Mrs Achuthan Pillai, who was warded at the University Hospital. She had a visitor there – her neighbour, who was introduced as Mr Nair. After a few moments of polite chatting and enquiring after her condition, Dasu took leave. As the story goes, Mrs Pillai then began enumerating Dasu's virtues to Mr Nair. She told him that Dasu was a model son to his mother, Mrs Gowri Panicker, and his family, and that he was an extremely eligible bachelor with no bad habits. She asked Mr Nair, "Is your daughter Ambika back from Manipal Medical College?"

"Yes, she is now doing her housemanship at the General Hospital," he replied.

She pressed on: "Dasu will be a good match for her. Shall I sound out Mrs Panicker?"

"No harm done," he replied. But as soon as he got home, Mr Nair excitedly announced to his daughter, "I have found someone with the qualities you are looking for. He is tall, handsome, and accomplished, and he does not smoke or drink. You have no reason not to meet him."

"Let me first meet him before you go any further," snapped Ambika.

A couple of weeks later, Gowri, in the company of Presenna's eldest brother and his wife – who lived close to the Nair family – went to visit them. Dasu remembered his mother saying, "She is tall and good-looking, with a long thick hair braid. They are from a good *tharavad*. When I mentioned our Ravi in Trivandrum, she remembered hearing of him as someone with a good voice."

This approval set the stage for the two of them to meet in late November, after it was verified that their horoscopes had matched. Dasu was accompanied by Aravind and Valsala and Mrs Achuthan Pillai's daughter and son-in-law when he called on Ambika. Aravind had just returned then from Edinburgh after completing Part 2 of the FRCS examinations and was working along with Venu at Sentosa Clinic. After a while, they all adjourned with Ambika to Hotel Jayapuri (now Petaling Jaya Hilton) for drinks, discreetly leaving Dasu and Ambika in a corner to themselves. Before they left the scene, Aravind ordered a Pimms No. 1 for Dasu. Later, when asked why, his reply was, "There is a genie contained in it that will help you to say the right things!"

Ambika found Dasu disarmingly charming and jovial despite a stern exterior. They exchanged their family history. She said her *tharavad* was called Numbreth, which was at Thiruvilwamala in the Thrissur District of Kerala, and her full name was Ambikadevi, although the "devi" part only appeared in official documents. Dasu said he had heard about the place but had never been back to India since his brief childhood stint there, where he had picked up the basics of the Malayalam language. He said he still recalled a nursery rhyme and wondered whether she knew it as well:

*Vaa Kuruvi, Varu Kuruvi, Vazha Thai Mel Iru Kuruvi, Nyaru Tharaam, Chakiri Tharaam, Koodendakkan Kudaivaram ..."*

Roughly translated, it goes as follows:

> Come little bird, come. Perch yourself on the banana tree.
> I'll give you twigs (and) give you coir. I'll come with you …
> to build a nest …"

It was meant as an indirect proposal to her, but it went totally missed.

Dasu and Ambika did get engaged on 16 December and were married on 6 April 1975 during the school holiday break. In addition to the wedding, there was triple joy in the year for Gowri with the birth of Valsala's first child, Sapna, in Kuala Lumpur; Ambi's second daughter, Rhitu, in Kuala Terengganu; and Venu's first child and daughter, Apsara, in Kuala Lumpur. The joy was marred only by the news received from her cousin Radha in Ernakulam, India, that Lakshmikutty Amma had passed away. Gowri grieved for her aunt who had faithfully looked after her and her sisters for many years at the Chandravilas abode in Palakkad.

The married couple with Dasu's side of the extended family.
Sitting cross-legged in the forefront is P. K. A. K. Menon;
Mrs Menon (Karthiyayini) is seated on Gowri's right.

Close on the heels of the three new granddaughters came other grandchildren, with 1976–1979 being the family's "baby boom" years. In order of arrival: Ashwin (Dasu's eldest child and son) and Sharad Christopher (Shivan's second son) in 1976; Gowri (Dasu's second child and daughter), Kiran (Valsala's second daughter), Govind Kishen (Venu's second child and only son, nicknamed Gopu) in 1977; and Nisha (Valsala's third daughter), Sathya (Dasu's third child and daughter), Vikram (Ambi's third child and only son), and Lavaniya (Venu's third child and daughter) in 1979. The Gowri clan was now something to reckon with. She had truly carried the torch of her husband's dream, settling down permanently in her country of domicile and becoming a citizen, and nurturing a second generation of offspring as home-grown Malaysians.

When Rhitu was born, Gowri flew to Kuala Terengganu to see her grandchild. Dasu and Ambika along with Valsala and Aravind decided that they would drive up to Kuala Terengganu in his Peugeot on the eve of the Hari Raya holidays on 6 October 1975. Ambika was then expecting Ashwin, and Sapna was less than a year old. They left in the evening around four o'clock. The present Karak Highway was not even envisioned then, and on the old two-lane single carriageway road it took them well-nigh nine hours to get to their destination. It was an eventful drive that found them travelling in a north-easterly direction to Temerloh and Kuantan and thereafter in a northerly direction via Chukai and Kuala Berang to Kuala Terengganu. As they took the turn-off to Kuala Terengganu just before Kuantan, the car stalled because of a puncture sustained in a back-wheel tyre. It was dark, and the torch they had with them was insufficient to manage the jack and fix the replacement tyre at the edge of the road.

Just then a car passed by. It stopped some hundred metres ahead and then started to reverse towards them. Having heard of highway robberies, they warily turned their heads in the direction of the approaching vehicle. A head popped out to ask, *"Kenapa awak punya kereta?"* (What's the matter with your car?) Dasu, still holding on to the lug wrench, pointed to the burst tyre.

"I shall reverse to the back of your car so that you have the benefit of my headlamps," said the man, speaking loudly in his native Malay language. Much relieved, they thanked him profusely. That road courtesy remained etched in their memories for a long time.

It was past one o'clock in the morning when they finally arrived at Kuala Terengganu. Gowri and Ambi had not slept and were waiting anxiously for them. The following day, after lunch, all of them went sightseeing. They visited the central market and the few batik and handicraft centres that were still open, making some purchases. Dasu bought a few long-sleeved batik shirts with pleasing geometrical designs and floral motifs for wearing at official functions. The ladies settled for some attractive batik paintings and scarves. Towards evening, they drove up to the picturesque Kemasik Beach, hoping to catch sight of the famous leatherback turtles that were known to come ashore for nesting. They couldn't spot any, as this stretch of beach was now too open to the public. But they enjoyed the scenic setting of the white sandy beach facing the clear waters of the South China Sea and the many palm trees that lined the shore. After a two-day stay, Dasu drove back with his passengers to Kuala Lumpur, deciding this time to leave early so as to arrive home before nightfall. Gowri returned by plane a couple of weeks later.

In early April 1976, Gowri felt the urge to visit Guruvayur in India and attend the *Bhāgavata sapthaham* by the learned Sri Anjum Madhavan Namboothiri. *Sapthaham* is the unfolding of the *Bhāgavatam* with all its essence and character over a span of seven continuous days. *Bhāgavatam* is an ancient Hindu text (Purana) consisting of 18,000 couplets (slokas) that eulogize the Supreme God Vishnu (Narayana) in his incarnated form as Krishna, and focusses on religious devotion (bhakti). It was compiled by the sage Vyasa, considered also to be the scribe of the Vedas and the Mahabharata.

Gowri coaxed Presenna's mother, Thilothamma, into going with her. They stayed at the *satram* provided by the temple *Devaswom*. They extended their stay by another two weeks to witness the various daily pujas performed at the temple and attend the various religious discourses and meditation classes that were being held. The seven day *sapthaham* ran through the Vishu New Year, which fell on 14 April. Gowri's prayers at the temple gained a new fervour at the news of the birth of Dasu's son Ashwin on 13 April.

☼

# OBSERVING VISHU

Back in Malaysia, Gowri's family severally observed Vishu, the start of the Zodiac New Year, in their homes in the traditional way with a *Vishukanni* ("that which is seen first on Vishu"). This involves arrangement, often in the family prayer room, before a large idol or image of Lord Vishnu a mix of auspicious items in a large *uruli* – a traditional cooking vessel made of bell metal – or alternatively on a large brass tray. The items include rice grains, husked and dehusked; some gold ornaments; gold and silver coins; some currency notes; a handheld mirror; vegetables such as pumpkin and yellow cucumber; and an assortment of fruits, in particular ripe bananas and mangoes, pineapple and jackfruit, and a halved coconut in which is placed some betel leaves and areca nuts. Kasavu mundu (traditional dress/*veshti* of Kerala) and a *kindi* (a traditional vessel with a tail used to keep water) are placed near the *uruli*. In some places, the mundu is made into a fan shape and inserted in the *kindi* along with the handheld mirror.

Yellow flowers are copiously placed in front of the deity. A particularly auspicious flower is the *konna poo*, flower of the golden shower tree, *Cassia fistula*. If accessible, it is usual to add other traditional flowers such as *thechi* (ixora), *mandaram* (*Caesalpiniaceae*), and *pichakam* (*Jasminum grandiflorum*) mixed with *thulasi* (holy basil). In the early hours of the morning, just before the break of dawn, the mother (or sometimes the father) in the household awakens to light the *Nilavilakku* (the traditional Kerala prayer lamp) and the joss sticks. She then brings each family member in turn with their eyes covered by her palm to the prayer room and tilts their heads so that when they open their eyes their first sight falls on the auspicious *Vishukanni*.

Set-up for *Vishukanni*

All the family members then sit around to recite collectively some prayers. Inevitably, the ever popular devotional songs *"Kani Kanum Neram"* and *"Thechi Mandaram Thulasi"* would be sung by one of the family members or played out loud on a cassette deck. As per custom, the elders in the family then gave monetary gifts to the younger ones. This is called *Vishu kaineetam*. Following an early-morning bath, everyone adorns new clothes. A celebratory lunch or *sadya* is prepared for that day.

*Vishu* in Sanskrit means "equal" and alludes to the equal number of hours of daylight and darkness that occurs on that day, which according to the Malayalam sidereal solar calendar marks the first equinox of the year. It is a traditional Kerala festival that comes usually in the second week of April.

## TRIP TO CAMERON HIGHLANDS

At the completion of the *sapthaham* at Guruvayur, both Gowri and Thilothamma decided to stay back to attend Ponnu's son's wedding in June 1976. Gowri spent the intervening time with Kamakshi Amma at

Puduserry. Kamakshi Amma had seen Venu and Ravi, but no other member of Gowri's large family.

"When will my other grandchildren come to see me? And my Suraj and Bindu, will they also come?" The questions poured out of Kamakshi Amma's heart.

"They will all come to see you soon. I promise you that," said Gowri, appeasing her and placing in her hands a recent photograph of Suraj and Bindu together.

"Is this for me?" Not waiting for a reply, she kissed the photograph several times and held it close to her chest, her face reflecting the pride and joy of being a great-grandmother.

Ravi, who was in his final term at the medical school of Kerala University in Trivandrum, came down to Pudussery in advance of the wedding to meet up with Gowri. He rendered a beautiful Malayalam song at the wedding reception.

Bindu and Suraj in 1975

Towards the end of 1976, Shivan and Shanti wanted Gowri and the rest of the family to join them at their multiroomed Tudor-style estate bungalow in picturesque Cameron Highlands, one of the country's most extensive hill stations. With an elevation averaging four thousand feet above sea level, it had a temperate climate throughout the year, with day temperatures rarely rising above 25°C and night temperatures dropping as low as 10°C. The families enjoyed the cool atmosphere and walked around the tourist spots wearing sweaters. They visited the famous Boh Tea plantation and walked around the orchards, nurseries, and strawberry farm.

Sharad and Ashwin were then less than 6 months old, and baby strollers were hired to cart them around. Shivan recorded the outings using his pocket Super 8 movie camera. Everyone developed a healthy appetite while in Cameron Highlands, and the cook at the bungalow rose to the challenge, even arranging a barbeque one night. The holiday trip was a memorable one for the entire family. Although the others were not game, Shivan also participated in a jungle trek while at Cameron Highlands to see the world largest flower, the rafflesia. He was in luck and captured the moment with his movie camera.

Indigeneous to Southeastern Asia, the rafflesia is a genus of parasitic flowering plants; it parasites on *Tetrastigma* vines. It lacks any observable leaves, stems, or roots – just a huge, leathery, speckled flower with five to seven petals. Rafflesia flowers can measure up to a hundred centimetres across and weigh up to 10 kilograms. The flower is difficult to locate, as it is only in bloom for seven days. The fresh-flower colour is orange-red; it turns black and disintegrates after five or six days. When in bloom, the rafflesia smells like a rotten carcass to attract insects.

A rafflesia flower in full bloom
*Source: https://www.flickr.com/photos/scornish/275469883.*
*photo by Steve Cornish and is licensed under CC BY 2.0*

☼

# SETHU LEAVES FOR LIBERIA

In early February 1977, Sethu and Uma left the service of Uniroyal at Harvard Process in Bedong to join the company's plantation in Liberia. It was a bold move, but it worked out extremely well for them; Sethu went on to serve there for twelve years. Prior to their departure, they made arrangements for Priya to study at an English-medium boarding school in India. Regularly every year, they would spend their vacation partly in India and partly in Malaysia. Almost invariably, the Section 17 house would be their place to stay and the focal point of visits with friends and relatives while in Malaysia.

Their stint in Liberia proved financially rewarding, and soon they bought a beautiful high-rise apartment on Penang Island at No.1, Persiaran Gurney (Gurney Drive), overlooking the sea. Following the purchase, they divided their time in Malaysia between Petaling Jaya and Penang. Gowri and her family sometimes would accompany them back to Penang from Petaling Jaya. They too liked the spacious apartment and tended to regard it as their Penang holiday resort. Uma and Sethu, on their part, enjoyed entertaining them very much.

On most occasions, Sethu would fetch for breakfast packed bundles of *nasi lemak*, a favourite among Malaysians. This is a combination of fragrant rice cooked with coconut milk and pandan (screwpine) leaves, with fried anchovies, roasted groundnuts, and a boiled egg. It is generally complemented by sambal, a spicy sauce which consists of a mixture of chili, anchovies, tomatoes, shallots, garlic, shrimp paste, tamarind, and lime juice. For lunch, Uma's favourite haunt was the Penang Golf Club, where à la carte Western and Chinese meals were regularly served. Sometimes in the evenings, Sethu and the children would take a leisurely walk along the Gurney Drive coastal esplanade to enjoy the sea breeze. Invariably, they would stop over at the Hawker Centre to tuck into their favourite savoury dishes of *char koay teow* (flat rice noodles stir fried in cooking oil or pork lard with light and dark soy sauce, bean sprouts, shrimp, sambal and egg on a wok set on high heat) and *asam laksa* (rice noodles in a fishy soup flavoured and soured with tamarind). The urge to head for the Hawker Centre for supper was irresistible for the children when they stayed at the Gurney Drive residence.

Uma, of course, was an excellent cook and normally would insist on preparing dinner for all her guests. Although she was a vegetarian like Gowri and Valsala, she was equally adept when it came to cooking meat dishes. She was a truly gifted individual. She had a melodious voice, and Gowri immensely enjoyed listening to her rendition of some evergreen Carnatic songs. Uma also captured the imagination of the Indian community in the country by her prowess at golf. She was a near-scratch golfer, frequently winning or becoming a close runner-up in club and state golf championships in the country. Her family was very proud of her.

A month after Uma and Sethu's departure to Liberia, Dasu had started preparing to leave for England on his second sabbatical. It was agreed that during his absence, his wife – who was then eight month's pregnant – would stay with her parents in Bangsar, a residential suburb of Kuala Lumpur. Dasu had already indicated to Ambika that if a daughter was born, she was to be named Gouri. Aside from the fact that it was his mother's maiden name, he found that name sufficiently modern and had, in point of fact, also encountered it in Australia in the person of the 1st Earl of Gowrie who was the longest serving governor-general of Australia. His good lady, Countess Gowrie, was renowned for her work in promoting the welfare of children in many parts of Australia. To Dasu, the name epitomized love and action, qualities he found in abundance in his own mother. He wanted her maiden name – which was never uttered by her children and grandchildren in addressing her – to be always called out loud and remembered. He reasoned that a daughter would present that opportunity, but suggested that the spelling be changed to Gouri.

Photograph of Uma and Sethu with Gowri in 1979

Popular Malaysian hawker's food: *nasi lemak* (*left*),
*char koay teow* (*top right*), and *asam laksa* (*bottom right*)

# A TESTING TIME

Just before Dasu's departure, the decision had been made that the family
would give up the Section 12 residence. Gowri was pained to leave the
house. Three of her grandchildren – Apsara, Ashwin, and Sharad – had
been born there over the period of December 1975 to October 1976. She

was perhaps naive to think that three daughters-in-law could coexist under one roof without irritations and misunderstandings. Whilst there was no open quarrel amongst the daughters-in-law, their spouses got an earful of their complaints, which of course reached Gowri.

Her three daughters-in-law came from different backgrounds. Presenna hailed from a large family and knew Gowri's family members from childhood. She had given up her job as a flight stewardess soon after she married Venu. Shanti had an unfortunate broken family background but had entered Gowri's family almost a decade ago. This was not the case with Ambika, who came from a small family and was in many ways a stranger in their midst at that point in time. She could not appreciate how overwhelmingly important the concept of togetherness was to her mother-in-law.

Gowri had been deprived of much-needed affection and emotional security when she was barely a teenager. Early widowhood had robbed her and her children of the joy of whole-family bonding. She was determined to create for her children as much as possible a *tharavad*-like existence in her adopted country. Dasu shared his mother's sentiment, although the practicality of it in modern living was to be tested for all concerned. It did not take Ambika too long to observe that her husband was continuing to bear the brunt of household expenses, with no containment efforts in sight. This bothered her – more so when her salary was being drawn into the pool as well.

Gowri was upset to hear of Ambika's dissatisfaction, as she was principally managing the household with Presenna's and occasionally Thilothamma's help in the kitchen. Ambika had her stressful work already cut out at the hospital, what with the night calls added on. Shanti was mostly busy minding Sharad and also trying to establish her modelling business. Although Gowri would have arguments now and then with Presenna and Shanti over some matters, she found her newest daughter-in-law was temperamentally more spirited and candid. Gowri took a myopic view of the sensitivities and discontentment that appeared to be brewing in the house and reacted by picking on Ambika, accusing her of trying to split the family. Ambika was visibly upset by the accusation and confided the matter to Dasu.

"Forget it. I'm sure she will herself realize that it was an overreaction on her part. She is incapable of not loving you, as you are already a part of me," was Dasu's comforting reply.

Mother and daughter-in-law reconciled their differences soon enough, but with Dasu about to take his six-month sabbatical leave and Ambika going to stay with her mother in Bangsar for the period of her delivery, the family was now forced to think afresh about the Section 12 house, which came with a high rental. Hari, having found employment with an accountancy firm in Penang, was already slated to move out. Shivan decided to take Shanti and his children back to Repah Estate in Negeri Sembilan to where he had been posted after his return from Indonesia just before Sharad was born. With that, Venu and Presenna too decided to move out.

For Gowri, who had always wanted her children to be together, this was a rather devastating moment. She brooded on it for several days and finally came to accept it as an artefact of life with extended families. She recalled her stay with Kamalam – a non-erasable event in her memory. She was also reminded of a saying in Malayalam that translated as, "Four testicles are more likely to get along than four boobs." Although the family decided to live as independent units, there was never any enmity between them; perhaps they all harboured individual disappointments at the failed experiment of living equitably under the one roof.

Venu and Presenna found a new dwelling in another part of Petaling Jaya and took Gowri and Thilothamma along with them to stay.

# [23]

At the end of May 1977, Ambika – leaving her newborn child in the care of her parents in Bangsar – came to London accompanied by Gowri. Dasu had already intimated his desire to Ambika to give his mother this unique opportunity to see a part of the world she had read much about in her novels. Dasu had remembered his mother humming many a time the tune with the opening lyrics "It was on the Isle of Capri that I found her ..." when he was a teenager. It was a hit song from the early 1930s that somehow had caught Gowri's fancy.

Before he left for London, he had told her, "Mum, when Ambika comes over to visit me, I want you to come along. We shall be taking a short coach trip across Europe. You will not be able to go to your favourite Isle of Capri, I'm afraid, but Italy will be included, and we shall definitely be visiting Venice for a gondola ride."

Gowri had a disbelieving look on her face, but her eyes gleamed with pleasure. She quickly asked whether Ambika minded her coming along.

"Of course not, Mum. She was all in support and thought it was the best present any son could give his mother. In any case, she being a doctor, I will also have peace of mind during the trip," replied Dasu.

Gowri wasted no time in informing others in the family, all of whom urged her to take the trip and offered to take her out shopping for the right garments. "It will be the spring season Mum, a lovely time to visit, but the weather can still be cold," was the general advice, and Gowri rightly heeded it.

☼

# A CHILDHOOD DREAM REALIZED

Dasu had booked with the Cosmos Europe Coach Tours for a sixteen-day tour of Europe from London towards the end of May. The trip covered seven countries: Belgium, the Netherlands, Germany, Austria, Italy, Switzerland, and France. Although hectic, it proved to be the most enjoyable trip ever for the trio, who found themselves in a mixed group of nationalities. They were, however, the only Malaysians. The others came from Iran, Singapore, Australia, New Zealand, Unites States, and Canada.

The guide on the tour was an extremely pleasant Italian lady who knew the history of every place inside out, and her camaraderie was contagious. Gowri had read a lot about the countries and historical places in Europe in her novels, and setting foot on some of these places on the tour really excited her. Mother and daughter-in-law bonded well, often trading jokes in Malayalam on the coach. They also got on well with their fellow tourists.

The coach drive across Europe was truly picturesque. They recalled passing medieval fortresses, castles, churches, and vineyards along the route. The Dutch countryside with rolling meadows of blooming tulips, daffodils, and hyacinths was a heavenly sight that simply could not be imagined. It was as if Mother Nature was putting on a special display just for them. The drive from Amsterdam to Innsbruck via the Rhine Valley was particularly exquisite. Everyone was thrilled to take the Rhine cruise with vistas of hilltop castles, half-timbered wine villages, and terraced vineyards.

Crossing over the Austrian border from Innsbruck via the Brenner Pass into Italy and heading to Venice via Carbonin, they were spellbound by the alpine scenery. The guide told them, "We are lucky to be taking this mountain pass. Only yesterday was it cleared of the heavy snowfall which had closed it for any kind of traffic for over a fortnight." There was still evidence of hardened snow on the ground on both sides of the pass.

Arriving at Carbonin for an overnight stay, they found fresh snow welcoming them in the morning. This presented everyone with the opportunity to frolic in the snow a bit before boarding the bus on its onward journey. Dasu and Ambika traded throwing snowballs at each other. Gowri, heavily clad in a coat and a head scarf to beat the chill, watched the scene from the sidelines ... but not for long. Not wanting to be left out of the fun, she joined them, throwing snowballs at both Dasu and Ambika and getting one right smack on her head courtesy of her regular seatmate. It was a unique treat for all of them to be handling the soft snow.

Picture-postcard scenery in the Austrian Alps

Arriving at Venice, they found the place a labyrinth of small streets, alleys, bridges, and canals – all very quaint and oozing with vintage charm. They walked around buying some trinkets and a couple of trademark Venetian masks. Most enjoyable was the gondola ride they took towards late evening on the Grand Canal, listening to the serenade by the gondolier.

"He is singing a romantic Italian song. We should respond by at least holding hands," said Dasu to Ambika.

"Yes, you must, but anything more might rock the boat!" quipped Gowri, smiling and looking away.

Although they had enjoyed very much the boat ride on the Rhine earlier on the tour, this was a new experience altogether – and under a full moon too.

*Top:* Snow-clad grounds at Carbonin and Gowri braving the cold
*Bottom:* View down the Grand Canal in Venice

Gondola ride on the Grand Canal in Venice.
*Source: https://www.flickr.com/photos/gnuckx/11645015125/;*
*photo by Gnuckx and is licensed under CC BY 2.0*

The next day, the tour bus made a stop at a Murano glass factory, where Dasu placed an order for some ornately decorated glassware to be sent home to Malaysia. Crossing over to Switzerland, they stopped at Lucerne, a truly picturesque city. They were equally enthralled with the stunning view they had of Lake Lucerne. While a few of the tourists availed of the paying option to take the night cruise on the lake, the rest fancied the Cosmos-added excursion of an evening of fun at a restaurant. Here they were served the famous cheese fondue, which Gowri and Ambika immensely enjoyed. They were also treated to traditional Swiss folk dances and yodelling. Some members of the tour party sportingly tested their ability at blowing the traditional Swiss horn.

The next day, as they entered Paris, the border authorities singled out the Malaysians for a thorough examination of their luggage. Gowri wore an understanding smile, but not Dasu, who felt that the security check was not routine and was carried out with some gusto, leading to considerable disarray of items within the bags.

Their stay in Paris was for two nights and three days. Some in the party took the Metro to other destinations for a quick visit, including the vineyards at Reims. Others favoured checking out gourmet French meals. Gowri recalled the New Zealand couple praising an exquisite restaurant they had gone to where they had enjoyed a delicious garlic-and-herb-flavored escargot dish. Dasu whispered, "They mean snails" to Gowri, who immediately wore a disgusted look and uttered a muffled shriek. Understanding her vegetarian habits, the couple took it good-humouredly.

The standout visits in Paris were to the Eiffel Tower, Notre Dame Cathedral, and the Louvre. They were somewhat disappointed at seeing the actual small dimensions of the famous *Mona Lisa* painting at the Louvre Museum; they had expected a large canvas portrait. Only upon returning to London did they explore its landmarks in turn, travelling by the underground tube on their own from their residence at East Acton. Dasu joined his wife and mother in one or two trips over the weekends, as he was at work during the week at the International Tin Research Institute at Perivale. Some weekends, they would pay a visit to their new-found friends the Bhanus, who were working with British Airways.

Their residence was at Hounslow West. Bhanu was the brother of Subadra Raghavan, a family friend of Ambika from her younger days in the oil palm estate in Slim River, Perak, where her father had worked. They were an extremely hospitable couple who also eagerly looked forward to meeting them both as friends and as fellow Malayalees.

On one early visit soon after their return from their European tour, Mrs Bhanu, whose maiden name was Indira, had asked them of their impressions.

"Never in my wildest dreams did I imagine I would be here on a different continent," answered Gowri. "Thanks to my son, I have now seen with my own eyes what I could but only read in books in my younger days. The places we went to all had a charm of their own. The tour was really a pleasant and memorable experience. Ambika and I have only a couple of complaints."

"About what, Aunty?" asked Indira..

"Oh, about the vegetarian meals that we were served, and the toilet and bath facilities at the hotels they put us in."

"The food was bland, was it?"

"That's putting it mildly! The standard meal of vegetarian cutlet, salad, and bread was giving us the creeps. Our teeth were refusing to bite into them. I wonder how anyone can eat anything without salt and chilli. We were pining for some plain rice and pickles, if nothing else."

"We should have taken a bottle of pickles with us, *Amma*" chipped in Ambika.

"Yes, indeed. Unfortunately, we found no Asian restaurants close by to the hotels we were staying in."

"Your lodgings were quite distant then from the main town areas?" ventured Indira.

"I would guess so, being budget hotels. The worst feature was their communal bathrooms located on each floor. They all had only bathtubs. Getting into them was a problem. And the toilets ..."

"Yes, Mum. I know what you are going to say," interrupted Dasu. "You were hoping that there would be a water tap and a ladle close at hand. You cannot expect that even in the posh hotels here, Mum." Turning to the others, he continued: "*Amma* once entered the bathroom immediately after the exit of a fellow tourist from his bath. She found the bathtub covered with a thick layer of dirt and foaming soap and quickly darted out. She found it unhygienic and unacceptable. I had to really coax the hotel management to wash the bathtub before she dared to re-enter." Everyone laughed and agreed on the items they should be taking along on any future trip.

Gowri returned home after four weeks, while Ambika stayed on for a further two weeks, squeezing in visits to Oxford and Edinburgh with Dasu.

Gowri in front of the Notre Dame Cathedral (*left*) and with Ambika at the Château de Versailles (*right*) in Paris.

Gowri posing with Dasu, Ambika, and fellow tour members on the European tour and relaxing on the grounds of Windsor Castle, London

☼

Dasu returned in August and stayed at Bangsar. He was meeting his daughter for the first time; she brought him luck, for within a month of his return he was promoted to associate professor, with the promotion being backdated to 1975, a step that was without precedent at the university. Dasu recalled a strong prediction by an astrologer he had consulted in 1971 that he would see his career prospects surge in 1975 and in 1980, but as the year 1975 had passed and nothing had happened, he had dismissed the matter as a fanciful interlude. Although his scientific mind attributed this to nothing more than coincidence, he couldn't help being sensitized to what might lie ahead in 1980.

"So, you still have some faith in astrology?" his colleague in the department had taunted him.

Dasu, who had been reading a bit about astrology, answered him in a measured tone. "I don't know if I can truthfully say I am a full believer in it, but I am tempted to believe that a properly constructed birth chart based on planetary positions may carry some clues about one's destiny. The prediction of my father's death to almost the exact date was certainly uncanny. Well, the astrologer has predicted something for me in 1980. Let us see if his prediction comes true once more!"

"Who is this chap you met?"

"He hails from Kerala and from a family of astrologers. He visits Malaysia quite regularly."

"And the basis of his predictions?"

"Yes, I did ask him about that. He said all his predictions come from a study of *Jyotishmati Upanishad*, the legendary first book on predictive Hindu astrology. In explaining the importance or otherwise of the positions of each of the planets in my birth chart, I recall he was largely reciting Sanskrit slokas and contextually interpreting them."

"Are you telling me that for each set of planetary positions there will be a different sloka?"

"I don't know whether that's how it is, but my guess is that these slokas in their totality contain the gist of yogic and tantric experiences of the entire human race – that is, experiences which are universal and inherited as described by Carl Jung."

"Wow, this is going a bit beyond me. And I had thought that I could quit chemistry and take up this trade!"

# [24]

With eligibility for a housing loan from the university, Dasu bought a double-storey, corner-lot detached house with a large garden compound in Section 17, Petaling Jaya. This was in February 1978. The house still stands majestically in its location, and its basic configuration has changed little over the decades. The ground floor has a driveway and car porches, a large living-cum-dining area that opens out into the garden, a bedroom with a bathroom beside it, a large kitchen, and an adjoining utility area (laundry) that has an exit door to the back of the house. Flanking the utility area on one side is a maid's bedroom, and on the other side there is a bathroom as well as a small store. From the utility area, there is an approach door to an entertainment room which shares a wall with the kitchen, and this opens out into the garden. The garden at the back of the house had rambutan, chiku, and star fruit trees at the time of purchase. The first floor has a landing hall with a balcony, a large master bedroom with an en suite bathroom and a balcony, and two other bedrooms connected by a shared bathroom.

Section 17 house that was to be Gowri's Malaysian *tharavad*

190

Moving in with his family on 26 May 1978, after completing some renovations, Dasu celebrated his birthday the following day in the house. Ambika, who was a registrar in the Department of Anaesthesiology at the General Hospital in Kuala Lumpur, welcomed the move because she hated negotiating the heavy traffic each day driving to work. She soon quit her government job and found a position at the Assunta Hospital in Petaling Jaya.

For both husband and wife, their places of work were now much closer to their home than previously. Dasu brought his mother to stay with him within a week of their move. She occupied the room on the ground floor. The bathroom adjacent to it was fitted with a modern toilet and a handheld bidet; a tiled shower seat was constructed along one side of the wall of the shower area at her request.

## THE MAKING OF THE MALAYSIAN *THARAVAD*

The Section 17 house soon became the meeting place of all of Gowri's children and grandchildren for many memorable functions. Many birthdays, *aranjanam* (naming ceremony of newborn), *choroonu* (child's first rice-eating ceremony), *vidyarambham* (child's first introduction to the world of learning; *vidya* means "knowledge and learning", and *arambham* means "beginning"), sangeet parties and wedding receptions were held in the house, and the beginnings of a Malaysian *tharavad* for Gowri was thus established.

The *aranjanam* ceremony is normally performed on the twenty-eighth day after the birth of the child when the *nakshatram* (birth star) of the child first repeats itself according to the Malayalam calendar. The infant is placed on the lap of the mother who sits cross-legged on the ground facing the east, where a lighted oil lamp is placed in front of the family deity. A black cotton thread, intertwined with a gold chain, is tied around the waist of the newborn; the infant's eyes are anointed with *kanmashi* (eye salve); and a black spot is placed on one cheek to ward off the evil eye. The child's chosen name is then whispered thrice by the maternal uncle (or father) into each ear of the child, while the other ear is covered with a betel leaf. He then takes a gold ring, dips it in a mixture of milk and honey, and brings the dipped end to touch the tongue of the infant. Other senior family members present at the ceremony follow suit.

The *choroonu* ceremony is performed when the child is a bit older, usually between the fifth and eighth month. In this ceremony, the father, following tradition, seats himself on the ground facing the east, and, with the child placed on his lap, feeds the child his first rice meal laid out in front of him on a plantain leaf. An auspicious day is chosen for this ceremony in consultation with a priest. As with the *aranjanam*, it is an occasion for celebration in the family.

*Vidyarambham* is the ceremony when the toddler, at the age of two or three, is initiated into the world of alphabets by the parents. Seated on the lap of the father in front of the family altar that includes the *murti* (sacred image) of Goddess Saraswati (the goddess of *vidya*), the child is made to write in a tray of rice grains the Malayalam script of the mantra, "*Om Hari Sri Ganapataye Namah*"("Salutations to Hari (Lord Vishnu), Sri (the goddess of prosperity) and Lord Ganapathy"). Parents may also elect to have this ceremony performed in a temple on an auspicious day chosen from the Hindu astrological almanac (*panchangam*).

Gowri was in the thick of these ceremonies for all her grandchildren, including in the preparation of the celebratory meals. No priestly help was needed as she was too well steeped in such traditions.

Whenever Uma and Sethu came on leave from Liberia, the Section 17 house would be their focal point in Petaling Jaya from which they would plan their visits to relatives and friends. For varying periods, some of Dasu's male siblings and their families also came to stay in the house. Whilst condescending to observe a *tharavad* style of communal living may not be the dream of every modern housewife, Dasu's wife, Ambika, who was *ettathiamma* (eldest son's wife) to his siblings, proved to be an extremely tolerant and understanding person. She accepted them wholeheartedly into the house in the spirit of the *tharavad* her husband was intent on establishing for his mother.

In terms of location, the Section 17 house was certainly very strategic. It was within easy reach of the University Hospital, the wet market, major shopping malls and supermarkets, the post office, schools, the airport, and access routes to major highways linking the north and south of the country. Also, the bustling Tuesday-night market (locally called *pasar malam*) in Section 17 spread along an entire stretch of road within a kilometre walking distance from the house; it thrives to this day as something of an institution. Despite causing a gridlock on the roads around it, it delights all those who attend with every imaginable item for trade. This is the place to go to for fresh produce at bargain prices, for savouring noodles and kebabs cooked on the spot at food stalls, and for buying at whittled-down prices ready-made garments, handbags, shoes, watches (often cheap replicas of brand names), sweets and savouries, and even VCR movies (many in pirated versions). The market starts around three in the afternoon and runs until after dark. Many an overseas visitor to the university was introduced to the sights and sounds of this night market by Dasu. They enjoyed the experience.

Over the years, the Section 17 house was the place Gowri's grandchildren would regularly flock during school holidays. Gowri counted those periods with them as among the happiest moments of her life. In addition to Dasu's children, she was nearly always surrounded by Venu's children and Sharad, who enjoyed her playful company. Gowri had a knack for creating her own special relationship with each of her grandchildren, so that every one of them felt like he or she was the favourite. A telephone call about the arrival of any grandchild would drive her to rush out of the house in her usual sarong and blouse, sometimes with only one slipper on in her haste, smelling of powder, eyes all lit up.

Up until the early 1980s, most of Gowri's grandchildren were under 12 years old. She would get them all to sit on the floor as she doled out mouthfuls of food to each of them in turn while telling stories. One of her favourite stories was Jane Austen's "Pride and Prejudice". Often, she would sit on her usual chair that had a pull-out footrest. The younger ones would vie to sit with her on the chair, nestled in her ample abdomen. Her tactic for keeping a restless young grandchild on her seat was to challenge the child to separate the fused fourth and fifth toes on her left leg. Though it was a bit unfair, it served as quite a fun game. Years later, Nisha would recall the scene: "We would sit there cross-legged on the carpeted floor, listening totally riveted to the unfolding story which took us back in time and to places that our minds could easily imagine simply because of the way she described them. It was also magical how her fingers created some strange alchemy with the rice, turning an everyday meal into something impossibly delicious."

If she wasn't telling stories, Gowri would engage her grandchildren in a word-building game or in reciting the multiplication table, which didn't quite end at the twelve-times table but stretched to sixteen. That's how she herself had learnt it, although its relevance had long disappeared, as the Indian rupee and its equivalent of sixteen annas was changed to the present decimal currency system.

Understandably, Dasu's children were the closest to Gowri, as she was with them the most through the various stages of their growth. As they got older, they would attend to some of her needs, whether massaging her tired legs at bedtime, turning on the television and VCR, or plucking flowers from the garden at prayer time. She would painstakingly explain to them the meaning of the *stotra* (devotional hymns) in both Sanskrit and Malayalam, which they would all recite collectively at prayer time in the evenings before dinner and soon after they had all taken their bath. She had not had the opportunity to teach this to her own children, who only knew the *stotra* but not their meaning. She subsequently wrote the hymns down in Romanized form and made them available to all her other grandchildren, and made it a point that they too should understand.

# TRAVEL BUG

Gowri just did not have the patience to await the school holidays to see her grandchildren who were not in proximate contact with her. She would frequently make trips to visit them. In the case of Ambi's children, this entailed just a two-hour trip to Ipoh, but it would take an additional three or four from Ipoh to get to Kangar in Perlis where Valsala and her children were staying. Aravind, upon deciding to rejoin government service after his postgraduate studies, had found himself posted to Kangar in 1976. It was while she was in Kangar around mid-September 1977 that Gowri had the opportunity to meet with HRH Raja Perempuan of Perlis, the consort to the ruler of Perlis. The Raja Perempuan had come with Toh Puan Muda, her daughter-in-law, to Valsala's house to see Kiran, who had just been born. Gowri found Her Royal Highness to be very affable and extremely down-to-earth. They struck up a light conversation on how, over time, delivery and postnatal care had changed, and on the re-emphasis that was now being placed on breast feeding.

The year 1977 proved to be a busy travel year for Gowri. Upon returning from Kangar, she paid a quick visit to Puduserry in India along with Kamalam, who had wanted her company on a visit to their mother. They found Kamakshi Amma in reasonably good health, except for her arthritic knees which still troubled her, preventing much mobility. Gowri bought her a two-wheel orthopaedic walker. This was an instant hit with the old woman, who started gleefully moving around the house.

One day the sisters decided to give their mother a royal oil bath. The oil was subsequently removed by applying copious amounts of scented soap lather on her body and shampoo on her still long hair, which they noticed was more grey than white. "Oh, my eyes, they are gone!" she screamed, pressing her eyelids tight all the time while the shampooing was in progress. After towelling, her reaction upon opening her eyes was childishly simple. "I can see much better now with my eyes."

While at Pudussery, Gowri and Kamalam spent some money improving amenities at their mother's place. This included getting a new pump and filtering system for the family well outside the house and refurbishing the bathroom with a water heater and a modern sit-down flush toilet. This, of course, added to their own comfort while they were there, as they intensely detested leaving the house premises to visit the old squatting-type toilet behind the house.

While in India, Gowri took the opportunity to source and purchase an embroidered, gold-threaded silk stole which she asked Valsala to present to HRH Raja Perempuan of Perlis as a small gift. Also before returning home, Gowri – in the company of Ponnu – took the opportunity to visit Dasu's father-in-law at Kadampat, his ancestral home near Thrissur. He had come to India to celebrate his sixtieth birthday. Gowri presented him with a silver cup.

Gowri kept in close touch with all her children's in-laws, who had much respect for her. They would unfailingly visit her if they came down to Petaling Jaya, and she would insist that they partake of food before leaving. She was particularly saddened to hear the news of the passing away of her daughter Ambi's father-in-law, P. K. A. K. Menon, in 1978. He was a jovial person who held to the view that "life was ours to be spent, not to be saved." His wife, Karthiyayini, who sought inspiration from Gowri's courage in bringing up her children as a widow, died suddenly one morning a couple of years later. Gowri had also sustained a personal loss in 1979 - her sister-in-law, Vilasini, in India, had succumbed to cancer. Bala Menon was badly affected by her death. Gowri had to keep in constant touch with him over the phone for several weeks to help him get over his sorrow. Bala Menon was much junior to Gowri in age, and he held his sister in great affection and esteem. At her insistence, he agreed to employ a maid to do the household chores and also look after Kamakshi Amma. Gowri undertook to meet the necessary expenses and send regular monthly remittances to Bala Menon.

## RAVI NURSES AN AILMENT

Ravi, who returned from his studies in India in 1977, completed his one-year housemanship at the Penang General Hospital. Soon thereafter, he was posted to the Melaka General Hospital as a medical officer. It was while on duty there that he started experiencing severe pain in his right leg and a growing numbness in his other leg. The combination badly affected his gait. He recalled being involved in a crash while riding a motor bicycle in Trivandrum, and he couldn't help wondering whether that fall had affected his backbone. A simple X-ray of the spine revealed nothing amiss, and the thought of a developing tumour gripped everyone's imagination.

Gowri was traumatized by the news. Her children were her most valuable asset, and she couldn't bear the thought of any one of them being afflicted. She prayed at the altar several times a day, beseeching the Almighty to transfer her son's pain and agony to her. Venu and Ambika, being medically trained, tried to downplay Ravi's ailment, assuring her that it was not life-threatening, but Gowri sensed that these were just words of comfort. Her agile mind wondered how his ailment could be corrected, be it in any part of the world.

The family consulted several medical specialists in Kuala Lumpur, and it was decided that an eminent neurosurgeon would perform surgery on Ravi's spine at the first opportunity to determine and, if possible, correct the cause. The operation, thankfully, revealed the absence of any obstructive lesion or growth. It was assumed that Ravi had a deep-seated neurological problem affecting the spinal cord, such as multiple sclerosis or demyelinating disease of the spine. Ravi before long had to resort to using a walking stick. Gowri was much tormented by her son's affliction, but Ravi was so positive in his outlook that he was able to cope with the handicap.

Kamakshi Amma with her daughters, son, and daughter-in-law in 1977:
(*seated, left to right*) Kamalam, Kamakshi Amma, Gowri;
(*standing*) Bala Menon and Vilasini.

One weekend in late 1980, Ravi went to visit Valsala and Aravind – who
had by then shifted to Alor Star – to discuss a proposal for marriage that
Aravind had earlier arranged through his good friend, Vanamali Menon,
a private practitioner in Kangar. Aravind had mentioned to Vanamali
Menon that he was looking for a bride for Ravi, who was nursing a medical
disability. Vanamali Menon had responded that he would approach his
unmarried niece, Susheela, who was a teacher in Ipoh, to see if she might
be interested. Valsala gave Vanamali her brother's horoscope details. Ravi

and Susheela met and had a frank discussion. He told her that multiple sclerosis is a progressive disease and that at some stage in his life he could be confined to a wheelchair. She had little problem with that projection.

Gowri was delighted to hear the news. The marriage took place in Teluk Intan in March 1981. Within months of his marriage, Ravi left government service and started his own private general practice in Melaka at Tanjong Kling. He developed it into a thriving solo practice. He bought a house close by at Taman Muhibbah, within walking distance of the seaside beach, which was considered by the landlocked members of his family as a resort place to visit.

Ravi weds Susheela. Standing second to the
bride's left is Susheela's mother, Rohini.

# THANKSGIVING AT THAIPUSAM

Prior to Ravi's operation, an intensely worried Gowri had vowed that she would carry along with him, upon his recovery, milk *kavadi* (shoulder weight of a pot of milk) on *Thaipusam* for three consecutive years.

*Thaipusam* is the Hindu festival dedicated to Lord Subramanya (Murugan) that falls on the day of the full moon in the Tamil month of *Thai* (January/February). In Kuala Lumpur, devotees negotiate 272 steps to reach the temple at Batu Caves, a limestone hill some 8 miles (or 13 kilometres on the metric system, which the country formally started to use in 1972) north of the city. On two occasions, Gowri – who was by then in her late sixties – and Ravi fulfilled the vow in Kuala Lumpur, and on another occasion in Penang. In Kuala Lumpur, they were accompanied by other members of the family.

*Thaipusam* is a colourful festival which attracts tourists from all over the world to witness devotees fulfilling their vows by carrying either a simple shoulder weight of a pot of milk or a massive *vel kavadi* – an altar assembled upon a steel frame decorated with flowers and peacock feathers up to a few metres tall, and attached to the chest and back of the devotee with hooks and skewers. Many of the devotees have either their cheeks or tongue pierced by a skewer. It is not unusual to find many of the pilgrims in drum- and dance-induced trance states while carrying the *kavadi*. The ritually conscious devotees observe a vegetarian fast and complete chastity for about a month before taking the *kavadi*.

*Left*: The Batu Caves, focal point of the *Thaipusam* festival in Kuala Lumpur. The 43-metre-tall gold-painted concrete-cum-steel statue of Lord Murugan was erected in 2006 at the entrance to the cave temple located 100 metres above the ground. *Right:* Close-up of Ambika's brother-in-law Sivalingam carrying a *kavadi* attached to his torso by hook-bearing metallic threads, and with his cheeks pierced by a skewer. (Photo courtesy of Dr R. Sivalingam, 2016)

Ponnu's daughter, Shoba, who had completed her studies, came down for a visit to Malaysia from Palakkad in late 1980 and stayed for a few months with Venu and Presenna. Hari, who had by then shifted back to Petaling Jaya from Penang and was staying with Dasu, went to see Shoba. She had grown up into a beautiful young lass. They began to see each other more often. At the back of their minds was the oft-repeated teasing within their families arising from the expressed desire by Hari's late father at Shoba's birth that she should one day become his daughter-in-law. Before Shoba left for India, Hari proposed to her.

Hari and Shoba had their engagement in November 1981 in India at Ponnu's house. In attendance were Hari's grandmother, Kamakshi Amma, and his uncle, Bala Menon. For Kamakshi Amma, the 7-kilometre car trip from her house to Ponnu's house in Chandranagar in Palakkad was probably the first in decades, and she was thrilled. At the conclusion of the function, she expressed a desire to go to Guruvayur temple, some 100 kilometres away from Palakkad, and pray for both of them. Hari arranged for the trip the very next day and also hired a wheelchair for her use. For Kamakshi Amma, it was a dream fulfilled, and her youngest grandson had helped achieve this for her.

Gowri and Thilothamma (*seated*) with the newlyweds Hari and Shoba, and Shoba's parents Ponnu and A. K. N. Nair (Nanu Uncle)

Hari and Shoba's wedding took place at the end of July 1982 in Petaling Jaya. The family sent for Bala Menon to be in attendance. He was a jovial person who bonded well with Gowri's children. He narrated to them all the historical happenings in his feud-ridden family, corroborating much of what they had heard from Gowri. He came alive when talking about the life he experienced in northern India when he left his home in Pudussery to join the Indian Army. "My stint in the army helped me to regain my sanity," he said unabashedly.

The grand-uncle proved a hit with his grand-nephews and grand-nieces. He had the uncanny habit of dozing off at short notice, if left to himself. And he was a terrible snorer. Gowri would reprimand the grandchildren for imitating his snore. Whilst at the airport, on his return trip home, he actually lost a piece of his hand luggage through this habit. It was stolen right from under his nose.

A few months prior to Hari's wedding, Gowri had found herself excitedly organizing the wedding event of Kamalam's son, Prakash, who was betrothed to her son-in-law Ravindran's youngest sister, Padmini. Gowri was responsible for bringing the proposal for the consideration of Padmini's brother, Balram, in the absence of their deceased parents. Prakash had qualified as a doctor from India and was attached to the Department of Public Health at the Kota Kinabalu General Hospital in Sabah. His parents had by then settled in Lahad Datu, a town in East Sabah, together with his married sister, Prabha. The entire Kamalam family came for the April wedding in Kuala Lumpur and stayed for the duration at the Section 17 house.

In July 1981, the Gowri family was saddened by the sudden death of Dasu's father-in-law, M. K. G. Nair. He had suffered a heart attack close to midnight in his Bangsar home, and before Dasu and Ambika could get there, he had passed away. Dasu helped with the funeral arrangements the following day. Ambika's few relatives, many of whom were acquainted with Gowri, came over to console the family. They included the family of K. Ramakrishnan, the sole relative from her father's side, and family members of her mother's Numbreth *tharavad* cousins V. N. P. Nair, N. K. Nair, and V. B. Nair.

Kamalam's family album picture with daughter-in-law Padmini
(*fourth from left*) and son Prakash (*extreme right*).

The approach of Deepavali in early November, combined with school holidays, prompted the family to plan for a holiday break out of town. They finally settled on the beach and holiday resort at Port Dickson, some 90 kilometres south of Kuala Lumpur. It was really an occasion for the grandchildren to bond. They enjoyed the frolic on the beach and the "treasure hunt" looking for painted shells and tennis balls hidden in the sand. Running barefoot after them on the slippery sand provided the elders with an unexpected burst of exercise.

The grandchildren coaxed Gowri to join them in the sea. She waded in knee deep, but this was done under the watchful eyes of both Dasu and Shivan, who didn't want a repeat of the incident that Gowri had experienced a decade back at Woodlands, Singapore.

One late afternoon, everyone was caught by surprise when a birthday cake was wheeled onto the beach with fanfare accompaniment and placed in the canopy tent where Gowri, wearing a large straw hat, was seated. Dasu announced that they were observing Gowri's sixty-sixth birthday early. Since the breeze wouldn't let up, it was not easy to get the candles lit, but the older grandchildren had a shot at it and managed finally to light them all. To everyone's delight, Gowri blew virtually all the candles out in one great puff from just where she was seated. Her puff appeared stronger than the breeze! She then had to cope with the inevitable mouthfuls of cake that each grandchild in turn was intent on feeding her.

Gowri with her grandchildren at the beach
resort of Port Dickson in 1981

# [25]

In February 1982, after observing *Thaipusam* along with Ravi, Gowri accompanied Ambika and her children on a month-long trip to India. Ambika had very much wanted to see her grandmother at Kadampat following her father's demise. Dasu arrived at Puduserry two weeks later. Kamakshi Amma was thrilled to see Ashwin, Gowri, and Sathya running round her house and making a ruckus. The sound of children laughing and crying had not been heard in her house for ages, and she seemed to be soaking up every decibel and savouring the moment. Bala Menon had no offspring and had lost his first wife to cancer in early 1979. Not a person to hold back his emotions, he cried on Gowri's shoulders when she asked him for details of the illness. Gowri sensed there was a need to find a second bride for her brother, and said to Dasu that she intended to seek Kamalam's support on the matter soon.

Dasu was meeting his grandmother Kamakshi Amma for the first time. Looking at her face, he saw a spitting image of his mother. She was jovial and wanted him most times to sit with her and chat. Sathya, seeing them together, would climb up to sit with them. She didn't quite fancy her father ignoring her and devoting his attention to someone else!

With Dasu's arrival, a trip was made to Guruvayur and Kodungallur, and thence to Pazhani, Madurai, and Rameshwaram for temple visits. Bala Menon accompanied them. Secretly, Gowri had long been harbouring hopes of a visit to historic religious sites in India. The Ramayana and Mahabharata, the two major Sanskrit epics of ancient India that she was very familiar with, contained geographical references to areas in present-day Tamil Nadu and Haryana where the mythological wars described in the epics had been fought. She wondered whether temples erected in their vicinity carried signatures of these ancient events. She was truly excited about the arranged temple visits. She felt that it was a God-sent opportunity and her good fortune that she was being accompanied by both her eldest son and her brother.

## VISITS TO GURUVAYUR AND KODUNGALLUR TEMPLES

The visits to Guruvayur and Kodungallur were accomplished on the one day. They left for Guruvayur first, arriving there for the afternoon pujas which commenced around midday. It was a cramped ride, but no one complained, as they were all gripped with excitement.

The Sree Krishna temple at Guruvayur is one of the most sacred and important temples in India. Non-Hindus are not allowed into the temple, which also observes a strict dress code. Men are not allowed to wear shirts or vests and must remain topless while inside the complex. They have to wear strictly Kerala *mundus* (cotton or silk garments worn round the waist), but are free to wear a shawl to cover the upper body. Ladies have to wear sarees. Knowing this, Bala Menon, Dasu, and Ashwin had already donned the *mundus* at the start of the trip. Following prayers, they walked around for a bit in the vast temple grounds. They left for Kodungallur immediately after partaking of some light lunch.

Their destination at Kodungallur was the famous Bhagawathy Temple (alternatively Kurumba Bhagavati Temple) there. This ancient temple stands out as among the first temples in Kerala which removed the caste and religious restrictions of worshippers. Gowri had always wanted to pray at the temple, and with that intention in mind had bought a red-dyed dhoti at Guruvayur to be given as the traditional offering to the goddess. Ambika had followed suit.

It was close to five in the evening when they reached Kodungallur. Surrounded by backwaters and the sea, Kodungallur is on the modern tourist map of Kerala for houseboat and backwater-resort tourism, but hordes of visitors also descend on this place for religious reasons. It is said to be the place where St Thomas first preached Christianity in India in 52 AD. It also boasts the first mosque to be built in India in 629 AD – the Cheraman Juma Masjid, which architecturally resembles a temple. Open to visitors of all religious persuasions, the mosque still keeps at its centre a traditional Kerala oil lamp. Kodungallur also once housed the world's second synagogue, but this was destroyed by the marauding Portuguese five hundred years ago and relocated to Kochi.

The Kodungallur Bhagawathy Temple was already open when they arrived. The idol of the deity, the goddess Bhadrakali, is an imposing one; it has eight hands with various attributes. One is holding the head of the evil demon Daruka, another a sword, next an anklet, another a bell, and so on. Gowri and Ambika offered the dhotis they had bought to the priest to be placed on the idol, and for the purpose of the prayer gave the names and birth stars of all relatives from both households written on a piece of paper. The prayer duly performed, the priest applied the sacred ash to the foreheads of all the children. Gowri and Ambika individually received the *prasadam* (offering) from the priest before leaving the temple. Conveniently, just outside the temple grounds, they found an eatery where they decided to have a quick dinner. It would be another four hours or more before they would arrive back at Pudussery.

The sun was already setting when they left Kodungallur – a huge red ball on the horizon. The oven-like heat of the afternoon had receded, and there was a gentle breeze that carried the unmistakable fragrance of jasmine. As the car sped on towards Pallakad, the sounds of the evening drifted in. First it was the cacophony of the crows returning to their nests on the top of the trees, but this soon gave way to a symphony of ringing sounds of temple and church bells, followed not long after by the muezzin's azan (call for prayer) from the minarets of nearby mosques. This uniqueness of Kerala – where the confluence of three major religions had not unleashed discord but rather fomented harmony and religious tolerance – has few parallels elsewhere. Kerala had also provided shelter to Jews whose first arrival and subsequent large settlement in Cochin dated back to over four millennia. History records no instances of antisemitism from the local majority Hindu population residing there.

Dasu's children, despite the somewhat bumpy ride, began to doze off, their heads pillowed against each other's shoulder. Left with her thoughts to herself, Gowri's mind went back to her younger days at Puduserry – those carefree days spent frolicking with her sisters and brother. They would watch the workers plant the paddy and sometimes jump in to help when no elders were around, and later in the season after the harvest they would take turns at thrashing the bundles of paddy stalks. Particularly enjoyable were those occasions when they would sneak out behind their house on dark nights to watch the bright canopy of stars in the cloudless sky and count the shooting stars that came by. Other than the soft chirping of crickets in the grass and the gentle rustle of the wind, the nights would be still and silent. They were conscious of the danger of slithering snakes, but they always felt emboldened stepping out in their togetherness. They would also stay on to witness the not-to-be-outdone dance of the fireflies lower in the sky, but rush back home in fright at the first sound of a screeching bird or the howl of some animal that to their imaginative minds were the sounds of prowling spirits. Most enjoyable of all, she reminisced, was the unbridled freedom of dips in their private secluded pond. She lingered on these memories that refused to dim with time.

It was close to midnight when they finally arrived at Pudussery, tired after the whole day trip, although the elders in the group had found it spiritually immensely satisfying.

## VISITS TO FAMOUS TEMPLES IN TAMIL NADU

The second phase of their temple visits started three days later. They had to travel some 100 kilometres to get to Pazhani (Palani, in Tamil), home of the famous hilltop Palani temple dedicated to Lord Subramanya (Murugan). It is approachable by the main flight of stairs cut into the hillside, but the family decided to take the funicular to make the ascent. The evening prayer bell call sounded as soon as they reached the top. They were able to witness the *abhishekam* (pouring of libations as an act of ritual purification) of the idol and pray to their hearts' content. They stayed overnight in Pazhani.

The next morning, they drove up to Madurai to visit the historic Meenakshi Amman Temple and pray to Goddess Parvati and Lord Shiva. Built some 2,500 years ago, it is one of the largest temple complexes in Tamil Nadu. The architecture of the temple is unique and something to marvel at. It houses fourteen gopuras (gateway towers) ranging in height from 45 to 50 metres and has four entrances facing four directions.

After spending the night at a hotel in Madurai, they left on the last leg of the journey to Rameshwaram, which together with Varanasi is considered to be one of the holiest places to Hindus. To get to Rameshwaram, which is located on an island, the family had to leave their car behind and use the railway for the crossing across the Pamban channel. The children were amazed to see hordes of people sitting on top of the train to earn a free ride.

Like a tour guide, and needed no prompting, Bala Menon narrated the history of the place. "The Ramanathaswamy Temple," he began, "is in the centre of the town. It was built in the seventeenth century. It is famous for its 1,200 gigantic granite columns and over 1,200 metres of magnificent corridors. According to mythology, this is the place from which Lord Rama built a bridge across the sea to Lanka, with the help of his *Vanara* (ape men) army, to rescue his wife, Sita, from her abductor, the rakshasa (demon) king Ravana. The temple is dedicated to Lord Shiva, although it has also shrines of Parvati Hanuman, and other deities. Legend has it that Lord Rama – along with his wife, Sita, and his younger brother, Shri Lakshmana – installed and worshipped here the Shivalingam (a form of Lord Shiva) to expiate their sin of killing Ravana, a Brahmin."

They were told that there were twenty-two wells around the temple with water that purportedly had medicinal properties. The family took copiously of the water from some of the wells to pour over themselves.

Returning to Puduserry from Rameshwaram, they next planned a short tour of South India. Bala Menon again served as their guide. They drove to Salem, where the spent the day with Uma's brother Krishna Kumar (fondly called Appan), who ran a medical practice there along with his wife, Kamala. From Salem, they headed towards Bangalore, where they spent two days at the residence of Usha Srinath, who was Ambika's friend from her medical college days. Usha's family was extremely hospitable. Gowri and Ambika enjoyed the company of Usha while doing a bit of bargain shopping at the textile shops. With Usha's help, Gowri located the residence of her cousin Chandra and paid a reunion visit.

Leaving Bangalore, they went 150 kilometres in a south-westerly direction to Mysore. Nearing Mysore, they stopped at the famous Chamundeshwari Temple (located on the top of Chamundi Hills) to pray. Their stay in Mysore was at the stately Lalitha Mahal Palace Hotel. They enjoyed sleeping in the spacious rooms. The morning after their arrival, they drove around to see the city and the Maharaja's Palace before stepping into the sprawling, beautiful Brindavan Gardens. The children were particularly excited watching the illuminated dancing fountains in the gardens that came on at sunset. Gowri and Dasu immediately recalled the hotel and the gardens as being part of the setting of the 1955 Technicolour dance-drama movie *Jhanak Jhanak Payal Baje* (meaning something like "jingle, jingle goes your anklet bell"), which they and the rest of the family had enjoyed watching in a theatre years back in Kluang. Later that night, Dasu was caught humming the melodious tune of a song from the film, *"Nain so nain, nahi milao,"* while putting the children to bed.

The next day, they left for Ooty, the famous hill station nestled in the Nilgiris (Blue Mountains) some 7,000 feet above sea level, at the south-western edge of the Deccan Plateau. On the way up, they saw tea estates, waterfalls, grazing deers, and a herd of elephants bathing in the wild in the sanctuary. They stayed at a comfortable cottage.

The next morning, they drove around sightseeing. They alighted to spend some time absorbing the sights at the rose garden, the tea museum, and the Ooty Lake. They spent two nights at Ooty before returning to Puduserry. Nearing Palakkad, they entered an eatery where Dasu – wanting a taste of non-vegetarian food for a change – ordered some egg curry to go with his parathas. This proved to be his undoing. For the next three days, he suffered from severe food poisoning, but Ambika nevertheless took him to see her relatives at Kadampat, near Thrissur, and to spend a night there. Soon thereafter, with their holiday over, the family returned home via Madras, where they had a day's stay with Prema, Uma's elder sister. The overnight train ride from Olavakkode junction in Palakkad to Madras was much enjoyed by the children. Back in Malaysia, Gowri was ecstatic about the trip. With photographs in hand, she entertained her other grandchildren with her narration of the Indian visit in the weeks that passed, including their uncle Dasu's reactions to his stomach upset.

# [26]

In the latter half of 1982, following double weddings in the family, Shivan took Shanti to India, primarily to see his grandmother and also to visit two important places of worship, Guruvayur in Kerala and Velankanni in Tamil Nadu, home to the famous Roman Catholic shrine dedicated to Our Lady of Good Health. The trip to Velankanni was arranged by Uma's brother Devidas and his wife, Aggie; Shivan had contacted them while in Palakkad. Shanti was a hit with Kamakshi Amma, who enjoyed being pampered and manicured by her granddaughter-in-law. Shivan brought back photographs of Shanti applying lipstick on his grandmother and spraying a healthy dose of perfume on her. Kamakshi Amma immensely enjoyed her make-up sessions and liked the perfumes very much.

One day, noting that their grandmother liked bitter gourd juice, probably on account of her taste buds being accustomed to *kashayam,* Shivan and Shanti gave her a half glass of beer. They told her that it was a fizzy form of bitter gourd juice sold in bottles. She enjoyed the taste. A picture of that mischievous act remains lodged somewhere in family albums.

While he was with Kamakshi Amma, Shivan noticed that she never failed to talk to him about her great-grandson Vikram almost every day. She scolded him for not bringing her his photograph. One day, Shivan asked her, "*Muthessi,* why are you not asking at all about my sons, Suraj and Sharad?"

She giggled and said in Malayalam, "It's not that, son. It is simply that he is the first Kollaikal Menon among my grandchildren."

Shivan understood that to mean a reference to the matrilineal descent system. While they were with her, both Shivan and Shanti took Kamakshi Amma at her request to Kadampat to see the late M. K. G. Nair's mother. When he was alive, M. K. G. Nair and his wife, Thangam, would never fail to visit Kamakshi Amma on their Indian trips. She found them to be a warm couple.

In November 1982, Venu and Presenna took their mothers and children on a short trip to Palakkad and Bangalore. Kamakshi Amma was overjoyed at seeing them and, in particular, her grandchildren. On their way to Bangalore, they stopped at Salem to meet up with Appan and his wife, Kamala. At Bangalore, Venu's intimate friend and university mate, Johar, was insistent that they all stay with him. Johar had a flourishing medical practice there. He and his family were extremely hospitable.

Returning to Palakkad almost at the end of their three-week trip, Thilothamma decided to stay back to spend some time with Ponnu while the others prepared to head for home. Venu brought back to stay with him his *valiachan*, Unnikrishnan, whom he found in a pathetic state of neglected health and undernourishment in his lonely abode in Palakkad.

Venu and Presenna with Kamakshi Amma in 1982

# A SUPERNATURAL EVENT

In late September 1983, Gowri received news from her brother Bala Menon through Ponnu that their mother was very ill and had expressed a desire to see her and Kamalam. Both sisters left immediately. Kamakshi Amma had a bad urinary-tract infection, and there was blood in her urine. She was admitted to hospital, but upon returning home she became weak and everyone felt that she was sinking. Hearing this, Gowri's niece Prema came down as well. The local doctor who was summoned to the home noted that the old woman's pulse was weak and her breathing was laboured. Shortly thereafter, he announced that he could detect no signs of life. The great matriarch of Kollaikal House, Pudussery, had departed.

No one resisted their tears. Finally, Gowri and Kamalam, subdued their anguish and sat down beside the body of their departed mother to recite some prayers while their brother went out to summon a Brahmin priest. The priest duly arrived, bringing with him a cow (considered a sacred animal in the Hindu religion, as it is the most pure and benevolent of all animals). Nobody said anything as they watched the cow being actually brought into the house. Following this quaint custom, especially prevalent amongst Brahmins, the hand of the deceased was raised to hold the cow's tail in the belief that the animal would guide her safely to the next life. Distant relatives in the neighbourhood, hearing the grievous news, began rushing to the house, all wanting a last sight of their beloved Kamakshi Amma.

There was a need next to bathe and prepare the body for cremation. The sisters rose to their feet, and while Kamalam went in search of a white saree in the cupboard, Gowri entered the kitchen to drink some water. Suddenly she froze. She heard the unmistakable loud voice of Kamakshi Amma asking for some milk. She rushed back to find her mother raising herself from the bed to a sitting position. Everyone was gobsmacked. Kamakshi Amma appeared to have come back from the dead – a resurrection. Gowri went and embraced her tight, shouting aloud "Guruvayurappa!" many times.

Kamakshi Amma looked around with glazed eyes but soon found her voice. "Some *sunderis* (beautiful celestial ladies) came to take me away," she said in a matter-of-fact manner. She continued, "I asked why they had come for me. They did not answer, but they guided my spirit away from my physical body to *Pitruloka*. They were stopped by Yaman (the Lord of Death in Vedic Hindu mythology). 'You have got the wrong person,' Yaman told them. They quickly brought me back."

Gowri could not immediately wrap her mind around what she was hearing. The story defied imagination. The fantasy of an old woman? Perhaps. But the Yaman tale sounded more plausible than a grave blunder being made by a practising medical doctor. In essence, Kamakshi Amma's recollection of her experience was a throwback to the old superstition, now the object of serious study by psychologists and psychotherapists, that upon death the soul migrates to an astral world with various levels, the entry to which is only possible upon some degree of fulfilment of one's past and present karma in the physical world. It was later discovered that at about the same time that Kamakshi Amma was supposed to have died, another death had occurred in her neighbourhood. Yaman obviously was not familiar with the local postal codes!

Both sisters were amazed to learn that their mother had taken care of her health all this while with disciplined consumption of some self-prescribed *kashayams* when needed and daily consumption of *dashmoolarishtam*. The *kashayams* are a concentrated bitter concoction of various herbs that often includes pepper, basil leaves, and dried neem flowers to treat cold, cough, fever, headache, obesity, indigestion, urinary calculi, oedema, etc. They are usually consumed diluted with water as prescribed, followed by a teaspoon of honey to get rid of the aftertaste. *Dashmoolarishtam* is a traditional Ayurveda formulation which contains fifty-five herbs as decoction, eleven herbs as powder, jaggery, and honey. It also contains five to seven per cent self-generated natural alcohol, which serves as a medium to deliver alcohol-soluble herbal components to the body. Bala Menon joked that it was the alcohol in the *dashmoolarishtam* that had caused Kamakshi Amma to be addicted to it.

*Dashmoolarishtam* is recommended by Ayurvedic physicians as a general health tonic to improve immunity and strength. It is an excellent tonic for convalescence and general debility, bronchial complaints, fatigue, digestive-tract disorders, rheumatic complaints, and generally restoring health and vitality. Kamakshi Amma always had more trust in traditional medicine than in Western medicine. She detested swallowing pills that had to be taken at prescribed times in a day.

Gowri and Kamalam returned from India some time in December, happy that their mother had a new lease on life. Gowri's humorous account of the cow and her mother's request for milk after coming out of her unconsciousness and presumably near-death state was quite entertaining for her children and her friends to hear, especially Mrs K. C. A. Menon (Thangam) and Madhavi. They were her regular visitors, although they rarely came together to visit Gowri. With Thangam, the conversation invariably centred around children, and Gowri recalled being consulted on Thangam's eldest daughter's marriage.

Because of the regularity of their meetings, they would often share their inner feelings on many family issues. Like Gowri, Thangam too was a widow and given to pious feelings. Gowri's children would fondly call her Aunty KCA. On the other hand, Madhavi was a much younger woman who reminded Gowri of Ponnu in many ways. Madhavi had her antenna on all the latest happenings among the Malayalee community, and she rarely arrived empty-handed. She would always bring along home-made *bondas* and *pakkavadas*, which went well with tea. Sometimes Ambika would sit in on their conversations and roll with laughter.

## OVERCOMING PREJUDICES

One afternoon, Padmini, another friend of Gowri, called her on the phone, bursting with gossip. "*Chechi*, did you hear the news? Remember Mrs Radha Nair, my new neighbour? Her son wants to get married to a Chinese girl who happens to be the daughter of your previous neighbour in Kampong Tunku, one Mrs Chin."

"Really?"

"Yes. She works in the same bank as he does. Radha is worried about the matter. Can I bring her over to see you?"

"No problem. Please come."

A couple of hours later, Padmini arrived with Radha, who wasted no time in opening up the subject. "My son brought her over one day to the house, only to say hello. The next I hear, he wants our permission to marry her."

"That sounds like a love marriage you have in your hands," said Gowri.

"Yes. It is the third case I'm hearing in our community," chipped in Padmini. "Our male children are being targeted by Chinese girls. They look for education and security, and find our Malayalee boys are well endowed with these."

"If you look at it like that, aren't our boys also to blame?" asked Gowri.

"I don't know. I wonder what their progeny will look like. Will they have Chinese eyes?" Radha wanted to know.

"Does it matter?" Gowri asked. "They may turn up fairer. I knew one family in Bukit Mertajam. The man was a Telugu and his wife was an adopted Chinese girl. Their children were strikingly beautiful, and even though they had more of a Chinese face-cut than an Indian one, they had bigger eyes."

"You may be right. But Radha has been entertaining thoughts of getting her son married to a girl in Kerala," said Padmini.

"Such arranged marriages may not always work favourably," Gowri warned. "The government, you know, is very tight these days about granting permanent residence quickly to foreign spouses, and if she goes to her mother's place in India to give birth, the newborn will not be eligible for Malaysian citizenship at all. Also, let us admit it, our children expect some modernity in the girls they are going to marry, like going out to parties and dancing. Girls from traditional families in Kerala may not readily fit the bill."

"Yes, I suppose so," noted Radha.

"Whether of mixed parentage or not, they are still our grandchildren," Gowri observed. "Nothing to prevent us teaching them about our language and religion, is there?"

"Yes, I guess that's true," conceded Radha.

"It's not that we have a shortage of Malayalee girls here," said Gowri.

"It's not that, *Chechi*," said Padmini. "Radha has unmarried daughters. We are not sure what determines the mindset of families when they are looking for marriageable girls."

"Are you saying that if a boy marries outside his race or caste, his sister's marriage will be jeopardized?" asked Gowri.

"We cannot be sure, *Chechi*," Padmini asserted. "It would be the case unless the girl's family is already well-placed in society."

"My son, Shivan, married a Eurasian girl," Gowri pointed out. "I had also reservations initially, having heard that mixed marriages seldom last. I now know this to be a ridiculous generalization. I had no problems whatsoever getting my two girls married to young men from excellent *tharavads* even before my boys reached their high station in life."

"We know that, *Chechi*," Padmini assured her. "Radha still cannot help worrying about her three girls."

"Don't be silly," said Gowri. "Life is full of surprises. To say that only our boys can fall in love with outsiders and not our girls is also a fallacy, particularly as our girls are also breadwinners."

"Yes, *Chechi*. I suppose that's a reality we have to cope with as well. You certainly have a way of balancing things up," said Padmini.

"Anyway," Gowri said, steering the conversation back to Radha, "has your son, what's his name, Raghav isn't it, already proposed to her?"

"He said to me he has. He wants to have an engagement first," replied Radha.

"If she has agreed, then she must have confided in her parents too. Let me talk to Mrs Chin. For all you know, she may entertain similar fears to yours."

The conversation ended, Gowri entered the kitchen to make some *vadai*, and before too long they were all seated to enjoy their evening tea.

The next morning, an hour before lunch, Gowri called upon Mrs Chin. "Come on in", beamed Mrs. Chin. "I haven't seen you for ages. How are you, Aunty?"

"I am fine and healthy enough to be mobile. I see you are looking well. I notice that this place has changed a bit."

"Yes, Aunty, but only after endless complaints to the municipality to do up the roads and prune the overgrown trees."

"Actually, I took a chance that you might be in," Gowri mentioned. "I had lost your contact number."

"I am glad you came, Aunty. I too wanted to contact you. I heard that you had moved to Section 17."

"Yes, it's not that far. My provision shop is still the same at Paramount Gardens."

"Aunty," said Mrs Chin, "can I ask you something?"

Gowri gave an understanding smile. It appeared Mrs Chin herself was going to open up the subject of her daughter.

"You know my daughter, Siew Moy. She wants to marry an Indian boy. She says he is a Malayalee, like you. His name is Raghav."

"Yes," Gowri admitted, "I heard about it from my friend who happens to be the boy's neighbour. She mentioned …"

"You know how it is, Aunty. My husband is upset about the marriage proposal. You know what he said? '*Sai eh*! Our grandchild is going to be dark.' I told him, 'The boy is fair-lah!' But he shouted back, 'The boy's father, Mr Nair, is still dark!' I told him, 'Not so dark one. Brown-lah! Look, Mrs. Panicker's children all fair-lo!' When I said that, he kept quiet."

Gowri was amused. She recounted the case again of the couple in Bukit Mertajam, and told Mrs Chin that her grandchildren would be fairer than their father for sure. She added that while there was a greater likelihood that the children would have more Chinese features, chances were also good that they might inherit bigger, expressive eyes.

Noting that Mrs Chin was in a receptive mood, Gowri continued, "Do you know that in a region called Assam in India, the many Chinese migrants who came during the British colonial period married local Indian women, and even after so many generations many Assamese actually look like Chinese? In any case, Mrs Chin, there are black- and brown-skinned girls in the world these days being crowned beauty queens. If your grandson or granddaughter is out there hurt or crying, you and Mr Chin, I'm sure, will be the first ones to rush out to get hold of the child and embrace him or her with your love, whatever the skin colour may be. God has cast us into different ethnic groups with different shades of skin colours, but internally we are all the same human beings with desires, feelings, and emotions, and we have also so much love within us to give, if only we would all open up."

Nodding and with a much-relieved look on her face, Mrs Chin got up from her chair. "Thank you, Aunty," she said. "I will tell my husband about our conversation. Now, what can I get you for a drink – white tea without sugar?"

"That will be fine. Thank you."

A month after her meetings with Radha and Mrs Chin, Raghav and Siew Moy were engaged. Gowri had a seat of honour at the function.

☼

# COUSIN RAMANI VISITS

In the early part of 1983, Gowri was thrilled to receive a visit from her cousin Ramani and Ramani's husband, Balakrishna Menon. They were accompanied by their daughter Maya, who was then stationed in Singapore with her husband, Jayapal. The cousins were inseparable in the few days they were together; they certainly had a lot of experiences to share. Dasu found time to take them to see the sights of Kuala Lumpur, including a visit to the Sri Murugan Temple at Batu Caves in Gombak and the Forest Research Institute at Kepong, where the country's oldest tropical flora and fauna can be found.

Gowri learnt from Ramani that almost all of her siblings had one or more children who had settled abroad, and that the indications were that the diaspora was likely to grow. A family get-together was arranged before the visitors left for Singapore, with Gowri promising to reciprocate their visit. This she did a few months later during a public holiday break in the company of Ambika.

Gowri relaxing on the garden swing with Ramani.

☼

# DEMISE OF UNNIKRISHNAN

In mid-December 1983, Venu and Presenna decided to make a short trip overseas. They left Unnikrishnan in the care of Dasu and Ambika. Gowri temporarily vacated her room downstairs in the Section 17 house for him and shifted upstairs.

On 28 December, Dasu woke up later than usual, as it was a national holiday honouring the birthday of Prophet Muhammad. He was preparing to come downstairs when he heard his housemaid screaming. Rushing down, he found out why. She had knocked on the door of the bedroom on the ground floor to bring morning tea for Unnikrishnan. Seeing no response, she opened the door slightly to see him sprawled face down on the bed with one foot dangling. Obviously, he had been to the washroom in the night and rushed back to the bed feeling faint. His body was cold.

Ambika came down and, examining him, knew at once that he had breathed his last. In the next hour, Venu – who had just returned from an overseas trip – arrived along with other members of the family. Gowri's daughter Ambi, upon receiving the news on the phone, broke down. She recalled being awakened in the early hours of the morning by the feeling of a cold hand touching her and a voice calling her "Ambili." She had instantly thought of Unnikrishnan, who was the only one who called her by that pet name. The premonition that something bad had happened to him was in her thoughts when the phone rang. She flew down from Alor Star, where she was then stationed.

Dasu also duly informed Mani *Ettan*, who came and telegrammed the news to Unnikrishnan's brother, Shankaran, who was then in Sabah. The deceased was embalmed in the house and prepared for cremation in the late afternoon. Dasu and his younger male siblings performed the funeral rites both in the house and at the crematorium. According to Hindu custom, the female siblings do not partake in the funeral rites. Ambi waited until the coffin was loaded onto the hearse before she re-entered the house and sat cross-legged on a corner of the floor. Her eyes were red and puffy. She carried her sadness like a heavy stone in her heart, and with her gaze transfixed on her beloved *valiachan*'s photograph hanging on the wall, she went into a silent prayer. She remained in this position for some time until she was ushered inside the bedroom, and the entire area was swept and cleaned with several bucketfuls of water.

## BALA MENON'S SECOND MARRIAGE

Towards late January 1984, Shoba gave birth to a bouncing baby girl, Nithya. She had been staying with Hari at Section 17 since their marriage. For Gowri, Nithya was a grandchild born after a lapse of nearly five years. The child instantly became the apple of everyone's eye. She grew up to be a mischievous but witty girl, very much attached to Dasu and Ambika. She started speaking well before she turned one, and her witty remarks in Malayalam often had Gowri and her children in stitches. In early October 1985, Shoba took her to Chandranagar and Pudussery. Gowri and her sister Kamalam accompanied Shoba as they very much wanted to get their brother Bala Menon married again. Nithya proved to be an instant hit at Pudussery. She had Bala Menon dancing to her tune, and bullied him into buying her different coloured bangles and toys. Kamakshi Amma was tickled pink listening to her endless conversation in broken Malayalam revealing nuggets of naughtiness.

While in Pudussery, Gowri and Kamalam used their persuasive skills to get a somewhat reluctant Bala Menon agree to a second marriage. He accepted, in principle, their argument that he needed someone to take care of him as much as Kamakshi Amma did. But he was adamant in not rushing into any alliance for the present, but promised that he would consider the matter a few years hence.

Gowri and Kamalam decided to stay back in Pudussery for a while, but Shoba and Nithya returned to Malaysia after about three weeks in the company of Hari who had come to fetch them. The day of their departure from Madras on 31 October was attended by tight security on the roads and at the airport. It was a day of mourning for the country, benumbed with the morning breaking news of the assassination of Indian Prime Minister Indira Gandhi at the hands of her own two bodyguards.

Not long after their return, Shoba and Hari decided to move into a rented house in a close-by locality at Subang Jaya. The impish Nithya told them they could go if they so wished, but she was not leaving "her home" which was with her "*Valiachan*" and "*Valiamma*" (father's elder brother and his wife). Nithya had her wish fulfilled when after a stay of three years in the rented house, Hari and Shoba returned to Section 17 where their second daughter Smitha was born in September 1988. They finally shifted in early 1989 to their own house which they had bought by then. However, prior to moving out, Hari and his family visited Kerala again to conduct the *choroonu* for Smitha at the residence of Shoba's parents in Chandranagar. Gowri accompanied them for she was very much wanting to get Bala Menon at least betrothed, if not married, on this trip. With Ponnu's help, a suitable bride for him was found at Chittalancheri, a village in the District of Palakkad. Following the marriage at the bride's abode a few weeks later, a wedding reception was held at Hotel Indraprastha in Palakkad city. Kamakshi Amma welcomed her new daughter-in-law, Jayalakshmi, with open arms, much to the delight of all.

Gowri extended her stay in Pudussery when she heard that Uma and Sethu were coming on leave from Liberia to participate in the *Lakshadeepam* ceremony at the Guruvayur temple. She joined them in the ceremony with Jayalakshmi. The *Lakshadeepam* is the festival celebration of the lighting of multi-tiers of traditional oil lamps that adorn the outer walls of the temple compound around the sanctum. With the lighting completed, all worshippers awaited the *seeveli*. This is the ritual in which the idol of Lord Krishna is taken in a procession of five caparisoned elephants around the temple, accompanied by the *panchavadyam* played by temple musicians. Witnessing the event, Gowri found it to be a spiritually moving experience.

Kamakshi Amma with her great-granddaughter Nithya in 1989

# A COSTLY MISADVENTURE

Sometime around mid-1984, Shivan lost his job with Plantation Agencies Pvt. Ltd. He rented a place close to Dasu's old Section 12 house and moved his belongings there while searching for a new job. Coincidentally, Venu was at this time contemplating opening a pub-cum-restaurant business with a friend of his, and he talked to Shivan about managing the enterprise. Gowri was not at all happy about the business proposition, knowing that both her boys, although not regular drinkers, were not disciplined enough to control their own alcohol intake once they got going. Dasu shared her views; all his siblings knew only too well his stand on drinking and smoking.

"You have a medical practice to run. Where will you have the time to look into the daily operations of a restaurant? A doctor with a business interest in a pub may give you a bad image. Do you want to risk it?" The questions flowed from Gowri.

"But I know of many lawyers who also have this side business, Mum. The restaurant business is quite lucrative. We can make money here. Anyway, Shivan is going to be there daily to manage the place," replied Venu.

Dasu, listening to this, was very sceptical. "Neither of you know anything about running a restaurant. Shivan will need to be in the kitchen and at the bar service counter in person to control waste and expenditure. It is by no means a pushover job managing a restaurant. I really do not know whether Shivan understands all this. Knowing him, he might find it beneath him to even enter the kitchen."

"Presenna's relative will be able to help out at the bar counter and keep an additional eye on the teller. My friend has identified a good cook. And Hari has agreed to scrutinize the monthly accounts. There is no need to worry. Anyway, I have found a place close to the University Hospital, which should attract a crowd," Venu concluded. "I have already paid the deposit."

There was nothing more to be said. Following renovations and the securing of the necessary licences, they had a grand opening. The signboard at the entrance read "Mayvilla Restaurant & Pub." Its signature version of the Bloody Mary, mixing local ingredients with the traditional tomato juice and vodka, proved a unique cocktail experience at the opening ceremony. Shivan had a hand in concocting it as he, more than any of his siblings, had refined taste buds for liquor and wines, which he had developed during his stint in the navy.

As was to be expected, the initial overhead was high, but even after several months, the business was slipping further into the red, with the break-even target elusive. As the restaurant's operation progressed into a second year, the very viability of the business came into question. The monthly revenue generated was grossly insufficient to cover operating expenses, let alone service bank borrowings old and new. It was clear that the lack of governance and controls, especially at the micro level, from the very start had led to the problem. Ill-defined accountabilities and responsibilities were partly to blame.

The brothers openly quarrelled and blamed each other, and their relationship soured. Gowri's heart sank. She was both angry and sad. "I told them many a time not to venture into this. Neither of them is financially stable. It was foolhardy," she muttered to the others around her. The words were said in anguish.

Dasu, taking Hari with him, saw each of his brothers separately and told them, "The business has clearly failed. Cut your losses before you have to declare bankruptcy. You have no choice but to come together to solve the problem by selling the business. I am going to be affected as well, as I have stood as guarantor for both of you. But more than that, you will be shortening our mother's life by this infighting."

Hari chipped in by saying, "Both of you are signatories to loans. You also have personal overdrafts to be serviced. You need to talk to your banks to make some protracted arrangements. I'll come with you."

The brothers agreed to patch up and move forward. They came to see Gowri and sought her forgiveness for putting her through the trauma. Dasu helped to settle some immediate payments to vendors who were threatening to close up the place. His wife, Ambika, was a silent witness to the fiasco, unable to comprehend how her husband would leave no stone unturned when it came to putting his mother's mind at ease.

# [27]

The family decided to honour Gowri on the occasion of her seventieth birthday on 15 November 1985. Dasu had put all his siblings on notice well in advance to ensure that all would turn up in full. Valsala and Aravind were then in Kuala Terengganu, Ambi and Ravindran in Seremban, and Shivan and Shanti in Negeri Sembilan. Prema's husband from India, Manohar Singh, was at that time visiting Gowri and family, and he joined the function.

The venue was fixed at the Fraser Hill Hotel. Fraser's Hill is a picturesque hill station located a two-hour drive north of Kuala Lumpur. It is a popular highland rainforest area, some 1,200m above sea level on the Titiwangsa Range, straddling the Pahang-Selangor state border. Dasu took charge of all the arrangements, with printed instructions for all to follow the moment they checked into the hotel on the morning of 14 November. The families were provided with details of the outdoor activities they could participate in until five in the evening at the very latest on that day. These included boating on the lake, horseback riding, and trail walking that would provide them a close glimpse of nature and the amazing variety of birds that would flock there, including some migratory birds from Siberia.

Towards evening, as expected with the sunset, a chill set in and everyone was glad to be indoors. Following dinner, a Scrabble competition was held over three games, with Gowri, Shivan, Aravind, and Ravindran participating. The large Scrabble board from Section 17 had been brought by the family for the occasion. It was purchased in the United States by Uma and gifted to her Scrabble-loving clan, headed by Gowri. The competition was keen. Gowri, Shivan, and Aravind won one game each, but as Aravind had emerged second in two games, he was adjudged the winner. A Scrabble dictionary was offered as the prize, but it was to be awarded by the birthday girl at the function the following day.

A strict conduct of the festive board was followed on the birthday. These included instructions on the dress code, punctuality of arrival at the banquet hall, the order of seating at the tables, the ushered entry of the birthday girl, the wheeling in of the birthday cake, and photography sessions. No one was permitted to retire from the hall until the function was formally declared over. More importantly, no consumption of alcohol was permitted from the moment of registration at the hotel until the birthday luncheon function was over. Dasu wanted to ensure that the occasion was a special one for Gowri, and he would tolerate no squabbles of any kind or overt boisterous behaviour to mar her happiness. He was confident of achieving this by discouraging liquor consumption over the entire period of the formal function. It was extraordinary that everyone complied.

By special arrangement, several courses of a variety of Chinese and North Indian dishes were served, with Bombe Alaska and fruit salad with ice cream for dessert. Everyone enjoyed the meal. After lunch, Dasu spoke affectionately of Gowri, stating that he and his siblings were most fortunate to be blessed with a mother like her. Quoting a line he had read somewhere, he said, "I believe in love at first sight, because I've been loving my mother since I opened my eyes!" He hoped that God would grant her an extended lease on life to see her great-grandchildren without needing another dip in the sea! He toasted her good health and long life.

In her response, Gowri thanked the Almighty for His continuing guidance of the family and said that nothing in life pleased her more than to see harmony and unity among all her children, sons- and daughters-in-law, and grandchildren. Gowri was then invited to present the Scrabble competition winner's prize to Aravind. The cake-cutting ceremony was performed with all her grandchildren holding hands and assembled in an arc on both sides of her. Ravi belted out the "Happy Birthday" song, joined by all family members. The photographs taken that day at Fraser's Hill with all members of her family present have not been surpassed for their total inclusivity at any subsequent family gathering.

Gowri with her children, children-in-law, and
grandchildren on her seventieth birthday

Gowri, assisted by her grandchildren,
blowing out the birthday candles

A month later, Ravi and Susheela treated Gowri to a holiday trip with
them to South India. They flew to Madras and then travelled by both
train and car to various destinations. At Palakkad, they stayed with Ponnu,
but they visited Puduserry almost every day to spend some quality time
with Kamakshi Amma and Bala Menon. In a hired tour taxi, they visited
Trivandrum, where Ravi had studied. They spent two days in Trivandrum,

with Gowri and Susheela meeting some of Ravi's friends and also paying a visit to the famous Sree Padmanabhaswamy Temple. The history of this temple dates back to the eighth century. Its presiding deity is Lord Vishnu, reclining on Anantha, the hooded serpent. Gowri enjoyed very much the tranquility she found at the temple.

Returning to Palakkad, they next visited Bangalore, again travelling by hired car with an overnight stopover at Salem, where they stayed with Appan. They booked their stay in Bangalore at the plush Windsor Manor Hotel. Gowri was very impressed with the English décor she found there.

*Top*: Gowri and Susheela with Sudarshan, wife Shanta and children (1985).
*Bottom*: Krishna Kumar and Kamala with son
Uday in their Trivandrum home (1996).

Upon arrival, Ravi wasted no time in contacting Babu and Venu's friend Johar, requesting them all to come to the hotel. Gowri was meeting Babu's wife, Shanta, and their two children Kavita and Kartik, for the first time. They quickly endeared themselves to her. In the days following their meeting with Babu, he took them around to view the various sights of the city. The sightseeing proved to be all the more enjoyable on account of the cool weather. They also visited a few well-known temples as requested by Gowri. Ravi and Susheela prayed for a child. Their prayers were answered – upon returning from India, they were blessed with a daughter, Dhanya, born in September 1986.

Gowri had an excellent relationship with her grandchildren, and in particular, her granddaughters. She was able to provide them with the closeness and emotional security they very much needed in their growing years and be the patient teacher they always wanted in helping to sort their study problems or learn home skills. Talking to them, Gowri felt that as many of them as possible should learn music and dance while they were still young. She persuaded her daughters-in-law, Ambika and Presenna, to enrol their girls in dance classes at the Temple of Fine Arts in the Brickfields area of Kuala Lumpur. This sanctuary for the arts was founded by His Holiness Swami Shantanand Saraswathi. Gowri had gone there once in the company of friends to attend a dance drama and was very impressed with the performance. Apsara, Gouri, Sathya, and Lavaniya had their training twice a week in the evenings at the temple. They had a choice to study Bharata Natyam, the Mohini Attam, or the Odisi dance.

"Which shall we choose, Mum?" Ambika had asked.

"The Bharata Natyam, of course!" Gowri had replied. "To me, it is the most graceful and most complete dance to watch. It is a dance of expression: the facial expression, the gestural movement of the arms and the associated foot movements, be it squatting, jumping, or twirling. All are integral to the dance. Every dance tells a story of a quest to unite with God."

"Yes, you are right about the movements," said Presenna, who had taken dance classes when she was young. "Western dance is more postural, but the Odisi is also a very expressive dance."

"I watched it once on TV, but I found the dance movements too sensual," said Gowri.

"Oh, Mum, which dance isn't?" replied Presenna.

Into the first week of dance classes, Sathya and Apsara both complained of headache following their return. Saying, *"Ende kuttigaluke kannu thattitunde"* ("My children have been struck by the evil eye"), Gowri immediately took a few red chillies and mustard seeds in her palm and rotated the clenched palm around each child from head to foot, thrice clockwise and thrice anticlockwise, and threw the contents into a saucepan placed over the lighted stove. Everyone could hear the spitting sound as the chillies and mustard seeds burst in the heat. She then threw the contents of the saucepan out in the garden. This was her way of removing the negative vibes and ill effects of the evil eye. This practice continues to be followed in most Indian households.

A couple of years into the dance lessons, Venu expressed disappointment at the progress of the children with their assigned dance teacher and suggested that they all shift their classes to the Ramli Ibrahim Dance Academy. Ramli, an ethnic Malay, had earned a reputation as an accomplished Indian classical dancer and choreographer, specialising in the Odisi. His bold fusion of Odisi with other dance forms had gained him favourable reviews. The children joined his academy but continued their classes in Bharata Natyam.

After the failed business at Mayvilla, Shivan sought the assistance of his close friend, the Malaysian ambassador to Papua New Guinea (PNG), to help him find a job there. He was successful in this and secured a three-year contract for a managerial job at a cocoa plantation at Rabaul. The rest of his family followed him some months later. They sent their eldest son, Suraj, the following year to the Rockhampton Grammar High School in northern Queensland, Australia. At the expiry of his contract and following Suraj's completion of his high school studies, they all came back to stay with Dasu at the Section 17 house for a few months around mid-1989. Shivan had applied to a number of other places in PNG before leaving the country and was hopeful of getting a new job, which he did. He returned to PNG in October with his family, but it was a lower-paying job. Suraj, in the meanwhile, returned to pursue his studies at James Cook University in Townsville. Dasu helped him meet the shortfalls in his term fees now and then while he was studying.

Gowri was not particularly happy at the prospect of Shivan's continued presence in PNG, and more especially so when she heard from him that in remote parts of western PNG, there were tribes who were still practising headhunting and cannibalism.

"Are you sure you are not going deep into the jungles to oversee the land clearance for your cocoa plantations?" she would repeatedly ask.

To this, Shivan would humorously reply, "All I know when I'm staying near the jungle outposts is that I'm served white cooked meat which tastes like pork. It could be human flesh!"

"*Narayana, Narayana!*" Gowri would exclaim, cupping her ears. The rest of the family would be in stitches.

Shivan would add spice to the ensuing conversation by narrating some queer incident or other that he had either witnessed or heard about during his stay in PNG. He recalled once being at a village not far from Rabaul where a fight was being staged between a venomous snake and a young mongoose whose hind legs were tied to a post. It was enthralling to watch. The natives were pushing the long deadly snake closer and closer to the mongoose, which managed to thwart the snake strikes by fluffing up its fur and still being incredibly agile. The snake only got a mouthful of fur on a number of strikes, but it slithered back each time before the mongoose could target its sharp teeth at the snake's head. The handicap eventually proved too much for the mongoose, which received several bites on its body. Although more resistant than most animals to snake bites, a mongoose could still fall sick or even be killed as a result of deep bites by a venomous snake.

The natives cut loose the tiring mongoose, which darted quickly into the forest. Shivan noticed that several natives were furiously running after the mongoose. He was told that they hoped it would lead them to specific plants whose roots it would get at and chew. The roots seemingly contained the antidote to the snake venom.

Gowri's grandchildren in the audience would remain spellbound as Shivan narrated such experiences. Sometimes he would amuse them with his smattering of Tok Pisin (pidgin English). He would set the mood by asking, "*Yu bai save long Tok pisin?*" ("Do you speak pidgin English?") They would in unison reply "*Ya. Liklik.*" ("Yes. A little.") It was a fun time.

# [28]

In the early eighties, the Section 17 house saw several parties hosted for international visitors to the university by Dasu. They came in their capacity as conference delegates or as external examiners. Accompanying them would be Dasu's research colleagues and students. Invariably, such functions would be held in the evenings, and the buffet reflecting various popular ethnic dishes always proved a hit with the visitors. Gowri, Ambika, and the children found them all a congenial lot. Among the regular visitors were the families of Robert Maggie from Australia and Moayad Attar-Bashi from Iraq. Both Robert and Moayad were brought in by Dasu for a period of service in the university.

Gowri in her garden with the late Professor Robert Magee,
his wife, Chris, and Dr N. H. Tioh.

One of Dasu's immediate neighbours was James Puthucheary, a brother-in-law of Chit Kuttan (Shivan's ex-navy mate from Singapore). James was a well-known trade unionist and lawyer, and a founding member of the People's Action Party (PAP) in Singapore in 1954. A champion of civil rights, he subsequently formed the Barisan Sosialis Party in 1961. James's wife, Mavis, was a member of the faculty of economics and administration at the University of Malaya. Dasu and Ambika would unfailingly attend the Christmas party they held each year at their house, which would draw many luminaries.

On one such occasion, while on the subject of food, James expressed a wish to eat some authentic Kerala dishes which he had enjoyed during his childhood. Dasu mentioned this to Gowri in passing a few days later. As soon as Gowri heard this, she cooked a few dishes and had them sent over to his house. James, ever the gentleman, promptly phoned Gowri and thanked her profusely in both Malayalam and English.

In October 1983, Dasu, who was then the Worshipful Master of Lodge Emerald in the East No.830 I. C., organized an informal evening get-together of the brethren of his lodge at his residence to mark the occasion of the visit of the then–Grand Master, the Most Honourable Seventh Marquess of Donegall, and his good lady, Marchioness Josceline, to Kuala Lumpur. It was a superb evening; everyone found the Grand Master and the Marchioness a very affable couple. One of the brethren was coaxed to sing "Danny Boy," a ballad closely associated with Irish communities. It was well received, and the Most Worshipful Grand Master promptly invited him to render it again at the Grand Lodge in Dublin. The Marchioness was curious to know about Gowri's background and her other children, and she was all ears when Gowri narrated a bit about her history.

"Have you been to Ireland?" the Marchioness enquired of Gowri.

"No, only to England, but I have heard a lot about Ireland from my son because of his connection with the Irish Lodge here. He has pointed out to me that the ancient Celtic society and the Vedic culture of the ancient Hindus have a lot in common."

"Indeed! I have heard that as well," the Marchioness agreed. "Apparently, it goes beyond the Sanskrit language into myths as well."

"Yes, the connection between Ganga [Vedic mother goddess] and Ganges parallels the story of Danu [Celtic mother goddess] and the Danube; *Danu* in Sanskrit means 'divine waters,'" Gowri explained.

'How very interesting," said the Marchioness. "You must visit us in Dublin."

The late Marquess and Marchioness of Donegall
with Gowri and her family at the garden party
hosted by Dasu at his Section 17 residence.

It also transpired from their conversation that the Marchioness was a lover of nature. Gowri promptly beckoned Dasu and relayed Lady Josceline's interest. Dasu promised to arrange a visit the very next day to the butterfly and bird parks in the Botanic Gardens, and for the Grand Master also a visit to the Rubber Research Institute at Sungai Buloh to try his hand at tapping a rubber tree.

Both Gowri and Dasu enjoyed entertaining their circle of old and new friends at Section 17, among them also many of Ambika's friends who found Gowri an affable companion and often would enquire about her.

An old bosom friend of Gowri from Bukit Mertajam days who used to visit her and stay with her a few days was Dr Meenakshi Nambiar. Other family friends, also known to Gowri, included P. G. Williams (Willie) and V. K. Ravindra Dass, Dasu's old schoolmates and neighbours from Kluang. Willie's father was the late Mr George, who was the senior hospital assistant in Mengkibol Estate, while Ravindra Dass's father, the late Mr Govindan, was the chief clerk there. Like Dasu, Ravindra Dass had also lost his father at an early age. Gowri was "Aunty" to them.

Both Willie and Ravindra Dass were good sportsmen in their younger days, and they were instrumental in introducing several games and sporting events for the estate community in Kluang, and particularly for the benefit of the children of the staff. Soccer, volleyball, netball, quoits, and badminton were among the games regularly played most evenings. In the days prior to the advent of television, it would indeed have been a dreary existence for the children in the estate without the infusion of such sporting activities into their lives.

In his working life, Willie was initially attached to the foreign ministry in Kuala Lumpur before earning a post at the information desk at the Malaysian Embassy in Moscow on account of his fluency in Russian. It was while in Moscow that he picked up his interest in Japanese shiatsu and Chinese chi healing massage techniques, which he practised at health centres there. Later, he added deep tissue massage and hypnotherapy to his roster of skills. He now runs his own clinic in Kuala Lumpur.

He would visit Dasu and Gowri every now and then, whenever he yearned for a good home-cooked vegetarian meal. At least that was what he would openly say, and Gowri, on her part, wouldn't disappoint him. She'd prepare some of his favourite dishes, including his favourite drumstick sambar. He would repay her after the meal with a gentle massage of her ever-aching feet. He enjoyed chatting about the old days and carried a good memory of the estate life as it then was.

Reminiscing about Kluang with him, Gowri recalled the occasion once when Willie's father George was in her house when he was urgently summoned to attend to a person who had been gored in his thigh by a wild boar. Apparently he was a new member of the hunting group from the labour lines which had gone in search of wild boars. In the process of capturing the animal, he was severely wounded. George had to insert several stitches on the wound to close it up. That same evening, Govindan Kutty received a parcel of meat of the wild boar that had been caught and slaughtered, and Gowri was put to the test making a really spicy dish with it. Her mind went back several times to the poor animal that had to suffer such a fate. Govindan Kutty loved the preparation, and he had a couple of friends come over to enjoy the dish with him and wash it down with a few bottles of beer and stout.

Ravindra Dass, after serving a brief spell as a trained teacher, joined the government service in the Valuation and Property Services division under the Ministry of Finance and rose to become its first director general. As a duly qualified chartered valuation surveyor, he was largely instrumental in pioneering the regulation of the real estate profession in the country. All those who hailed from the humble homes in the estates around Kluang looked upon him proudly as a role model. A charitable person, he was the driving force behind the establishment of a welfare centre in Petaling Jaya, under the management of the Guru Dharma Society, providing free medical service among other welfare activities for the underprivileged from all racial groups. Ambika helped out at the centre on some weekends.

Gowri also visited her friends fairly often, thanks to Ambika's employment of a driver to take her to work and the children to school. His name was Albert. When Ambika started her private practice in 1983, Albert's wife was employed and trained by her as a nursing assistant. They were a loyal couple who endeared themselves to the family.

Gowri's Section 17 *tharavad* continued to be the permanent postal address for all her family. Both official and social letters to individual family members would arrive there, and Gowri would painstakingly sort them out. These included summonses for traffic offences and reminders for unsettled bills. She knew without being too inquisitive who were the offenders and the procrastinators in the family.

Gowri would often rest in the living room of the Section 17 house, which had a clear view of the front gate, typically reading a Mills & Boon paperback or watching a Malayalam movie. Despite the riveting and dramatic plots of Kerala's finest film writers, little that happened on the street would get past Gowri's keen eyes. Having noted unsavoury characters darkening the driveway with increasing frequency, Gowri immediately issued an edict that the main and back doors of the house were to remain locked at all times, and similarly for all bedroom doors and windows before retiring for the night. This was seen as a precautionary measure, as anyone could climb over the garden fencing and gate. Indeed, that directive proved a blessing, for not long afterwards, there was an encounter, and Gowri was in the thick of it.

☼

# STRANGER IN THE NIGHT

It was a Saturday night. Shanti had come up from Seremban, and so also Uma, who was en route to Liberia after her visit to India. The family chatted until quite late. Close to midnight, they all retired to their rooms. Uma occupied the bedroom downstairs with Gowri, and just before retiring to bed she wheeled in her large suitcase from the dining hall. Sitting on the bed, she quickly rearranged the contents of the suitcase, wherein she now placed her jewellery, as she was planning to stay for a few days in Malaysia. She was talking to Gowri while doing the repacking when she heard Gowri start to snore on the bed next to hers. The packing incomplete, she decided to switch off the lights and sleep as well, and leave the suitcase unlocked in the room.

In the very early hours of the morning, Gowri woke up hearing a light thud. The sound was not repeated. She then decided to go to the washroom. Coming out of the washroom, she switched off the lights and was about to re-enter the bedroom when she heard descending footsteps on the nearby staircase.

"Is that you, Shanti?" she asked, turning back to look up the stairway which was lit by a dim ceiling light. Almost instantly, her eyes fell on a stranger in a black long-sleeved T-shirt and jeans. The man froze for a moment but reacted quickly. Uttering *"Tak, tak!"* ("No, no!") he sprinted down the stairs in a flash. Gowri flung herself into her room and locked the door, and with Uma now awake, they both banged on the door, shouting at the top of their voices, *"Kallan! Kallan!* ("Thief! Thief!") Dasu! Dasu! Come down!"

Dasu, hearing the commotion, jumped out of bed and, still in his sarong, dashed down the stairs, only to catch a fleeting glimpse of someone escaping through the louvre window. With all the lights in the hall switched on, and armed with a *parang* (big knife) from the kitchen, he went over to the window. The thief had used a crowbar to sufficiently bend the external grill railing of the louvre window to allow for entry and exit. Dasu deduced that the thief must be a small-sized man. Opening the main door of the house, he went into the garden. Hari, who had come down and then gone up the stairs to fetch his spectacles, followed him in the search. But the man had already escaped through the fencing, in which a hole had been cut. It was clear to everyone that he was a petty thief and, in all probability, a drug addict who had come alone in search of small items that he could sell.

Shanti and Shoba, who were still at the top of the stairs, were seen laughing loudly when Dasu re-entered the house.

"What's so funny?" Dasu asked.

"It's the way Ambika came down the stairs," explained Uma. "She slipped and came *thud, thud* down the staircase in a sitting posture, shouting 'Thief! thief!'" Everyone, including Ambika, joined in the mirth.

"Was anything stolen?" Dasu asked.

"I don't think he had the time. When he heard the downstairs toilet flushing, he must have decided to abort his mission," observed Gowri.

"I'm glad that I locked the bedroom door before I slept," said a relieved Uma, who was thinking of her valuables in her suitcase. They would certainly have been easy pickings for the intruder.

Dasu called the police to inform them of the break-in. While waiting for them, everyone became suddenly seized by hunger pangs brought on by the relief that they had managed to scare away an intruder. They all tucked into a heavy early breakfast. At daybreak, the police arrived to take photographs and fingerprints. The man was not in their files, and that was the end of that episode. Dasu and Ambika decided to replace the louvre windows in all the rooms downstairs with more modern windows with better security grilles.

## TOUCH OF GANGA – VARANASI AND BADRINATH

Some years later, in September 1989, Dasu and Ambika took their mothers on a pilgrimage tour of North India. Ambika's youngest brother, Achuthan, accompanied them. The children were kept in the care of family members while they were away. It was a two-week guided tour for just the five of them, arranged by Hamsavahini Travel and Tours.

The tour was truly amazing, covering Delhi and the holy towns of Varanasi, Haridwar, Rishikesh, Jyothirmath, and Badrinath. Arriving at Delhi for an overnight stay, they flew to Varanasi (Benares) for an unforgettable dip in the sacred Ganges River (Ganga) after participating in prayers conducted by a priest at a less crowded spot on the river bank. Varanasi on the western banks of the Ganga is famous for its temples and *ghats* (flight of steps leading to the river).

According to Hindu scriptures, the touch of Ganga cleanses one of all sins, and a dip bestows heavenly blessings and *moksha* (salvation). They all took their ritualistic dips, holding hands and wishing for reconnection in their next life.

Gowri and Dasu, uttering names of their dead ancestors – and the name of their aged Kamakshi Amma, who was still alive – and praying for their *moksha*, symbolically dipped again in the waters. They saw half-burnt corpses floating in the middle of the river along with partially burnt pieces of wood from the funeral pyre and floral garlands, all carried by the strong current. The hallowed river struck them as highly polluted, but that viewpoint changed as they moved to its upper reaches along the route where the waters were sparkling clear and fresh. The Ganga originates from the Gangotri glacier in the Indian Himalayas and travels more than 2,500 kilometres across the plains of northern India to join the Bay of Bengal in the east.

Views of Varanasi: (*left*) Gowri in an attitude of prayer facing the sun after her ritualistic dip in the Ganga; (*right*) the submerged Shiva temple.

After they returned from Varanasi to Delhi, their journey to the remainder of the pilgrimage towns, all of which are in the state of Uttarakhand, was by car. They had a Nepali driver whose competency was increasingly appreciated as he drove them up the winding and misty mountain roads with hairpin bends to the holy town of Badrinath. They likened him to a sure-footed mountain goat. The scenery kept them astounded. Badrinath, with an average elevation of 10,000 feet, owes its significance as a major pilgrimage site to Adi Shankara, the revered Hindu theologian and philosopher who was responsible for giving a unifying interpretation of the whole body of Upanishads. *Badri* refers to a berry that grew abundantly in the area, and *nath* refers to Vishnu.

On their way up to Badrinath, they halted at both Haridwar and Rishikesh, where they took ritualistic dips in the Ganga and prayed at the temples. Their stays overnight at these places were prearranged at tourist lodges, but they were in for a surprise when they arrived at near dusk in Badrinath. There appeared to be no vacant place in the lodge they had been booked in (it appeared to be a case of overbooking) or in any of the hotels near to the temple. They didn't relish the idea of descending in the dark to lower levels in search of hotels. Finally, the driver spoke to the authorities of the Badrinath Vishnu temple and managed to get them shelter for the night in the temple *satram*. The water was icy cold, and Dasu's request for hot water in pails still meant a cool bath before they retired for the night.

The room was cold. The one blanket available for each person was insufficient to provide the desired warmth. They regretted not taking the advice of their driver at the start of the journey to buy and consume honey to combat the cold. The request for hot water was repeated the next morning, but only Dasu and Gowri availed themselves of it, as it was slow in coming. Ambika, her mother, and her brother decided to take a cold bath rather than wait. Ambika almost had a cardiac arrest when she poured the cold water over her body, an experience she would remember for a long time. None of them knew of the presence of hot water springs near the temple.

Badrinath Vishnu Temple, as seen from far and near.

The temple sits on the banks of the Alaknanda River. It stands approximately 50 feet tall with a small cupola on top, covered with a gold gilt roof. The architecture resembles a Buddhist temple. The facade, built of stone, is brightly painted and has arched windows. A broad stairway leads up to a tall arched gateway, which serves as the main entrance. As they walked towards the temple, they saw two eagles circling lazily in the deep blue sky.

"They are *garudas*," said Gowri. In Vedic mythology, the *garuda* is the celestial eagle-mount of Lord Vishnu.

They prayed at several *murtis* in the temple, and Gowri and Ambika's mother, Thangam, both had *archana* (special, personal, abbreviated puja done at a devotee's request by the temple priest) performed at the main shrine that housed the 1-metre-tall black shaligram stone statue of Vishnu as Lord Badrinarayan. After prayers in the temple, they had breakfast and walked around the temple precincts, relishing the cold mountain air.

Following an early lunch, they descended almost four thousand feet below to Jyothirmath – one of the four cardinal institutions established by Adi Shankara – and spent the night there. On the way down, they stopped at several places to take photographs. The view was breathtaking. At one point, Dasu walked a few yards from where their car had stopped to take a good shot of a deep ravine close to the road edge, but he had to endure the screams coming from behind him.

"Dasu, be careful! Don't go so close to the edge," called out Gowri.

'Dasu, wait. Wait. You might slip. Let Achu hold you from behind," screamed Ambika.

But before Achu got anywhere close, Dasu had already retraced his steps after taking several snapshots.

At another place downhill, the car was again halted at the sight of a sprouting spring. Everyone got down to taste the water.

"It's simply gorgeous. So cold and so fresh," was the general verdict. The words uttered in Malayalam this time came first from Ambika's mother, who was generally soft-spoken and not much of a conversationalist.

Ambika collected some of the water in a drinking bottle and, looking at Dasu, quipped, "Don't worry, you can have a bit of it to take back for testing its pH and bacterial content."

As the car slowly descended the narrow road to a lower level, an unusual sight met their eyes. A young Uttarakhand woman was seen walking uphill on the road edge carrying a huge pumpkin on her bare head. It was an extraordinary balancing act, and the woman appeared hardly conscious of the load on her head. Elsewhere along the road, a common enough sight was of men covered in wool wraps squatting at wayside stalls drinking piping hot tea. It was funny watching them spew steam from their mouths in the cold air.

Returning finally to Delhi, they spent two days there sightseeing and shopping. Jayam, who was in the Indian civil service and stationed in Delhi, came to see them at their hotel with his wife, Leela. Gowri had not seen him since his escape from the Changi Prison in 1942 and the brief interim shelter that she had given him at Labis. They traded a lot of news about their families.

On the sixteenth day of their sojourn in India, they took a flight back to Kuala Lumpur. Both mothers were extremely happy that they could perform the much aspired to once-in-a lifetime pilgrimage to holy sites on the Ganga before their mobility or senses departed them. Gowri carried a pictorial memory of that trip for a long time, and she would never tire talking about it to her friends.

Upon arriving home, Dasu – who had risen to the rank of professor in 1980 – found himself immediately immersed in organizational efforts for the international chemical conference which he had been planning for the past year. Sponsored by both UNESCO and ISESCO, the conference was held under the distinguished royal patronage of the Yang Di-Pertuan Agong, DYMM Sultan Raja Azlan Shah, who was then also the chancellor of the University of Malaya. Held in October about the time of the Commonwealth Heads of Governments Meeting, the conference helped put the Department of Chemistry at the University of Malaya on the world map. In the same year, Dasu won the coveted National Science Award. The family was proud of his achievements.

Gowri with Jayam and his wife, Leela, in Delhi (1989)

Dasu presented the cash prize that came with the award to Gowri. Her eyes welled up with tears, but she promptly gave back the cheque, after bringing it to touch each of her closed eyelids. For Dasu, the pride in her eyes meant much more than the cheque, and it vindicated somewhat the guilt he was carrying for his selfish overstay in Australia to pursue his PhD degree. He insisted that his mother accept at least a small portion of it to settle her debts with Guruvayurappan. She couldn't decline when Dasu put it like that, as she had the habit of pledging some monies to the temple at Guruvayur whenever anyone in her family encountered health or other problems that needed quick recovery or a safe solution. Only she knew what the mounting unsettled quantum was. Dasu was later to learn that she had provided for *annadanam* and some cash donations.

Scenery along the narrow 42-kilometre stretch of
mountain road from Joshimath to Badrinath.

# [29]

In December 1989, Ambika took her mother and children for a ten-day stay at the ashram of His Holiness Swami Bhoomananda Tirtha near Thrissur, where a special *homam* (ceremonial Hindu ritual) was performed to ward off health afflictions and other negative energies from her ancestral Numbreth *tharavad* in Kerala and bring in divine and auspicious energies. As Ambika would be going to Puduserry thereafter to see Kamakshi Amma, Gowri took the opportunity to send the bottled Ganges water that she had specially bought from Varanasi for her mother. While in Guruvayur, Ambika managed to perform the *sayana pradakshinam* (circumambulation around the temple by rolling along the pradakshina path).

A few weeks later, it was announced by the temple authorities that no female pilgrims would henceforth be allowed to perform this rigorous rolling circumambulation ritual. Ambika was happy and relieved that she had been able to fulfil the vow that she had made many years ago to perform this ritual to ward off health afflictions and negative energies on both sides of her family.

Gowri with her growing-up grandchildren in 1989. Flanking her are Suraj
and Bindu, her eldest grandson and granddaughter. Perched on the sofa
is her youngest granddaughter, Smitha. Not in the picture is Dhanya.

Around January 1990, Aravind, who was then working at a private clinic
in Teluk Intan in the State of Perak, successfully secured an attachment at
the RIPAS Hospital in Bandar Seri Begawan, the capital city of Brunei.
Valsala sought a transfer to a school in nearby Labuan to fulfil the required
months of government service that would qualify her for optional retirement
and pension. While in Labuan, she would come to her Brunei home in
Bandar Seri Begawan only on weekends, taking a boat cruise.

Gowri went over to stay in Brunei to look after the kids, as they had
started school there. This was the second time that Gowri found herself
in some intimacy with Valsala's children. The first occasion was some
four years back in Teluk Intan when Valsala took a two-week break to
visit Kamakshi Amma in Pudussery who had longed to see at least one of
Gowri's daughters.

Staying in Brunei, not a day was missed by Gowri and her son-in-law
playing Scrabbles. They sharpened their skills in the game, particularly
in configuring seven-letter bingo words which would earn a fifty-point
bonus. Gowri's key strategy was to aim for a stem word comprising of three

consonants and three vowels so that picking up another word would in most instances immediately generate the bingo word. One stem word she would constantly aim for was SATINE.

After her optional retirement papers were approved, Valsala sought and landed a teaching job in Brunei in February 1991. Brunei is a tax-free country, and expatriate staff then also enjoyed the privilege of a tertiary education subsidy for their children. Aravind and Valsala stayed on in Brunei for almost twelve years. Their children all opted to study in New Zealand following their secondary school studies in Brunei.

# DEMISE OF GOWRI'S MOTHER

Gowri returned to Petaling Jaya from Brunei in early March 1991. On 20 March, Dasu received news that Kamakshi Amma had passed away. He simply told his mother that she was gravely ill and arranged for Ravi to accompany Gowri to Puduserry the very next day. On their arrival at Coimbatore by plane via Madras, they took a taxi straight to Puduserry. Only when they were nearing the house did Ravi break the news.

Surprisingly, Gowri remained composed; it was as if she had anticipated it from Ravi's body language. However, she cried her heart out when she saw Bala Menon and Kamalam, who had arrived there as well. Kamakshi's funeral had taken place on the same day as her death. The practice of embalming the body is seldom observed in villages even to this day, and cremation is traditionally performed before the next dusk or dawn, whichever comes earlier. Gowri was glad that at least Bala Menon had been there at her deathbed and had managed to give her a sip of the holy Ganges water that Gowri had sent earlier.

Both Ravi and Gowri stayed back until the *adiyantharam* was observed on the twelfth day following Kamakshi Amma's demise. An *annadanam* for a thousand people was arranged by Gowri in memory of her departed mother on that day.

A few months after Gowri's return from India, she received news that her nephew Prakash, who had been stricken with Parkinson's disease not long after his marriage, had died in India, where he was undergoing treatment at an undisclosed healing centre. Gowri and her children grieved for him and his family.

The events of her mother's death and that of her nephew all within a span of a few months visibly upset Gowri, and this began to affect her health. Her blood pressure and diabetes were out of control, and she was diagnosed as having heart failure. She had to be hospitalized on a few occasions to stabilize her health condition.

On one such occasion, Dasu was in East Germany on consultancy work with Uniphoenix Corporation Bhd., which had invested in a tin chemicals plant at Bitterfeld. He was urgently summoned back, but he found upon arrival that his mother was out of the woods. Deep down, he had felt that she would recover her health, for despite being not entirely drawn into it, he had some respect for astrology. Insofar as he was concerned, the predictions about him made by a visiting astrologer from India in 1971 had thus far been proved correct to the point of wonder. Going by the same astrologer's readings, his time to perform funeral rites for his mother was still some years away. Psychologically, this was a comforting thought.

As she recovered from her hospitalization, Gowri refused to remain idle at home. She was the chief instructor to the local and Indonesian maids on how to cook various Kerala dishes. Mariah binti Mistun (Su, as she preferred to be called) turned out to be the family's longest-serving maid, attending even to the great-grandchildren Gowri did not live to see. She was an excellent cook and had an uncanny memory when it came to likes and dislikes of individual family members. She was a caring person and was regarded by the Gowri clan as a virtual family member. Su was the envy of many of Gowri's friends who found their foreign maids grossly inefficient in the kitchen, often mishandling modern electrical appliances. Gowri's remark that this was a case of *"Kurangante kayil poomala!"* ("Placing a garland in the monkey's hand!") aptly described their plight.

At times, Gowri would summon Albert during mid-mornings to take her to her favourite shop owned by Harbhajan Singh in Jalan Masjid India. This area in Kuala Lumpur is like a mini-India, filled with stores selling Indian ethnic wear, especially colourful sarees, scarves, and trinkets; jewellery shops; and a variety of restaurants. Gowri knew Harbhajan from her early days in Bukit Mertajam. An enterprising man, he would periodically make trips in his van, lugging bales of newly arrived sarees to his customers in the northern and southern states. He would make it a point to stop at Gowri's place in Bukit Mertajam on his way up to Penang and Kedah on each such trip and tempt Gowri into purchasing some sarees and children's clothes, and allowing credit terms as well. They got along very well, and he would offer *mataji* special discounts on every purchase.

Close to his shop, there was a small videotape-rental kiosk which Gowri would also unfailingly visit. She enjoyed watching new Malayalam film releases. One of her favourites, which she particularly enjoyed watching over and over again, was the 1990 award-winning Malayalam musical comedy *His Highness Abdullah*. The story revolves around Abdullah, who is hired by the members of a wealthy royal family to assassinate the family head, Maharaja Udayavarma. Abdullah comes into the royal palace disguised as a Hindu Brahmin classical singer and tries to use this mask to softly kill the maharaja by imprisoning him. Abdullah then wards off the maharaja's enemies, and in the process exposes his true identity. The grateful maharaja learns that Abdullah is the son of his old friend and forgives him for masquerading as a Brahmin. He also bestows on Abdullah the hand of his daughter.

Gowri generally confined her movie watchings to the afternoons, often dozing off for sizeable portions of the time and then asking someone now and then to rewind the movie. Sometimes she would invite the grandchildren to sit on her lap to watch the movie – a clever move to get them acquainted with the language. She was never an early sleeper and, indeed, would occupy herself until sleep came with a Scrabble game or two with her daughter-in-law Ambika. A large-sized Scrabble board was at hand, and the game would be substantially enlivened whenever Shivan or Hari was present, as newly coined words would suddenly emerge out of the woodwork that were often received with sceptical resistance.

# EMBRACING VISION 2020

The year 1991 stood out in the annals of the country when under the steadying hand of his political leadership and with his out-of-the-box thinking skills, Premier Tun Mahathir Mohamad promulgated Vision 2020 for the country's emergence as a fully developed nation within thirty years. Gowri rarely engaged in cerebral conversation on political matters, but everyone knew that she was a keen follower of nightly news on television that kept her updated on developments. She was the first to point out to Dasu that Vision 2020 was smartly put to refer to visual acuity – a sharp vision. To her, Tun Mahathir was more than a harbinger of change and development; he was also the catalyst for the same.

Gowri watched keenly his proactive efforts to strengthen the country's infrastructure to attract investments and foster growth, and she openly admired his many achievements. Among her standouts were the national network of expressways and federal roads regarded by many as the best in Asia; a world-class international airport at Sepang, the Multimedia Super Corridor – in the mould of Silicon Valley – near Kuala Lumpur, the development of the country's indigeneous car, Proton; and finally the iconic Petronas Twin Towers.

Tun Mahathir, of course, is also credited with the development of Putrajaya as the home of Malaysia's public service. Among his other bold measures was the privatisation of education in 1996, which saw the rise of private colleges and universities as well as branch campuses of foreign universities in the country. English was allowed as the medium of instruction in these institutions. All this could not have happened without political will, but external factors such as the exposed vulnerability of the country to the economic recession in 1985-1986, the demand for university graduates created by the growing presence in the country of multinational enterprises, and the new Vision 2020 Policy also helped hasten its realization. Although Gowri was not to know this, Dasu's extended service in higher education for another decade following his retirement in 1999 was a direct consequence of Tun Mahathir's national policies favouring educational liberalization.

While in office, Tun Mahathir stood tall as the Father of Modern Malaysia. He was the fourth prime minister of Malaysia, and he went on to serve the nation for twenty-two years following his appointment in 1981. He took the helm of office when his immediate predecessor, Tun Hussein Onn, retired on health grounds in 1981. Although he was not very forthright on his mixed ancestry, the Malayalees in the country counted him as one of their fold as his grandfather, Iskandar Kutty, hailed from Kerala.

Gowri had an apt comment: "He has Malayalee blood in him, all right. Look at the boldness of his action in the "Buy British Last" campaign[8], and his follow-up Look East Policy which was to learn from the experience of Japan and Korea in nation-building."

# PRIYA'S WEDDING

In March 1991 Uma's brother Devidas, his wife, Aggie, and their son Dinesh came to Penang along with Uma and Sethu who were on their return trip to the Unites States from India. Following Sethu's retirement in 1989, both he and Uma would stay from spring through fall with their daughter Priya in the States, with the remainder of the year spent near-equally between Trivandrum in India, where they had bought a house, and their Penang home at Persiaran Gurney. While her parents were still in Liberia, Priya had moved to the United States in 1978 to further her education. Graduating *summa cum laude* from Post University in Connecticut with BSc in Accounting, Priya landed a job with the Hartford Financial Services Group, and invested in a home at Hartford. She had by the time of her father's retirement already obtained permanent resident status in the United States.

Gowri and her children were overjoyed at seeing Devidas and family when they came to Petaling Jaya, accompanied by Uma and Sethu. As Suraj's birthday had already passed on 12 March and Dinesh's twenty-first

---

8    This policy stemmed from a number of British aggravations, including their tightening of London Stock Exchange Regulations in specific retaliation towards Malaysia's control over the Guthrie Plantations Group, and the hike in tuition fees for foreign students - the majority being Malaysians - studying in UK.

birthday was around the corner, Dasu decided to hold a joint birthday party lunch in their honour at his house on 16 March. The function was well attended by all of Gowri's children and grandchildren. For Dinesh it was his first meeting with his Malaysian cousins.

Uma and Sethu returned to Malaysia in the month of October from the United States with the news that Priya was betrothed to Keith Palmer and that the couple, following their marriage in November, would be visiting Malaysia en route to Australia for their honeymoon. Both Priya and Keith arrived in early December at Petaling Jaya with Uma and Sethu. They all opted to stay at the Section 17 house where everyone thronged to see the newlyweds. One evening soon after their arrival, Dasu arranged for a family get-together over dinner at his house.

The occasion was also used by the family to cajole the recently married couple, Priya and Keith, to participate in a garland exchange ceremony, an important ritual performed in Indian weddings. They did that to the sounds of traditional Indian wedding music played briefly on tape and earned a loud cheer. This was followed by Ambika performing the *aarti* (light from ghee-soaked wicks arranged in a platter) and applying vermillion on their foreheads. Gowri, Uma, and Sethu were then summoned to bless the couple.

Shortly thereafter, dinner was announced. All were surprised to see Keith enjoying the spicy dishes and using his right hand adroitly to eat the food. The function was full of merriment, with vocal renditions by Venu, Ravi, Uma and Venu's children, Apsara and Lavaniya. It was a reunion to remember.

Gowri with Devidas and Aggie

Priya and Keith Palmer in the company of Gowri

# MALAY WEDDING

With the approach of the end of the year, as is generally the case in Malaysia, the wedding season began in earnest for all communities, coinciding as it did with the school holidays. Gowri had never previously attended a Malay wedding, although she had heard that aside from the essentially Islamic *akad nikah* (marriage contract) ritual, there were some wedding customs and ceremonial procedures which the Malays culturally shared with the Indians. She'd had the chance to witness the *akad nikah* and the *bersanding* (ceremonial seating of couple on dais) ceremonies of their neighbour's daughter, Aisha Tajuddin, while she was staying in Kampong Tunku. Aisha was Valsala's colleague at school. She came with her mother to hand-deliver to Gowri the wedding invitation card. Aisha explained that her fiancé's name was Bakar and their *adat meminang* (engagement ceremony) had taken place some six months ago.

"What was the engagement like?" a curious Gowri wanted to know.

"Oh, it's a serious ceremony, Aunty. Bakar came to my house with his party on the appointed day and time. They brought with them gift trays containing items that were previously agreed upon by both parties when the conditions for the engagement were discussed, including the quantum of the wedding expenses, *wang belanja*, which will be borne by the bridegroom. The items brought for me were a gold ring; a betel-leaf container filled with betel leaves, arecanut, and other ingredients; a complete set of clothes; a shawl; a handbag; a cosmetic set; and a pair of shoes. All the items were handed over to representatives from my side of the family except for the ring, which Bakar's eldest sister took in her hand."

"Didn't Bakar's parents come along?"

"No, they don't get involved. So also my parents. Only family elders take part from both sides."

"Did you give gifts from your side?"

"Yes, Aunty. In fact, we have to give them more gifts. Not only that, the number of trays and number of gifts must be odd-numbered. I don't remember everything on our trays, but I know there was a *songkok* (velvet cap), a prayer mat, a pair of new clothes, and a digital watch among them. After the exchange of gifts, the date and time for the *akad nikah* were confirmed."

"And the gold ring?"

"That was placed on my finger by Bakar's eldest sister. I met Bakar only after that, and all the guests were treated to a meal in my house before they left."

The *akad nikah* ceremony was a week away. It was held at Aisha's house in the morning, and Gowri went along to witness it with Valsala. The *Kadi* (state-appointed religious official) officiated the simple ceremony. Aisha was given away by her father in the presence of two witnesses, and Bakar had to recite in one breath the *lafaz nikah* (marriage vow). The *Kadi* then gave the couple a brief sermon on their rights and responsibilities from the Islamic perspective. Following the ceremony, the bride and groom signed the marriage certificate issued by the *Kadi*, which was attested by the witnesses present. Gifts were then exchanged between both parties. The couple were ushered to sit on a specially decorated *pelamin* (dais) and henna was applied to their hands by members from both sides of the family. Rice-flour paste was also applied to their palms and foreheads as a sign of blessing and protection from evil or malicious influences.

The follow-up *bersanding* ceremony and *kenduri* (feast) were held at the Kampung Tunku Municipality Multipurpose Hall towards mid-morning the next day. The bride's party arrived early to welcome the guests and await the ceremonial arrival of the bridegroom. The bridegroom, looking dashing in his cream-coloured songket dress and traditional headgear, arrived at eleven thirty in the morning, led by womenfolk. Behind him came musicians beating the hand-held kompang drums and bearers of *bunga manggar* (decorative flowers). Once seated, a welcoming *pencak silat* (martial arts display) was performed in front of the bridegroom.

The bridegroom and the bride – who appeared from her chamber looking radiant in her traditional pearl white kebaya (wedding dress) and veil – were then invited to sit on the specially decorated dais, which was centrally located in the wedding hall so that the guests seated at the prearranged tables could have a clear view. The couple were then blessed by elders and close family friends with scented water, henna, sandalwood paste, and rice flour paste. Following the *bersanding* ceremony, which publicly ratified their union, a sumptuous wedding lunch was served at the site.

Gowri was pleasantly surprised to note that they had specially ordered vegetarian dishes for her and Valsala.

In August 1994, Gowri's niece Sathya (her cousin Radha's daughter) accompanied by her husband, N. K. Menon, and sister Krishna, visited Malaysia. Dasu and Ambika took them around Kuala Lumpur, including the Genting Highlands mountain resort and casino on the outskirts. Sathya's husband had a happy outing at the casino playing roulette, though not the others, who concentrated merely on the slot machines.

Gowri with Sathya and N. K. Menon
(*third and fourth from right*) and Krishna (*third from left*)

The following day, Ravi and Susheela came down from Melaka and took them away for a couple of days' stay with them. The visitors enjoyed their trip very much, soaking in visits to historical and interesting sites, including the Portuguese-built A'Famosa fortress; the Stadthuys, the imposing red town hall and governor's residence of the Dutch; and Jonker's Street, the prime *baba-nyonya* heritage site of the state, well-known for its antique shops. The

Babas and Nyonyas are Chinese of noble ancestry who have adopted much of the Malay culture into theirs. Likewise, a community of Indians exists in Melaka who have adopted Malay cultural practices. They are the Chitties. They speak Bahasa Malaysia (Malaysian Language or Standard Malay) and dress and act as Malays but retain their Hindu religion.

Ravi arranged for his driver to drop them back at Section 17 after the Melaka visit. That evening, all of Dasu's siblings and their families came over to meet them over drinks and some Chinese food, including vegetarian Chinese dishes they were tasting for the first time. They liked the vegetarian noodles, but their taste buds did not quite accept the soya-based "mock meat" preparations. The conversation drifted to their interesting visit to Melaka and the developments they saw around Kuala Lumpur. They were full of praise for the recently constructed national north-south expressway.

"The privatisation of the highway project on the BOT mode is the right strategy the government has adopted. The tolls collected for use of the highway will ensure its effective maintenance," explained Dasu.

"Well, I must say that your roads are very clean, even in the towns," observed Krishna.

Dasu and Gowri exchanged understanding looks. Smilingly, Gowri turned to Krishna and said, "That's because littering in urban areas invites a heavy fine! Because of that, I have noticed that one bad habit among the population also seems to have nearly disappeared. And that is spitting at will on pavements and roads. It was so disgusting to see this habit in the old days."

Following a further day's stay at Section 17, Sathya and family flew to Singapore, where they planned to do some major shopping with the money won at the Genting casino before finally heading back to India.

A month after their departure, Ambika's mother, Ammukutty Amma (Thangam, as her husband fondly called her), suffered a heart attack and came to live at the house in Section 17. She was a companion to Gowri. Like Gowri, she was a strict vegetarian and enjoyed her solitude reading her many prayer books. While her sons, Radhakrishnan (Unni) and Achuthan, both younger than Ambika, would come to see her regularly at weekends, she also enjoyed the visits now and then of her nieces (her elder sister Subadra's daughters), Indira and Susheela (Sushee for short), and their spouses whenever they came to Petaling Jaya. Indira had a medical practice in Kota Bahru in Kelantan where her husband, Gopakumar, was working as a civil engineer. Sushee ran a dental clinic in Kota Tinggi in Johor.

With Subadra unwell in India, Thangam and her husband played parental roles in getting Indira and Sushee married in 1975. Both Sushee and her husband, Ronnie Sivalingam, a medical practitioner, had pious leanings. They were active in the Sri Amman temple affairs in Kota Tinggi, and they found in Gowri a person with whom they could discuss spiritual matters. Gowri came to learn that on several occasions at temple festival prayers, Sushee would break out into a trance, such was her devotion. At Ronnie's request, Gowri taught both of them several slokas.

Gowri also got to know well Thangam's close friends the Raghavans, whom Thangam had known from her days at Lima Belas Estate in Slim River, where Mr Raghavan and Thangam's late husband were colleagues at work. Gowri found the Raghavans delightful company; they often shared with her the latest happenings in Kerala.

## NATURAL/SUPERNATURAL

On one visit to Kuala Lumpur, Sushee narrated an astonishing account of a problem she had encountered on her right forearm, just below the shoulder. She had been experiencing needle-like pricking pains for almost three weeks which affected her work at her dental practice. Although she did suffer from cervical spondylosis, she was sure that this pain was different.

At her insistence, an X-ray was taken and then repeated. This confirmed the presence of two foreign bodies in the shape of broken nails embedded in the subcutaneous layer of the skin. A surgical procedure successfully removed the foreign bodies, which were identified to be metallic. The doctors were baffled. They looked like charm needles (*susuk*). Such charm needles were once inserted to act as talismans for protection against injury or accidents as well as a facial-cum-body art among women in the Malay Archipelago before the advent of Islam, but this practice had long been banned. That such needles were found in Sushee's arm was hard to fathom.

Sushee then made the decision to consult an astrologer to figure out the mystery. The astrologer told her that because of the planetary positions in her birth chart, she was currently going through a bad phase in her health and professional life, but that this would soon pass. Abruptly, he turned to her and asked, "Did you undergo any surgery recently?" Seeing her hesitate, he continued, "You have to be truthful."

"Yes, I did."

"Was there anything odd?"

Sushee explained about the surgery and the implanted charm needles that were removed from her arm.

"They have been put there by a bomoh [shaman]. Someone jealous of your practice is behind it. Your birthchart shows you will be the object of much envy. But you will never experience the full impact of this bad charm because of your overpowering faith in God. The worst is over."

Gowri, after hearing all this, wrote down a Romanized Sanskrit mantra and gave it to Sushee. "There is power in this prayer verse. Recite it daily," advised Gowri.

# [30]

In May 1995, Dasu had to take formal retirement from the University of Malaya, as the compulsory retirement age in the country then for those in service in government and statutory bodies was 55. But the university extended his services until 1998 and then by a further year to 1999. He continued his deanship of the science faculty over this period. He went on to serve in the educational field for another decade or more in the private sector thanks to the changes in the government's educational policies.

In November 1995, Gowri turned 80. The family decided that her birthday party would be held in Melaka. Valsala and Aravind could not get leave to come from Brunei, but all of Gowri's other children were present. Among her grandchildren, the only absentee was Ashwin, who had left a year earlier to study at King's College, London. Gowri had, however, a new grandchild by then, as Shoba had delivered her second daughter, Smitha, in 1988. She was to be Gowri's last grandchild, who along with Sathya and Nithya qualified as the Section 17 *tharavad*-born children.

Of Gowri's seventeen grandchildren in the 1990s, twelve were girls. All the grandchildren would descend on Section 17 for a get-together at the flimsiest excuse. They enjoyed each other's company, and the girls, in particular, shared common interests for singing and dancing. Gowri's joy knew no bounds when they were around her. Now and then, they would all dress up for a group photograph with Gowri on the lawn of the house. They also had fun dressing up their grandmother in fancy costumes when it came to parties. Gowri with her sense of humour would almost always oblige.

Gowri's bevy of granddaughters as they looked in 1993.
*Clockwise*: Bindu, Smitha, Nisha, Sathya, Rhitu, Gouri, Apsara,
Lavaniya, Kiran, Nithya, Sapna. Absent: Dhanya.

Gowri in a frolic pose playing up to her grandchildren.

# GOWRI'S EIGHTIETH BIRTHDAY

The family celebrated Gowri's birthday at Melaka at Ravi's suggestion. Everyone stayed at the Klebang Beach Resort. The day prior to the function, beach games were organized by Ravi. All the grandchildren wore T-shirts bearing the words "*Ammama's* 80th Birthday Bash" that were specially ordered by Shivan. The younger members of the family had secret practise song sessions, while for the older ones there was a choice of pool, dart, and card games after dinner. Because of stinging jellyfish, no one ventured into the sea; those who fancied a swim took to the swimming pool at the resort.

The birthday function was held in the evening of the following day. Delicious seafood fare was served from the kitchen at the resort, but Gowri and other vegetarians in the group had specially ordered dishes brought in from another restaurant.

Gowri's grandchildren sang a special birthday ode which they had composed for her. The lyrics of the ode entitled "Love Is the Answer" were by her eldest grandchild, Suraj, and went as follows:

> There comes a time when a mother's love
> Burns a message that is heard above.
> A heart so bold, and a will so strong,
> One woman's life reflects in this song.
>
> Seven children and a raging war.
> What brings tomorrow, what shall I do?
> What lies behind my future's door?
> Oh, my children, all I have are you.
>
> Gather up my strength now.
> I know what I should do now.
> Words rise up from within
> Blowin' in the hot summer's wind.

And she said:

*Chorus*
Love is the answer,
Love is the way,
A family that loves will forever stay, yeah,
Through times of trouble,
Through times of woe,
We'll have each other and need nothing more.

All her children are grown up and workin',
All married and have children of their own.
Times have been hard, times have been trying,
But her words of wisdom have been sown deep within,
And as they face their troubles now,
They know what they should do now.
The secret to survive
Is written in the hot summer's wind.

And they hear her say ...

*Chorus*

The ode was sung with such gusto to guitar strumming by Sharad and
Gopu that all the audience joined in for the chorus. Gowri was moved by
the reverence with which everyone in the hall held her. A birthday cake
was wheeled in, and everyone stood up to sing the birthday song. With the
assistance of her youngest grandchildren, who were standing closest to her,
she managed to blow out the eight candles in two puffs.

Gowri was asked to say a few words. She rose to her feet and accepted
the cordless microphone that was passed to her. She was smiling, filled with
pleasure. Brushing aside a strand of hair caught on her lip, she brought the
microphone close to her mouth, her eyes half-closing. Her voice was loud
and clear, and the verse that she began to recite immediately struck a chord

with the audience. It was the Gayatri Mantra, familiar to all of Gowri's children and many others in the audience:

*Oṃ bhūr bhuvaḥ svaḥ*
*Tát savitúr váreṇ (i) yaṃ*
*Bhárgo devásya dhīmahi*
*Dhíyo yó naḥ prachodáyāt*

Translated, it means:

Oh God! Thou art the Giver of Life,
Remover of pain and sorrow,
The Bestower of happiness,
Oh Creator of the Universe,
May we receive thy supreme sin-destroying light,
May Thou guide our intellect in the right direction.

She thanked all the members of her family and those of her extended family who had come to partake in the function and make it such a memorable one for her. Pausing for a moment, she continued, "A mother should not be lost for words. But I am today. I did not think I would live to this age when I lost the father of my children thirty-seven years ago. But God, although He took my husband away, has played a merciful hand in getting all of us to where we are today. Never lose your faith in Him. He is all around us. With faith, you will find the courage to move on and make your destiny.

"My fervent wish will always be that you, my family, remain united and love each other. Celebrate each other's success and help each other when the need arises. Remember that my blood runs in each and every one of you, my children and grandchildren. God has blessed me with all of you. I cherish you all, as I do also my sons-in-law and my daughters-in-law who have borne me my grandchildren. You have not come into my life by accident but by divine blessing. You must always love and support one another. Generosity of the heart has to be cultivated, and therein lies the seed of true happiness. If any one of you are going astray, the onus is on all the others to bring him or her back to the right track. Life is always a challenge, but meet it. It is too precious not to fight for it. Looking at my own life, it has, indeed, been one hell of a fight."

She paused for a sip of water and then continued. "To my grandchildren, I have only this to say: Love each other. How many of you have read *The Three Musketeers*? You know what their motto was? 'One for all, and all for one.' That's how your relationship should be. *"Ikyamathyam maha balam"* ("Unity is great strength").

"Be proactive in your learning habits. There is an old Chinese proverb which says, 'Don't curse the darkness – light a candle.' In other words, ignorance is no excuse. Focus on your studies. Learn to motivate yourself and remain dedicated. Strength of character comes from focus and commitment. You will all do very well in your studies. Don't give up if success doesn't come immediately. Have the courage to follow your dreams. Courage matters a lot. That applies to all of us as we journey through life. Also, we need to be morally strong. Our family should brook no disrepute. I know all of you will succeed well in life. Chant the Gayatri Mantra everyday of your life. There is power in it to bestow happiness on you. I love you all."

Everyone clapped, cheered, and came to hug her. The grandchildren present were invited to say a few words. They all did, one by one, speaking impromptu and mixing their words, which elicited much mirth as well. Sharad spoke in pidgin English, saying *"Hepi berthde, Ammama. Mi lavim yu."* Everyone understood the words.

The evening went on with more merriment. There were vocal renditions by Venu, Hari, and in particular Ravi, whose renditions of the popular Malayalam songs *"Maanase maine varu"* and *"Thamasamenthe varuvaan"* were simply superb. All Gowri's grandchildren were familiar with the tunes, as in their encounters with Uncle Ravi they rarely escaped "sing along with me" sessions. Towards the close of the function, Venu's children Apsara and Lavaniya chipped in with a lovely duet, choosing for the song the Barbra Streisand classic "Memory" from the 1981 musical *Cats*.

Before everyone dispersed, they had a photography session. Gowri insisted on a photograph of Gowri alone with her grandchildren. She had special affection for each of them. They were the reason for her continued living, she confided in Dasu. Indeed, every Thursday morning, she would unfailingly recite the *Vishnu Sahasranāma* (literally the thousand names of Lord Vishnu). She believed that the chanting of this *stotram* would benefit the entire family, giving relief from all sorrows, lessening the negative impact of fated events, reducing stress, bringing peace of mind, and ushering in auspicious things in their lives.

The next morning, after a hearty Malaysian-style breakfast of *nasi lemak*, almost all of them left on the return journey to their respective homes. Gowri stayed back to spend a few more days with Ravi, Susheela, and Dhanya. Ravi was, by this time, confined very much to the wheelchair, but that neither prevented him from fulfilling his professional duties in his clinic nor indulging in social activities. He was very active in the Melaka Theatre Group and even helped write the lyrics of a few humorous plays, all of which were held at leading Melaka hotels. The theatre group was the first to introduce dinner theatre in the state. Gowri had attended one of these plays in an earlier visit and was impressed by the performance of the local actors. It reminded her of her visit to the West End theatre while she was in London many years back.

Gowri celebrating her eightieth birthday with her family at Melaka

Gowri in the company of her relatives through marriage on her birthday. *Left to right*: Rohini (Ravi's mother-in-law), Thilothamma (Venu's mother-in-law), Gowri, Subadra (Ammukutty's elder sister), Ammukutty (Dasu's mother-in-law).

# [31]

With the approach of the New Year in 1996 came the news that Gowri's eldest grandchild, Suraj, had asked for the hand of Presenna's niece, Sajitha, in marriage. The family decided that he would have a temple wedding in Kluang where Sajitha's parents were residing, followed by a church wedding a few days later in Petaling Jaya. Presenna's sister Ponnu came down from India for the occasion. The temple wedding was on a Friday morning in the month of April.

A motorcade left Section 17 for Kluang on Thursday afternoon, with Suraj travelling with his parents Shivan and Shanti in the one vehicle. Accompanying them was one of Shanti's stepbrothers, George (Uncle George to the kids), who had endeared himself the most to Gowri's family. He was then working with Malaysian Airlines in the baggage handling division and was invariably contacted by one and all in the family on outward-bound trips to help manage their excess baggage problems. Gowri went in Dasu's car, while Thilothamma travelled with Venu. The family were all put up at the Merdeka Hotel in town – except for Thilothamma, the bride's grandmother, who stayed at the bride's home.

## SURAJ'S WEDDING – A TOUCH OF TRADITION

The temple wedding was held in the *kalamandapam* adjacent to the temple. It was a simple ceremony conducted in Kerala style with far fewer religious compulsions than other Hindu weddings. Based on the auspicious time for the tying of the nuptial knot or *thalimala* (necklace with gold

272

pendant), the entrance times of the bridegroom and then of the bride were fixed. Suraj, dressed in a cream silk shirt and cream silk mundu, entered the *kalamandapam* with his family at the appointed hour to the tune of *nadaswarams* (long wind instruments). At the entrance, Suraj had his feet washed by the bride's younger brother, Virojan, to whom he presented a gold ring.

Pankajam, Presenna's older married sister, performed the *aarti* for Suraj. With the *nadaswarams* playing, the groom was then escorted to the *mandapam (raised marriage platform)* where the priest was seated by two rows of young girls – the *thalam* girls – walking in pairs. Suraj's cousins were among them. The lead girl in the first row carried the *changala vatta* (sacred oil lamp), while the lead girl in the second row carried the *ashtamangalyam* (eight auspicious articles). The girls behind them carried platters of rice, turmeric, and flowers on which lit oil lamps were placed. The *mandapam* was beautifully adorned with flowers and a *nirrapara* (a vessel filled to the brim with paddy) with a flowering coconut bunch inserted into it, and surrounded by three *nilavilakku* (traditional oil lamps). Suraj seated himself on the right side of the dais.

The bride, resplendent in her traditional off-white saree with a golden border and wearing gold ornaments, was next escorted by the *thalam* girls to the dais to the sounds of the *nadaswarams*. She sat on the left side close to the bridegroom. The priest then conducted the Ganapathy Homam. After this, the priest – having conducted the puja – handed to Suraj at the precise moment the *thalimala*. Suraj tied it around Sajitha's neck to the accompaniment of the sounds of the *panchavadyam* (five types of Kerala music). The couple stood up to garland each other, the bride garlanding first. This was followed by an exchange of rings, the bridegroom placing the ring first on the bride's finger. Sajitha's father, Vasudevan, then took her right hand and entrusted it to the right hand of Suraj, and held both their right hands together with his hands while the priest recited some Vedic prayers. This solemnized the wedding.

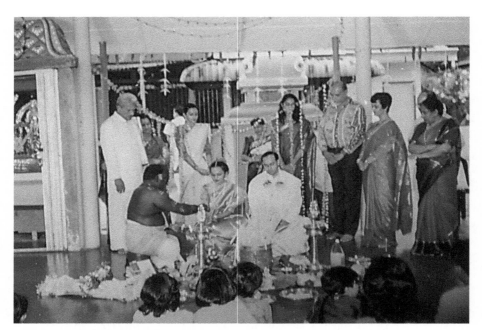

Solemnization of the marriage of Suraj, Gowri's eldest grandson, and Sajitha at Kluang. Shivan and Shanti are standing behind Suraj; Sajitha's parents are on the extreme left.

The newly-wed couple next took three rounds of the *mandapam*. Suraj then gifted his new bride with a saree and a blouse on a platter. Shanti in turn gave her new daughter-in-law a gold chain, which she placed around her neck. The bride and groom separately gave their *dhakshina* (token amount in reverence) to the priest in betel leaves. This concluded the marriage ceremony.

The couple then sought the blessings of the two grandmothers, their parents, and their uncles and aunts on the *mandapam*. This was followed by the senior-most members of the family, beginning with the bride's parents, feeding both the bride and the groom a spoonful of sweetened milk mixed with plantain fruit. The newly married couple then went to pray at the temple and sign their marriage certificates at the temple office, after which a vegetarian *sadya* was served at the temple premises.

A formal wedding reception was held in the evening at the Banquet Hall of Merdeka Hotel, where the toast to the bride and groom was given by Dasu. Although it is traditional for the nuptial night to be spent in the bride's home, in a touch of modernity, the bridal suite at the hotel served the purpose for Suraj and Sajitha. A few days later, they were married according to Christian traditions at the Assumption Church in Petaling Jaya. Gowri and her family and Shanti's mother, Violet Ambrose, and family were all in full attendance.

A month or two after their wedding, Uma, Sethu, and Priya came down with Priya's son, Sethu Jr. Gowri was delighted to see her great-grandnephew. They stayed for a week with Gowri.

# WORRIES RETURN

The months of September and October 1996 were very disturbing ones for Gowri – first with the news that Shanti had developed breast cancer and then that Valsala was experiencing stroke-like symptoms on one side of her body.

Shanti came back to stay with Suraj and to undergo radiotherapy, making only intermittent trips to PNG, where she had initiated a modelling and boutique business which was being handled by Shivan in her absence. Gowri was immensely worried about Shanti, having read about this dreaded affliction. She was genuinely fond of her daughter-in-law, and Shanti reciprocated this love. Shanti once confessed to her eldest son, Suraj, that she found in Gowri the mother's love and closeness she seemed to have lost with her own biological mother who remarried and left her with her grandparents.

Shanti opted not to undergo mastectomy. This proved a fatal mistake. The cancer that could have been arrested progressed, and she developed secondaries. She succumbed to the disease four years later.

Apsara, Gouri and Lavaniya (*seated*)
modelling the boutique Indian outfits designed by Shanti in PNG.

Valsala's ailment could not be addressed in Brunei, and she had to come down to Singapore for a thorough diagnosis. The test showed that she had incurred a bleed in the brain due to an arteriovenous malformation. A gamma-knife radiosurgery was decided upon and performed. It proved to be successful, restoring substantially her agility and health.

"Despite its name, there is no knife or scalpel involved in the procedure," explained Valsala. "Instead, a number of precise beams of high-energy gamma radiation are directed to the treatment area. For this I had to wear a head frame surgically fixed to my skull so that the treatment area remains stationary at the target point of the gamma rays. I didn't have to shave my head." The teacher in Valsala came through well in the explanation.

Towards the close of the year came the news that Bala Menon was diagnosed as having lung cancer. He stubbornly refused to undergo radiation treatment. Gowri contacted Uma's bother, Krishna Kumar, then in private medical practice in Trivandrum, to coax Bala Menon to undergo treatment. Bala Menon obliged for one incomplete spell of treatment at a private hospital, but he discharged himself, as he could not endure the discomfort that attended the treatment. "If death comes, let it come," was his resigned stand on his health problem. The only concession he made was to cut back on his heavy smoking.

He went back to Puduserry to devote full time to serving on the management committee of the Sree Kurumba Bhagavati Temple that was situated just across the road from his house. The temple is famous throughout Kerala for its colourful annual festival, the Pudussery Vedi, celebrated at the end of February. His ancestors had long been the keepers of the temple. It was his *tharavad* temple. The cancer, which was already in its third stage when detected, soon reached the terminal stage. He died a few months into 1997.

Gowri broke down on hearing the news. She was consoled to hear from Ponnu that Kamalam and Uma's elder sister Prema were there at his deathbed, and Kamalam stayed for the duration of the *adiyantharam* and a bit longer. With the demise of Bala Menon, the surviving portion of the once extensive Pudussery Kollaikal *tharavad* home of Kamakshi Amma's mother, Ammalu Amma, in Kerala has sunk into oblivion, as her lineage of female descendants entitled to carry the *tharavad* name nurtured no ambitions to preserve it as a symbolic heritage. Only some of the descendants of Ammalu Amma's sister, Devu Amma, and her brothers continued to live in the locality and helped to oversee the ancestral shrines that are now visited by the general public as well. Devu Amma's great granddaughter, Thangamani, often visited her aunt Kamakshi Amma when she was alive and had in the process endeared herself to Gowri's and Sarawathi's children. She remained the first point of contact for them in Pudussery.

Upon Bala Menon's demise, none of his nephews and nieces had any objections to their aunt, Jayalakshmi, taking ownership of the Pudussery abode. The house has since been renovated by her relatives to a modern two-storey bungalow. The old faithful well that was at the side of the house remains untouched, the only historic relic standing to this day of the bygone *tharavad* home of Ammalu Amma.

The Sree Kurumba Bhagavati temple at Pudussery

The remaining portion of the once extensive Kollaikal *tharava*d house at Pudussery where Gowri's mother, Kamakshi Amma, lived (*left*), with (*right*) the century-old well beside it.

Ambika and Prema with Gowri's second cousin, Thangamani (*third from right*), and her family.

☼

Uma and Sethu returned for their annual visit to Malaysia in early April 1997 and once again met all family members while staying at the Section 17 residence. Dasu recalled Uma saying goodbye to Gowri and walking away, only to stop abruptly and rush back to hug her again and cry. It was as if she had a premonition that she might not see her aunt again. Gowri, holding her in an embrace, comforted her and asked her in jest, "Do you by any chance feel I won't be around when you come next?" Others gathered around giggled. Uma laughed through her tears and, planting a kiss on Gowri, left the scene in a somewhat happier frame of mind.

In the month of May 1997, Gowri went to stay with her daughter Ambi, who had by then moved to Bandar Sri Damansara, a nearby precinct in Petaling Jaya following Ravindran's retirement from government service in 1996. Gowri's diabetes was giving her problems, and the family felt Ambi would have more time on her hands to give Gowri the constant nursing attention she now seemed to need. In the matriarchal system, it was a norm that daughters would care for their mother, and this pleasure was quite denied to Ambi and Valsala because of their heavy work schedules while in service. The opportunity only arose for Ambi upon her joint retirement with Ravindran from government service. Gowri's shift meant that she was now missed very much by Dasu, who had been looking after her for almost nineteen years, and he would visit her with Ambika and the children several times a week.

Gowri had a downstairs room in the Bandar Sri Damansara house, with an attached bathroom. An air conditioner was fixed in the room by Hari, who also arranged for an Indonesian maid to look after her needs. Nor was the maid's name, and she slept on a mat in the same room. Gowri was steady on her feet and had no difficulty walking around the house. She was able to take her bath and dress herself independently. Nor's duty was mainly to make sure her meals and medicines were served on time and to attend to the daily massage Gowri needed for her aching legs and feet, and occasionally for her neck and back.

Hari would visit his mother most weekends and amiably engage her and everyone else there in lengthy conversations. It was through Hari that the family learnt about the July 1997 shocker of the Asian financial crisis, triggered by speculative attacks on local currencies, that threatened a global financial meltdown. Thailand was the first casualty in Southeast Asia; it was forced to devalue the baht. Malaysia's defence of the ringgit was a bold one, with much of the credit for it going to Tun Mahathir. He went against the International Monetary Fund (IMF) guidelines of observing reduced government spending and raising interest rates. Instead, he increased government spending and pegged the ringgit to the US dollar. Malaysia recovered from the crisis faster than its Southeast Asian neighbours.

While staying with Ambi, Gowri missed the friends who often would drop in at the Section 17 house, and once asked her daughter why she had to buy a house so far out. She would talk to Thilothamma, her friend since her Johor days and now multiply her relative, almost every day to get over her boredom. Often, she would sit and play Scrabble, laying out the letters for herself and a virtual opponent. Thus she would play and time would soon pass.

Sometimes she would rope in her son-in-law, Ravindran. He was often slow in his game, and Gowri would grow impatient and say, "Why Ravi, come on! Stop thinking too much and put down the word!" When Ravindran was still hesitant, she would peek at his letter rack and say, "Why don't you put down this word. I am sure you have the right alphabet letters there!" Ambi would once in a while sit down to have a game with her, only to get reprimanded. "You are an English language teacher and yet you can't come up quickly with a word!" Gowri's frustration was understandable. As an avid player, she would easily come up with words with top scores, and she couldn't bear to see her opponents still labouring for a word.

Most times after her morning bath and prayers, Gowri would enter the kitchen and cook special dishes for her son-in-law. In the process, she taught Ambi's maid the intricacies of authentic Kerala cuisine. Gowri did not fancy using the microwave oven for cooking curries, but she found it useful for cooking potatoes in a jiffy for *aloo bondas*, her favourite teatime snack.

Occasionally, Ambi would invite Gowri's friends over for tea. Gowri also had a frequent visitor in Mrs N. G. Nair, who would sometimes stay on for a few days. They shared a strong interest in Hindu scriptures and often would recite verses from them together.

☼

# GOWRI, THE SPIRITUAL MENTOR

One weekend, Bindu and Rhitu, having heard Gowri's devotional prayers, approached her.

"*Ammama*, what's so special about our religion? Is it because we have many gods? Is the Bhagavad Gita our equivalent of the Bible and the Koran?" The questions were jointly posed.

"Why the sudden interest?" Gowri asked them, hiding her amusement.

"Not sudden, *Ammama*. We found the books on Hinduism a bit confusing and difficult to follow. We thought you will be able to tell us about our religion in an easily understandable manner," Bindu replied.

"Actually, *Ammama*, it would be best if you could write it down for us in a nutshell so that we can share it with our cousins as well," added Rhitu.

"Hmm! I will see what I can do," replied Gowri. "Let me have a look first at the books that you have been reading." Rhitu went up the stairs and soon returned with a bundle of books. Gowri looked through these and others in her own collection.

Mrs N. G. Nair said that she too had some good books in her possession which she could loan to Gowri. "It is commendable that your grandchildren are taking an interest in their religion. There is formal religious education for the young at the school level who follow the Christian or Muslim faith in this country, but not for the Hindus. I wonder why this is so?"

"I guess with the Hindus, they have stuck to the traditional method of imparting religious knowledge to the young in the home, which is through the elderly womenfolk in the family," Gowri observed. "Often this happens at dusk soon after the family prayers have been performed, when all the children are gathered around the altar. But the many Hindu immigrants who came here were younger people who had less time on their hands to teach their offspring anything more than the importance of following the path of righteousness and indulging in daily prayers to the Almighty through the recitation of the limited hymns they knew."

"Perhaps the temples could play a proactive role here, and there is really no paucity of them in the country," mused Mrs N. G. Nair.

Gowri smiled and nodded affirmatively while turning the pages of the books now in her possession. She found a book titled *The Hindu Mind* by Bansi Pandit, which had several passages in it worthy of quote. She set down to work, and within the week had penned a draft which she asked Dasu to edit and print out, to be given to all her adult grandchildren. The contents, written in a question-and-answer format, ran into three pages (see Appendix 1).

Rhitu came in to see Gowri as soon as she read the contents. "Wow, *Ammama*, you missed your calling. You should have been a scholar. That was a very erudite summary. Thank you so much." This simple insight into their religion has been clung to tenaciously by them all.

## GOWRI'S PRIDE IN HER GRANDCHILDREN

Gowri liked her children and grandchildren to be around her at all times. She looked forward to weekends when the family would come over to see her, especially Dasu. She was sad Venu could not visit her as often because of his clinic and told her daughter to tell him a patient wanted to see him – she being the patient!

In Vikram, she found a good listener. She related her childhood stories to him. She was elated to hear the news at the end of May that Sapna had graduated from the University of Canterbury with a master's degree in engineering management with distinction. She sent her granddaughter a congratulatory telegram followed by a letter – both now cherished keepsakes for Sapna. Bindu, she recalled, had graduated with a bachelor of commerce in accounting degree from the University of Canberra in 1995, and Suraj with a degree in economics from James Cook University two years earlier. Her three elder grandchildren had done her proud.

The others, she knew, were already pursuing their tertiary level education – Rhitu in electronics engineering; Ashwin in mechatronics; Kiran and Sharad in commerce; and Nisha, Gouri, Apsara, and Govind in medicine. They constituted the second wave of graduates to come from the family. Closely behind them were Sathya and Vikram.

Gowri was not surprised by Sathya's desire to read law after watching her glued to law programmes on television. Vikram, she sensed, had leanings towards a degree in business. She wished circumstances had been different so that her Shivan, Ambi, and Valsala could have been similarly provided with the opportunities for higher education that they merited.

Suddenly she got excited by a passing thought: now that Suraj was married, there was a need, yes, surely a need to prospect for suitable life partners for Bindu and Sapna! She knew she had to revisit her neglected links with her old contacts in the country. This proactive mood prevailed for some time, keeping her mentally busy.

As the year drew to a close, the country was blanketed for some three months by a terrible haze that severely affected horizontal visibility and caused widespread health problems on account of the alarmingly high content of fine particulate matter in the air. The haze was caused by the rampant slash-and-burn practice of farmers and the peat fires blown by the wind from Indonesia, especially Sumatra. Gowri suffered an upper respiratory infection as a result and had to seek attention from the hospital. She was asked to wear a respiratory mask for a while and keep indoors. The haze only cleared when the delayed monsoon showed up in early November to quench the fires.

ഓം

("Aum" in Malayalam: The sacred syllable stands
for Brahman, the Ultimate Reality)

# GOWRI'S DEMISE
# 25 MARCH 1998

*"Soft with love are our thoughts of you.*
*The light you have lit still burns bright to illuminate our paths."*

# [32]

January 1998 saw the iconic eighty-eight-floor Petronas Twin Towers open to the public at the Kuala Lumpur City Centre (KLCC). These were the tallest buildings in the world at the time, and they held the record for six years. They still remain the tallest *twin* towers. The towers with their steel and glass façade are connected by a double-decker sky bridge. Outlets at the Twin Towers, such as Suria KLCC (an upmarket retail centre) and the Petronas Philharmonic Hall, were open to the public. Gowri went to see this new architectural marvel along with her daughter Ambi. She came back somewhat shocked at the prices of goods even at their discounted offer prices.

The Petronas Twin Towers
*Source: Copyright 2012 Laurus Creations. Reproduced with permission.*

At her granddaughter Bindu's birthday in early February, Gowri insisted on making *avial* and *payasam* dishes. As it turned out, it was to be a special occasion, as unknown to Gowri, Rakesh had asked for Bindu's hand in marriage on that day. In the weeks that followed, Gowri met Rakesh several times. She knew his grandfather and grandmother well from her days in Johor and was happy that there was going to be a union between the families.

In early March, Gowri's family members who were around came to observe the annual *shradham* for Govindan Kutty at Ambi's house in Bandar Sri Damansara, as Gowri was staying there. *Shradham* – ritual prayer for a departed parent – is an important ritual in Hindu Dharma. It is held that there is a subtle energy in the *shradham* prayers that deceased ancestors present in the *Pitru* region may avail of to progress to a higher sub-plane of existence. Suraj came with Sajitha, who was in her early stage of pregnancy. Gowri was overjoyed that a great-grandchild was on the way. The *shradham* also included prayers for Sathiabhama and Unnikrishnan. Little did anyone realize that Gowri would soon be counted among the departed souls.

A week later, around 21 March, Dasu's daughter, Gouri, who was doing part of her medical degree programme at Manipal in India, came down for the holidays. She had brought with her two pure silk sarees, one for each of her grandmothers. Dasu took her to see Gowri as soon as she arrived, and the granddaughter presented her grandmother with a pastel green saree. Gowri liked it very much.

When they had left, Gowri told the housemaid, Nor, "Gouri thinks I may not be around by the time she finishes her medical course. So she has given me the saree early. I'm going to wear it now." After donning the saree, she went round the house showing it to everyone.

## THE SPECTRE OF LIFE'S END

On the late evening of 24 March, Sushee and Ronnie came down from Kota Tinggi to enrol their eldest child, Sheena, for a diploma course in mass communication at the Lim Kok Wing Institute in Kuala Lumpur. Dasu, seeing Sushee, remarked that Gowri was having problems with her new dentures.

"Come, let us go and see her," responded Sushee without hesitation.

"It's a bit late now, Sushee," said Dasu. "She could be resting. We shall call on her first thing in the morning."

They all sat up chatting for a while, and then everyone retired to bed. Dasu, as was his usual habit, was at the computer for a short while before he slid into bed. But no sooner had his head touched the pillow than, for no apparent reason, he developed an episode of hiccups.

Ambika, noticing this, said, "Someone is thinking of you."

"Maybe some jealous guys are wondering why I have been reappointed as the dean even after my formal retirement," quipped Dasu.

"No, it could be your mum. You better call."

Dasu used the extension phone in his room. His sister Ambi came on the line.

"How is Amma?" Dasu enquired, still hiccupping.

"She was not feeling quite well earlier in the day. She is okay now and sleeping, I think. Let me check." A moment later, Ambi returned. "*Etta*, she hasn't slept yet. She is coming on the line now."

The subsequent conversation between mother and son was in the vernacular.

"How are you feeling, Amma?" Dasu asked.

Gowri's reply was, "I'm tired, son. My stomach is feeling a bit queasy. Wish I can throw all this medicine away. I have this constant pain in my legs."

"Shall I come over? Perhaps you need to go to hospital."

"No, no. You take rest. You are hiccupping. Drink some water. I'll try and sleep it off."

"You do that, Amma. I will come tomorrow morning anyway. I love you."

Dasu laid back in bed, worried about his mother. The light pitter-patter sound on the roof was intensifying with every passing moment. It had started to rain at the same hour as it had done the previous two nights. The frosted panes of glass of the closed window lit up on and off as streaks of forked lightning slashed across the sky.

Dasu pulled back the curtains. The rumbling sound of thunder could be heard in the distance. A car alarm went off, and the wailing sound filled the night air. A dog barked. Dasu pulled both edges of the pillow closer to his ears. He resisted giving in to negative thoughts and closed his eyes.

Back at Bandar Sri Damansara, Ambi continued sitting with Gowri on her bed, lightly massaging her aching legs. Gowri asked for a glass of Milo (a chocolate beverage). Nor made it quickly and brought it to her. After a while, Gowri told Ambi to retire to bed, as she had to leave for her school early in the morning. Ambi left after instructing Nor to call her if Gowri was feeling unwell.

At two in the morning, Nor knocked on Ambi's door saying Gowri was unwell. Ambi sprinted downstairs. She found Gowri restless and wanting to go to the restroom. She got up only to fall back into bed, struggling for breath. Ambi yelled for Ravindran. She could sense her mother was slipping. She quickly got out the holy Ganga water from the adjacent prayer room and sprinkled some into Gowri's mouth while reciting prayers.

Gowri's eyelids lifted for a second, and there was a look of appreciation in those clouded eyes.

"*Mollae* …" Her voice was only a breath. "*Nee karayanda.*" ("Don't you cry.")

Ambi cried into her ears, "*Ammae, Ammae. Yenne vittupokanda.*" ("Mum, Mum. Don't leave me.")

But Gowri's eyes had already closed.

Ravindran, coming down and, seeing Gowri's condition, immediately began chest compressions, pumping the chest hard and fast, and then blowing into her mouth. Ambi wanted to call the ambulance, but Ravindran shook his head, indicating there was little or no life left in the body. Suddenly, they heard Gowri exhaling a long breath, and she was gone. Ambi ran immediately to call Dasu.

Dasu took the phone. It was an odd hour, and his hand trembled as he took the mouthpiece. It was Ambi, and she was crying. "*Etta*, our mother is gone. She is gone."

Fighting back tears, he said to her, "I'm coming now. Be brave." He put the phone down and was immediately hugged by his wife, tears sliding silently down her cheeks. She had been a dutiful daughter-in-law to his mother, and although she had occasional tiffs with Gowri on some issues, being herself a spirited woman, they had shared many happy and golden moments. Gowri was her spiritual guide as well and had taught her many Sanskrit hymns.

Dasu and Ambika dashed to Bandar Sri Damansara, leaving Sushee and Ronnie in a dazed state to break the news to relatives and close friends. When they arrived at their destination, Dasu tearfully embraced Gowri while Ambika checked the body thoroughly for vital signs. She detected no pulse. Her face confirmed her clinical findings. Dasu then pumped his mother's chest several times, hoping against hope that she would stir to life. She remained lifeless. The light of his life had gone.

Dasu went into a corner and sobbed on his sister's shoulders. By then, Hari and Shoba had arrived. Ravi and Susheela were contacted in Melaka. Gowri's other children were away from the country at that point in time: Valsala and Aravind in Brunei, Shivan and Shanti in Sydney, and Venu and Presenna in India visiting their two children who were studying for medicine at Manipal. They were all contacted. And so too, all the extended family members and Gowri's circle of friends.

Dasu immediately arranged for the University Hospital ambulance to come down and take the body to his residence at Section 17 and to have the embalming done there. His sister was in full agreement with this move, as she felt that Gowri always viewed her son's house at Section 17 as her rightful place, her Malaysian *tharavad*. Dasu also contacted the person knowledgeable about Kerala Hindu funeral rites, who gave him some instructions on how the body was to be handled before the coffin arrived.

By the time the body was embalmed, it was around seven in the morning. The two Ambikas bathed the body and applied *bhasmam* on the chest, hands, and all the joints of the body before clothing it in a white Benares saree with a gold border. This was the saree that her husband had bought her way back in 1957 and which she had preserved well. She had many a time told her daughters that on her final journey to meet him, she wanted to be clad in it. Ambi wept as she draped it around her mum. It was a poignant moment. She reflected upon the fact that Gowri had always remained a romantic at heart and this saree, the last her husband had bought her before his demise, was very special. "She was only 42 when he died. So young still, and she has journeyed, traversed life with fortitude, taking his place at the helm. How lonely and bereft she must have felt without her life partner."

Finally, upon application of sandalwood paste to the forehead, the body was laid in state on a full banana leaf placed on a white linen cloth on the floor of the large living room, which had been cleared of its furniture. The head of the deceased was placed in the south. A mixture of *thulasi* leaves, some earth, and rice grains were sprinkled around the leaf. An oil lamp carrying a single lighted wick was placed at the head end, and on either side of it an *ari kizhi* (a cleanly cracked half of a coconut containing oil into which is immersed a small piece of white cloth containing rice grains, which is folded to yield a spout that could be lighted). Lighted joss sticks and *sambrani* (benzoin resin) were placed near the body. An audio cassette player was turned on; the sounds of the prayer hymns emanating from it filled the air.

With the arrival of the coffin, the body was raised and placed in it. The ceremony proper awaited the arrival of all of Gowri's children from overseas. The cremation was set for Thursday at four in the afternoon. The hearse was arranged to take the body to the crematorium at Kampong Tunku around three o'clock. Valsala and Shivan arrived by Wednesday evening, but Venu could only come the next morning.

# THE VIGIL

That night, Gowri's children who were around kept vigil, each tearing up as they remembered instances in their lives with her, as children growing up and as adults. They had always valued and sought her advice on all things happening in their lives. They had continued to share their joys and troubles with her. She was always just a phone call away. It was as if she held a magic wand that helped dispel their worries and woes. She had always had this capacity to soothe with her storehouse of experience and wisdom.

Shivan then said to all his siblings, "Let us not weep in silence. Amma is still in this room … at least her spirit is. Let us speak of her aloud, each of us recalling our special moments with her, episodes that others of us may not be aware."

"Yes, I agree," said Valsala. "Let us not be morose. Amma won't like that. Amma many a time told us, 'When I die, release my spirit, and don't hold me back with wails. It makes it easier for me to leave the material world when everyone wishes me farewell with smiles.' It is a journey home she had long been waiting."

Pausing to clear her throat, she continued, "Let me share this with you all. In Brunei, none of us in government service can leave the country without first getting permission from the relevant higher authority. I told Amma this once, and her response was, 'That means if I die you can't come immediately and may be not even stay for the *adiyanthiram*?' I told her not to think along those lines and that I would come for sure. You know what? I am here, and it seems to me more like a miracle. Only just yesterday, the education ministry closed all schools for three weeks because of the terrible haze caused by forest fires in Kalimantan. I had decided to fly in today by the evening flight at any rate and surprise Amma, as I was not expected. How I wish I had phoned her to say that I was coming. It would have made her happy. Odd, isn't it? The haze had to happen to bring me home sooner, only to be around to attend her funeral and *adiyanthiram*," said Valsala, choking with emotion.

Then she stood up and walked slowly to the coffin. Bending over it and with tears sliding down her face, she spoke to her Amma, almost in a whisper. "You had a hand in causing the haze, didn't you? You were summoning me home, weren't you? Nothing is beyond you! Bet you interceded with Guruvayurappan to make this possible!" Her siblings, listening, were moved again to tears.

"You know, for me, the most traumatic and most exalting experience was when she fell into the sea and I brought her up alive," said Shivan. "I had shudders thinking I could have been the cause of her death. Lord Shiva must certainly have guided me to reach her that quickly. Dasu mentioned that her *jathagam* had noted that she was fated to experience a life-threatening crisis in midlife, and if she survived that she would go on to live a long life. I am glad that I had a hand in deciding that."

Dasu nodded. "Yes, that's true. Mum always used to say, 'People with good intentions will always have fate on their side.' For me, when I was away in Australia, there was never a day I would not pray to Lord Krishna to keep our Amma alive till I came back to fulfil my filial duties. Do you all remember the large framed photograph of Lord Krishna as a baby that we had at our altar in Kluang? My closed eyes will visualize Him every time I prayed for His blessing. I am more than grateful He has been merciful. My most gratifying moments were when I took Mum to see the sights of Europe and the pilgrimage to Varanasi, where I held her hand and we both dipped in the Ganges, praying our bond would continue into our next lives."

Ravi, who was in his wheelchair, then started to speak, his voice on the edge of breaking. "She has been a great mother to all of us. We will always hold her in our hearts. For me, my special moments were when Mum braved to climb with me to Batu Caves. I remember especially the third time, when I was using a walking stick. I couldn't steady myself on my feet, and I told Amma that having done the penance twice, I might want to skip this. She wouldn't hear of it. That evening, at the temple close to the caves, I had a bucketful of cold water taken from the river behind the temple poured over me and the priest came and chanted something. He then smeared my forehead with *bhasmam* and some of it also on Amma who was holding me. I put the milk urn on my left shoulder and reached for the walking stick. Suddenly I felt I didn't need it. Amma was right behind me chanting some verses. Some of you also were there. You might recall when we reached the foot of the hill, you were all amazed that I began climbing the steps with unbelievable ease. It was as if I had been charged. I cannot medically explain it. Mum too appeared to have little difficulty although her climb was not as swift. Her intense devotion and the physical and mental suffering she endured for me will always remain in my memory."

The youngest sibling, Hari, then spoke. He was initially inaudible as words strangled in his throat. But he collected himself. "No woman could ever be a loving and understanding mother like our Amma. In her eyes, I was the one who was the most doted upon by our father and the one with whom I had lesser years to share than others. I could, therefore, sense the extra attention she always had for me. Whenever she looked forlorn, I would instantly try to bring her back to normal. Often, her distress was caused by us confiding our woes to her. My solution was to bring Nithya to her. It was like a tonic. She would become so engrossed with what the chatterbox was saying, especially her witty childish remarks, that she would come out of her gloom and laugh, calling others nearby to come and listen to Nithya's utterances. She was an extraordinary human being. We were blessed to have her as our mother."

Ambi remained too distressed for words. She was glad that God had given her the opportunity to attend to her at her deathbed and administer the holy Ganges water.

Ronnie was the last to speak. His voice was scratchy and hoarse. "Aunty was very close to me and Sushee. She regarded us like her own children and used to say that if she departed we would have to be there with the others to perform the funeral rites. That we were here on the eve of her death could only be by God's grace. Let us all pray for her *moksha*," he concluded, referring to the release from the cycle of rebirth impelled by the law of karma. The chant of the mantra *"Om Namah Shivaya. Shivaya Namah Om"* then filled the air, with all others joining in

## CREMATION AND *PINDA DANAM*

The celebrant came early on Thursday morning with materials for the cremation ceremony at home and at the crematorium. Relatives and friends from all walks of life came in large numbers to offer their condolences. Counted among them were many non-Malayalee Indians, Malays, Chinese, and Eurasians – friends of her children and grandchildren – who had come to pay their respects to a simple grand old lady. The crowd overflowed from the living room to the garden and onto the road. A taxi driver was heard to enquire whether it was a politician's funeral!

Gowri had, in the space of over twenty-five years in Kuala Lumpur, become a well-known figure, particularly within Malayalee circles – not because of who her children were but because of her own graciousness. Many stopped to speak to her children of how positively she had impacted them. Little did they realize how many lives she had touched. The many garlands and wreaths that arrived needed even the space behind the house to contain them. In keeping with Gowri's wishes, no one wailed in their grief, just silently sobbed as they bid her farewell. It was an extraordinary tribute to a simple housewife whose grit in bringing up her children as a widow was much admired and respected.

The cremation rituals having being dutifully performed by Gowri's sons, sons-in-law, and her eldest grandson, Suraj, the ashes were ceremoniously collected from the crematorium the next morning by Dasu. A portion was kept in a small urn hung in the porch of the house with a small lighted lamp facing it. The remainder of the ash, collected in a bigger urn, was immersed in the sea at Morib, some 65 kilometres away, on the same day. Priya flew down from Connecticut in the United States and stayed a few days until the post-mourning rituals were over on the eleventh day. All of Gowri's children and immediate family members observed complete chastity, the male members remained unshaven, all consumed only vegetarian meals, and the prayer lamp at the altar remained unlit over this period. There were daily prayers in the evenings, attended also by Gowri's close friends, performed in front of a large garlanded framed photograph of Gowri. On the third day, the glass frame of Gowri's photograph suddenly broke after the prayers. An elderly person who was in attendance remarked, "Gowri's soul is now no longer with us and has happily departed to join her *pitruloka*" – that is, the astral world of her ancestors.

On the twelfth day, Dasu and Hari took the small urn containing Gowri's ashes to Gaya in India's Bihar state to participate in a prearranged Vedic ceremony called *pinda danam* for the salvation of departed souls. The ceremony was conducted by a chief priest who came from Prayag. Thereafter, the chief priest took custody of the urn containing Gowri's ashes to be immersed at the confluence of three rivers – the Triveni Sangam – in Prayag (Allahabad). Before they left Gaya, both brothers visited Bodh Gaya, some 16 kilometres away, where they offered oblations to the lotus feet of Lord Vishnu at the ancient Vishnupad Temple. Bodh Gaya is also the most holy place for Buddhists, as it is where Gautama Buddha is said to have obtained enlightenment (*Bodhimandala*) under what became known as the Bodhi Tree. This sacred fig tree is located in the Mahabodhi Temple Complex, the foundations of which were first laid by Emperor Asoka in the third century BC.

Hari and Dasu at Gaya for the *pinda danam* ritual for Gowri

Views of Mahabodhi Temple Complex (*left*)
and Bodhi Tree (*right*) in Bodh Gaya

Thus ended the life's journey of one great soul, a warm human being who showed her family and the world at large the true meaning of fortitude, love, and the courage to live life by meeting its challenges head-on, accepting the struggle, confronting the tragedy, and always keeping faith in the Almighty to show the way forward.

# THE ENDURING LEGACY

One of twenty-four exquisitely sculptured wheels of the
Chariot of the Sun God at the thirteenth -century Konark
Sun Temple, Odisha, India, now a World Heritage Site.

# [33]

Gowri's death came as a shock to the family, as she was not in any emergency health situation that would have alerted them to expect an adverse outcome. It took many weeks for the family to get over their grief. They felt enveloped in a sphere of emptiness. This included the grandchildren, for whom Gowri was at once their counsel and confidant.

## GOWRI'S "VISITATION"

Dasu's daughter Gouri recalled that her *ammama* had appeared in a dream the night she died, with her coffin yet in the house, and had told her granddaughter not to be sad and that they would meet again. "She mentioned the name of the place. It starts with *G*, that's all I can remember," she told her mourning parents.

"*Ammama* is certainly watching over you and all of us," said Dasu, appeasing her.

"I remember, *Acha*, when I gave her the saree, she asked me what I wanted for my coming birthday in April. I said I didn't want anything, only her love and kisses. 'Maybe I shall write a poem,' she then said to me. And, *Acha*, Ambika *Achema* (Aunty Ambi) showed me the poem that she had actually started on, scribbled on her note pad." Weeks later, Dasu had access to this note containing the unfinished poem, which was among his sister's memorabilia on their mother.

Don't grow soon
Don't fly far
I want you near
My Gowri dear.

My love plus kisses,
Blessings lots
Bundled here
To get you near.

Another find was a *Bhagawati* stotram written in her own handwriting in
Malayalam.[9]

Meanwhile, Valsala's children, who were all in New Zealand, had only
themselves to console as they reflected on their grandmother's death. It was
as if an ecplise had set in and they were all under cover of darkness, with
but a slight glimpse of the receding light of their beloved *ammama*. They
observed a vegetarian diet for the duration of the mourning period and
kept in constant touch with their parents and some of their cousins. Even
after two weeks, it didn't seem real to them that they would never see their
*ammama* again. "It made sense to my brain, but not to my heart," wrote
Kiran in her diary.

Kiran recalled an eerie episode that happened sometime around the
period of mourning. She had come from Christchurch to spend the start
of her university vacation with Sapna in Auckland. Since Sapna and Nisha
were sharing the double bed in the one-bedroom apartment, Kiran elected
to sleep on the couch in the lounge. In the middle of the night, she woke
up with a start, her heart pounding. Seeing nothing, she was about to close
her eyes when she heard a voice – a soft approaching voice.

"Ma … ma … ma," it called.

Her heart skipped a beat. She squeezed her eyelids tighter.

"Ma … ma … ma," it called again.

---

[9]   This and its English transliteration are given in Appendix 2 for the benefit of
relatives and other interested readers fluent in the language.

Knowing she had to confront the voice, she opened her eyes. She saw a strange dancing, flickering light in front of her. It had a silhouette – one that she knew all too well. She realized instantly that she was not dreaming, as she could see the room, the windows, and the TV in the corner. The light was still there. Her *ammama* was there, bounded by and alive in the white light. The light quivered to reveal her saintly face, her pursed lips, her smiling kind eyes, and then the rest of her. She was clad in a white saree.

Kiran couldn't move. She was gripped by fear and longing. Longing made her move towards the light, but fear paralyzed her. She tried to open her mouth. "Am … ma … ma" was all the sound that she could manage. The amazing light-like silhouette flickered. The silhouette moved as though to touch Kiran's head, but didn't and instead clasped its hands together as if in prayer … then just disappeared. It was ten seconds of sheer awe and fear. Kiran then suddenly found that she could move. She bolted into Sapna's bedroom and jumped into bed, startling her sleeping sisters.

## BINDU'S WEDDING

Aravind's mother, Bhargavi Amma, who had been in a coma before Gowri's demise, passed away almost a month later. She was a soft-spoken lady and respected by all in the family. She preferred to stay with her second son in Subang Jaya most of the time, as this was a central place where she could be close to her other children as well. Valsala's children were very much attached to her.

Once Valsala and Aravind brought their two older girls Sapna and Kiran to Dasu's house while they went to attend a wedding function. Within moments of their departure, both of them started crying. Gowri and Dasu had a tough time comforting them. "I wanna go to Bhargavi *Ammama*'s house!" they wailed. Dasu had little choice but to take them to their grandmother. It was only when they were much older and when Gowri went to stay with them that they endeared themselves to her. Both Gowri and Bhargavi Amma would have been proud to learn that Kiran and Nisha had emulated the success of Sapna in their studies; Kiran graduated in 1999 with a bachelor of commerce degree from the University of Canterbury and Nisha in 2003 with a medical degree from the University of Dunedin.

Gowri with Bhargavi Amma, holding Nisha in her hands

Gowri, before her death, had told her daughter Ambi that if anything happened to her before Bindu's marriage, her earthly absence should not be an excuse to postpone the marriage (on account of the customary twelve-month mourning period). The family accepted her wish and conducted Bindu's marriage to Rakesh in December 1998. Bindu's sister, Rhitu, who had just graduated with a degree in electrical engineering from Universiti Teknologi Malaysia, shared the floor with Rajini, Rakesh's sister, as the master of ceremonies. At the reception, Dasu in his toast to the newly married couple noted that Bindu's maternal grandmother and her paternal grandparents, although not physically present, were from their heavenly abode also witnessing the function and showering upon them their blessings. He offered the following words of advice to the newly married couple:

"As an elder in the family, perhaps it would be in order for me to offer a few words of advice to our newly-weds. They expect it. The audience perhaps also expects it. There's no such thing, of course, as a perfect marriage, but that doesn't mean your marriage can't be fulfilling and happy. Building a strong marriage takes hard work and commitment. It takes two people who are willing to say to each other, 'I know that there will be tough and testing times ahead, but I promise to stay with you, no matter what.' When life gets hard, even the best marriages are tested. Someone once observed, 'Marriage is like a game of cards. It starts with two hearts and a diamond and ends with clubs and a spade.' Yes, there will be fights in any marriage. If a couple doesn't argue, it is a sign of distrust. All healthy relationships have hiccups. But that same someone also said, 'A happy marriage is the union of two good forgivers.' Combine that advice with mutual respect and trust, and you have all the ingredients for a happy married life. It is our hope and wish, Bindu and Rakesh, that you will apply God to your lives and that your love for each other will grow from strength to strength, or as my Armenian friends would have me say, 'May you grow old on one pillow.'"

He also alluded to the marriage eligibility of the bride's sister, his niece, and quipped that any proposal bypassing him would not be entertained.

Wedding photograph of Bindu and Rakesh

☼

# THE FIRST DEATH ANNIVERSARY

The family observed Gowri's first death anniversary in March 1999 with a *shradham* at Dasu's house. Thilothamma; Rakesh's mother, Rekha; Mrs K. C. A. Menon; Mrs A. V. G. Menon; and some of Gowri's other close friends in Petaling Jaya joined the family for the prayers. In the absence of Gowri, the mother figure of Thilothamma seemed to fill the void. All of Gowri's children had known her since they were small. She lived to the ripe old age of 93 and was with Venu and Presenna when she died in September 2007. Her eldest daughter, Ponnu, who had returned to Malaysia after her husband' death in 2006, was around to mourn her loss.

Not all of Gowri's grandchildren were present at the *shradham*. Sapna, Kiran, and Nisha were still in New Zealand. Suraj, Bindu, and Rhitu attended the function, and so did Ashwin, who had completed his three-year course in mechatronics at King's College, London, in 1998, and Sharad, who was in his final months of study for the bachelor of commerce degree that was being offered locally by the University of Tasmania.

Gouri, Apsara, and Gopu were all away doing their preclinical studies at Manipal, having already joined the medical degree programme of Melaka-Manipal Medical College in 1996. Lavaniya joined them in Manipal soon after the *shradham*, as she had also gained entry into the medical programme. Also present to witness their *ammama*'s first *shradham* were Sathya and Vikram, and the much younger group of grandchildren comprised of Nithya, Dhanya, and Smitha, who were still in school. Sathya had enrolled in September for her law degree at Help University College, which had a twinning arrangement with the University of West of England. Vikram had also enrolled for a twinning degree programme in business management, with his final year to be done at James Cook University. Gowri had envisioned that all of her grandchildren would take to their studies well and come up in life. She had while she was alive instilled in them that vision, taught them how to recite prayers, and shared with them the importance of keeping faith in the Almighty.

☼

# TRIBUTE FROM GRANDCHILDREN

A couple of days before the anniversary function, Dasu had alerted the grandchildren that they would be called upon to say a few words in memory of their ammama. He could see that some of them carried written notes when they arrived on the day for the *shradham*. Following evening prayers and the *shradham* puja, and before anyone partook of the food, Dasu invited the grandchildren to speak about their ammama.

Rhitu was the first one to speak, and her words were eloquent: "*Ammama* to me is the epitome of strength, resilience, and beauty all rolled up into one magnificent human being. A hug and kiss from her is like chicken soup for the soul. Whether she's giving a witty remark (which is ever so often) or reprimanding with fiery, passionate eyes the ones she loves, every memory of her brings a smile to my lips. She's my *ammama*. I am privileged to be her bloodline."

Bindu followed suit. Her words were set in poetic prose:

> A true matriarch you were
> A blessing to us all
> You lived life with vigour
> For you saw the world through our eyes.
> The love and bond you created
> Was indeed the legacy you left us with.
> You remain a true inspiration to me.
> The epitome of strength, beauty, and grace
> My *ammama* … my hero!

They were followed by the younger ones – Lavaniya, Vikram, and Sathya – all of whom echoed Bindu's sentiments with the words, "*Ammama*, you are always in our hearts, We miss you."

Then Sharad, in his typically straightforward manner, said, "Having spent much of my childhood abroad, the act of 'returning home' for me, whenever time and money permitted, was never fully achieved until I found myself in my grandmother's loving embrace. In her arms, this oft-confused and thoroughly lost young delinquent would instantly remember who he was, where he came from, and where he belonged. In her arms, I was home, I was found, I was safe. For so many of us, *Ammama* was simply … true north."

Ashwin followed next with words he had penned: "Thinking of you, *Ammama*, conjures up a smorgasbord of memories, sensory cues, and, of course, teachings. Powder puffs and the whiff of scented talcum powder, the sensation of skin being scoured with a Pears soap-infused loofah, and the oh-so-glorious aroma of your chicken curry all remind me of you. If I can speak our mother tongue, Malayalam, it is because of you. If I have in me an affinity for Kerala and our culture, it is because of you and the tales you told. If I can pick out and understand more than a smattering of Sanskrit, it is because of you. Yet for me, the lasting lesson you impressed upon me, on more than one occasion, and which adequately captures you and your life ethos in a nutshell, has been this: that to be happy, we cannot live merely for ourselves; we must live to serve others."

Valsala then got up to say that she had received from Nisha in New Zealand her reminiscence about her *ammama*. She then read out these words:

> I don't know how you did it, *Ammama*, but each of your seventeen grandchildren felt like your personal favourite. In a family where it would have been so possible to be lost in the crowd, you created a unique relationship with each of us. In the years to come I know we will always remember what it felt like to be so fully, unconditionally, uncompromisingly loved. If God had to take you, *Ammama*, I hope He looks after you as lovingly and gently as you looked after all of us.

Suraj was the last to speak, choking with emotion as he did so. "I was the first to call her *Ammama*. I didn't have much competition, even when Bindu arrived. She doted on me. I often felt that she treated me more like her youngest son than her first grandson. As I grew, she heaped on me more and more affection, rarely raising her voice in trying to get me to focus on my studies, as my grades were but average in the early years, given my Mum and Dad were not always with me. She would tell me not to worry when *Acha* lost his job and my studies in Rockhampton appeared to be heading for the rocks, and finally imparted some of her inner courage to me when Mum was diagnosed with cancer. It was in fact her perseverance and courage that led me to pull up my socks, be independent, and focus on my studies in the State of Queensland, gaining entrance into university and graduating with high marks. I can still remember the pride that she wore on her face when I got my degree. She said to me then, 'I want you to be what Dasu has been to his siblings, a pillar of support and encouragement, not just to your brother Sharad, but also to all your cousins.' She was the epitome of love. Our best tribute to her is to spread that love among us all and keep it there. *Ammama*, I know you are watching us from above. We are all blessed to be your grandchildren. Rest in peace, *Ammama*. We love you, especially me, your Suraj Mon."

In October 1999, Venu underwent a heart bypass surgery at the National Heart Institute. The surgery went off well, but it was still a traumatic experience for everyone in the family. They prayed hard that the next thirty days would fly past, as the doctors had told them that all patients have to live through a potential risk of heart attack during this recuperative period. Venu was advised to alter his lifestyle. All his siblings also became acutely aware of their genetic predisposition to coronary heart disease.

As soon as he graduated in mid-1999, Sharad left to join his parents in PNG, but he came back to Section 17 before Christmas with his mother, who needed to undergo chemotherapy treatment.

As in most parts of the world, Malaysia was not spared the confusion and concerns that attended the dawn of the new millennium (also known as Y2K, which stands for the year 2000). Many maintained the twenty-first century began on 1 January 2001, but already on 1 January 2000, predictions were afoot that there would be a computerized Armageddon as the practice of representing the year with two digits would cause date-related processing problems with logical error(s) arising upon rollover from x99 to x00. This made the year 2000 indistinguishable from 1900. There were also attendant apocalyptic jitters about national and international catastrophes happening on that date that would signal the end of the world. Luckily, apart from some minor computer glitches, the world survived an unnecessary scare.

But the year 2000 did indeed start badly for Gowri's family with the passing away of Dasu's mother-in-law, Ammukutty Amma, who was staying with him. She suffered a heart attack on 1 January and succumbed to it on 29 January. Her grandchildren Ashwin and Sathya were at her deathbed, but not Gouri, who was still at Manipal in India completing her preclinical studies.

Shanti bravely fought her cancer, but agonisingly for the family the end was in sight. She died on 5 November. Shivan was shattered. They had been a loving couple. He had always pampered her dream of establishing a boutique-cum-modelling school. Her efforts in Kuala Lumpur and Johor Bahru had only gained her mixed success, but her business appeared to be more rewarding in Port Moresby, PNG. Unfortunately, Shanti's ill health intervened and the business lost ground on account of her intermittent absence. Within weeks of her demise in early November, Sajitha gave birth to her second son, Adharsh. Shivan took some solace in nurturing his new grandson, but he remained crestfallen. He wound up his business in PNG and settled down with Suraj.

Ashwin, who had returned from his studies in late 1998, had some difficulty in adjusting to the two desk jobs that he found around Kuala Lumpur, which gave him few career options. He prevailed upon his parents to let him accept a position that he was offered at Sun Microsystems in Dublin. His parents were aware that he was influenced in his choice of Dublin by the presence there of his girlfriend, Gillian Horgan. He had got to know her while they were both studying at King's College in London. She qualified as an ultrasonographer.

Ashwin proposed to Gillian in mid-2002. When they heard the news, Dasu and Ambika urged them to get married as soon as possible. Both of them had met Gillian when she came on a holiday to see Ashwin in 1999 and stayed with them. She was tall and strikingly beautiful, but rather shy; she only engaged in conversation when talked to. She had an extended family in Ireland, and from his brief question-answer conversation with her, Dasu gleaned that she was very liberal-minded and really a simple person at heart. She was at home with the informality she found at Section 17. Although English was generally spoken in the house, she found the Malaysian English or Manglish spoken by the children and visitors somewhat amusing with the added flavours of exotic words and syllables. "Can u off the fan? The food will get cold-lah. Gill, you've never before tasted the chillie one?" were her first introduction to Manglish at the dinner table. It was charming creole, but it fell flat when she tried to imitate it to Ashwin. In the days preceding her departure, she wore moist eyes. Both Ambika and Dasu knew then that she was passionate about their son.

Early in the new millennium, in February 2001, Dasu and Ambika left for Sungai Petani, where they were to stay for six years. He was tasked as the vice chancellor and chief executive to establish a new multi-faculty private university – the Asian Institute of Medicine, Science, and Technology. The university was the brainchild of Datuk Seri S. Samy Vellu, the visionary president of the Malaysian Indian Congress, a component party of the Barisan Nasional coalition government. Ambika worked in the university as the medical officer at the staff and student clinic. They would come down to their Section 17 house on at least two weekends a month until they rented out the premises in 2002 to an advertising agency. They only returned to live in it following renovation around May 2009. Until then, they would reside mostly at Ambika's family house in Bangsar whenever they came down to Kuala Lumpur.

Dasu's youngest child, Sathya, returned from her law studies in Bristol in 2002 and found an immediate job placement with the reputable firm of Shearn, Delamore & Co. in downtown Kuala Lumpur. Ambika saw to it that she had a room to herself at the Bangsar house.

In September 2002, Dasu and Ambika decided to conduct Ashwin and Gillian's marriage at the Lakshmi Narayan Temple in Kuala Lumpur according to Hindu rites. They made all the arrangements for it working from Sungai Petani, assisted by Dasu's sisters. Gillian's mother came for the occasion with her friend from Hong Kong and enjoyed very much the ceremony and the grand reception that followed. The video recordings of the two functions were taken to Ireland for Gillian's father and family members to view. A follow-up church wedding was held in Cork, Ireland.

Joining Dasu's family on the trip to Ireland were Apsara, Gouri, Dhanya, Rohan (Ambika's nephew), and Ambika's sister-in-law Jenna Lau. Apsara and Gouri stayed on to do their one-month pre-arranged elective postings in medicine at St James's Hospital at Dublin, which Gillian had helped arrange.

## SHIVAN'S DEMISE

A new addition to the Gowri *tharavad* came in the form of her great-granddaughter Tara, who was born to Sajitha in mid-March 2007. But the good tidings were marred by the news received several months earlier that Shivan had contracted colon cancer. When first diagnosed following colonoscopy, he was said to harbour a third-stage cancer. Aravind and Venu tried to prevail upon him to undergo surgery and not to settle for just chemotherapy, but in his despondency he preferred to live through his karma without being a burden to anyone. Progressively his ailment worsened, with secondaries in the brain that started to give him hallucinations. Dasu and Ambika remembered receiving a distress signal one morning from the rest of the family about his critical condition when he had to be rushed to the Sungai Buloh Hospital. They drove straight down from Sungai Petani to the hospital upon hearing the news. Shivan had the premonition that his time was up and was already bidding goodbye to all his friends and loved ones at his hospital bed when Dasu arrived. They hugged each other, sobbing.

"I know I'm leaving," he said to Dasu.

"Don't say that, the call is only with God. Be brave. Don't entertain negative thoughts."

"I already had a tryst with Mum. She is expecting me." Then uttering *"Aum Namah Shivaya"* thrice, he closed his eyes.

Dasu wiped his tears and held his brother close. Within half an hour of their meeting, Shivan suffered a massive cardiac arrest. It was as if he had been waiting to see his eldest brother before he departed the world. Although Shivan had long ago left the Royal Malaysian Navy, his ashes following cremation were scattered at sea from a naval ship with full funeral honours accorded him by his colleagues who were still in service. This was, in part, in appreciation of his significant contributions in compiling the history of the navy.

Rear Admiral (Rtd) Datuk Danyal Balagopal, a close friend of Shivan, had this to say in tribute to his ex-naval mate: "Shiva Prasad, as he was fondly known amongst the naval circle, was ever ready to lend a hand when needed. When the idea to form the Brittania Royal Naval College (BRNC) Alumni was mooted in early 2000, he was the automatic choice to be the first secretary and started the groundwork, which he accomplished within six months. During the same period, he also assisted me in researching and compiling the historical perspective of the book *Serving the Nation* for the Royal Malaysian Navy. He was an accomplished writer with an extremely good sense of humour. Unfortunately, his untimely demise prevented him from witnessing the launching ceremony of the BRNC Alumni. May God bless his soul."

Dasu left AIMST University in 2007 after completing two terms in office. It was while in service there that he was conferred in April 2005 the Award of Darjah Setia Dirajah Kedah (D.S.D.K.), which carries the title Dato', by His Royal Highness, The Sultan of Kedah, for his contributions to higher education in the state.

After finishing his stint in Sungai Petani, Dasu found his assistance sought in a similar capacity to establish an international university in Ipoh, Perak. He went on to serve this university - Quest International University Perak- for six years until his retirement in March 2013. It was while he was in Ipoh that he conducted the marriage of his daughters Gouri in November 2007 and Sathya in May 2008. Just prior to these events, Dasu and Ambika had rented a double-storey house in Bangsar close to Ambika's family house. Their Section 17 house was still being rented out then. It was ironic that this *tharavad* house which was the meeting place for the prenuptial ceremonies of a number of Dasu's nephews and nieces was not to be the wedding house for any of his own children.

# RAVI'S DEMISE

On 13 July 2011, Dasu received word that his brother Ravi had died in his sleep at age 64. The previous evening, after leaving his clinic and getting into the car, Ravi had given the clinic a lingering look. This is what his nurse told Susheela. His daughter, Dhanya, who had returned from Manipal in December 2010 after completing her dental degree, shed more light. "*Acha* called me to his room and showed me the cheques he had written out for payments to various vendors, and he also signed three blank cheques to cater for other payments. I asked him why he was showing me all these. He didn't answer. I then asked him whether he was feeling okay."

"I'm all right, *Mollae*," he said, using the term of endearment for a daughter. "Sometimes I feel I should retire."

That night, he watched a DVD in his room and retired to bed. Just past midnight, Susheela was sleeping in the adjoining room with Dhanya when she heard a loud sound. Rushing in, they found Ravi breathless, complaining of pain in his back. He indicated that he wanted his back to be rubbed. Susheela held him while Dhanya applied the massage, but while she was at it, he slumped and died in their arms. Dhanya tried to resuscitate him but failed. The ambulance was immediately summoned, but the paramedics in attendance knew he was beyond help. This was confirmed by Ravi's medical colleagues who also rushed to the scene.

"He certainly had a premonition, like Shivan," said Venu, who was the first sibling to arrive the next morning. Suraj and Vikram did the funeral rites at Melaka, assisted by Dasu. Vikram found it hard to accept his uncle's demise. Suraj wading with him into the sea to immerse the urn of ashes, consoled him: "Not everyone dies of old age. People get run over by cars. People choke on peanuts or fish bones stuck in their throats. There are no guarantees about one's future; life departs whenever God beckons."

With a sigh, Vikram – holding firmly the urn on his head – moved farther forward to catch the tide that had started to recede. When he was chest deep in the sea, he turned to face the sun, and uttering *"Aum Namah Shivaya,"* immersed himself thrice in the water. On the third dip, he released the urn, the cloth cover of which had previously been ripped open so as to discharge its contents. He saw the ashes being dispersed by the tide. The act accomplished, both he and Suraj suddenly found their mundu coming off them. "Ravi Uncle is playing tricks with us! He is pulling our mundu," they cried as they hurriedly tried to grab their floating garments. Dasu and others watching the frantic scene from the shore couldn't resist a hearty laugh.

In early June 2009, with the renovations completed at the Section 17 house, Sathya and Prem Kumar moved in. Sathya was near full-term. Dasu remained in Ipoh with Ambika, as he was still actively engaged in establishing the new private university. Gowri's *tharavad* house was blessed once again when Sathya delivered her first child, Anishka, on 23 June 2009.

# [34]

Well into two decades after her demise, Gowri's memory still remains etched in the hearts and minds of her surviving children, her daughters-in-law and sons-in-law, and her grandchildren. The third generation that has sprung up continues to be united in joint family get-together functions. Leading the pack are Gowri's eldest great-grandson Akhil (Suraj's son) and her eldest great granddaughter Ekta (Bindu's daughter), who was born in 2004. Back in India, Gowri is also fondly remembered by her only surviving cousin Chandra and her nieces and nephews.

As this final chapter is being written, except for Nisha, Vikram, Nithya, and Smitha, all of Gowri's other grandchildren have married, as follows:

- Sapna to Uma Shankar in 2000
- Kiran to Raiyo Nariman in 2001 (child: Shohreh)
- Ashwin to Gillian in 2002 (children: twins Jaya Ambika and Anjali Elizabeth)
- Sharad to Michelle in 2004 (child: Arielle)
- Rhitu to Vibin Menon in 2005 (children: Adhya, Ashta, and Virath)
- Apsara to Dharminder Singh Chopra in 2006 (children: Anushri and Arav)
- Lavaniya to Capt. Selvakumar in 2007 (children: Esha, Arshan, and Mayuri)
- Gouri to Kesavan Nair (Dinesh) in 2007 (child: Sahana)
- Sathya to Prem Kumar Nambiar in 2008 (children: Anishka, Rhea, and Sameera)

- Govind Kishen (Gopu) to Rena Menon in 2013 (child: Lakshmi)
- Dhanya to Arvind Raj in January 2016

Gowri's *tharavad* has indeed grown and, in the Malaysian context, now combines both the matrilineal and patrilineal components, as depicted in the Gowri Family Tree (Appendix 3).

Gowri's sister-in-law, Jayalakshmi, passed away at the start of the new millennium, not fully benefitting from the coronary by-pass surgery that she underwent some five years earlier. Gowri's sister Kamalam passed away peacefully in Lahad Datu, Sabah, around 2001. Her daughter Prabha, who had long isolated herself from the rest of her cousins, did not inform them of the demise; they heard the news many weeks later from a visitor. Some nine years before Kamalam's death, Dasu and Hari had gone over to Lahad Datu upon hearing the news of their uncle Shankaran's demise. As Prabha's only brother Prakash was deceased and both her husband , Balan, and son, Pradeep, were away from Sabah at that point in time, Dasu and Hari dutifully performed the funeral rights for their uncle. Prakash's wife, Padmini, was by then already in Kuala Lumpur with her two children, Vivek and Divya, having rejoined her working life as a biochemist.

More recently, Sethu and Uma, who were so intimate with all of Gowri's children from their young days have also departed from the scene, both dying of cancer. Sethu passed away in India in 2011, while Uma – who returned to the United States for advanced treatment on her cancer – died on 31 December 2014. Their lives have so interwined with Gowri's children and grandchildren that their irreparable loss continues to be mourned by them as this chapter is brought to its conclusion. Gowri's legacy of deeply held faith, fortitude, generous attitude to life, and unfettered love – in essence, a portion of herself – is what she has left behind for future generations.

Ekta

Akhil

Adharsh

Tara

Anushri

Anishka

Rhea

Sameera

Arielle

Arav

Shohreh

Arshan

Adhya

Esha

Sahana

Jaya

Ashta

Mayuri

Lakshmi

Anjali

Virath

GOWRI'S GREAT-GRANDCHILDREN

# APPENDIX 1

## Gowri's Brief Script on the Hindu Religion

(Edited for better readability, with supplementary content added in italics. The original simplicity of the explanations is essentially maintained; the discerning reader is referred to the many scholarly texts on the Hindu religion that exist; this includes the References cited below.)

The important thing to note about Hinduism is that it is both a religion and a way of life– *"a free and open culture encouraging self-realization … It does not require that we hold to a single belief or saviour to gain salvation."*[10] Ours has been a yogic culture from the earliest pre-Vedic times in the Guru–Chela (teacher-disciple) tradition. The sole purpose of yoga for thousands of years was the attainment of the highest spiritual goals: self-realization, enlightenment, and the liberation of the individual soul, but it has since come to embody physical practices such as asana (postures) and pranayama (breath control) and become more mundane in its ambitions, yielding much of its spiritual ground to the Vedas.

There is a multiplicity of beliefs within Hinduism, with utmost freedom of thoughts and actions, but there is one common denominator which resonates with all, and this is proclaimed in the Rig Veda as follows: *"Ekam sath, Vipraah bahudhaa vadanti"* ("The Truth [God, Brahman, etc.] is one, scholars call it by various names.") The original Sanskrit name for Hinduism is *Sanatana Dharma*, meaning "eternal religion".

---

[10]    D. Frawley (Vamadeva Shastri), *How I Became a Hindu: My Discovery of Vedic Dharma* (New Delhi: Voice of India, 2001).

Despite the broad set of traditions that exist, there is one other common ground that connects them all. This concerns the view on life. It is widely held that life is a moral progress toward an eventual liberation from reincarnation, with death acting only as a momentary hiccup between incarnations. *As per the Puranas, in Hindu eschatology, the universe itself is seen as a living being, experiencing the same cycle of rebirth, life, and death.*[11]

**Q: Doesn't the myriad of beliefs then present difficulties in achieving uniformity in the practice of the religion?**

**A:** Yes, but not in a dysfunctional sense. Hinduism is not a regimented religion bound by ideology and rules. While there may be no uniformity in Hinduism, celebration of diversity is its very essence. Inasmuch as there are different sects within the religion reflecting different schools of thought, there is also the admission into its fold of people who reject it, as well as atheists.

**Q: Does this explain the reason for the many types of religious activity in Hinduism and the worship of many gods in the form of idols?**

**A:** *"Everything that we find in human religious activity from primitive rites to insights of pure consciousness can be found in the religion."*[12] As described by Bansi Pandit,[13] one can liken Hinduism to "a huge tree with its numerous branches representing various schools of thought. The tree itself is rooted in the rich soil of the Vedas and Upanishads. The Vedas represent the religious traditions while the Upanishads represent the philosophy upon which the traditions are based."

Many forms of worship are allowed in Hinduism, and therefore, the worship of *murti* (images) or idols is neither prescribed nor proscribed. As an external symbol used for worship, the *murti*, after the divine has been

11    D. M. Knipe, "Hindu Eschatology," in *The Oxford Handbook of Eschatology*, ed. J. L. Walls (Oxford University Press, 2008).
12    Frawley, *How I Became a Hindu.*
13    B. Pandit, *The Hindu Mind: Fundamentals of Hindu Religion and Philosophy for All Ages* (Dharma Publications Inc., 1996).

invoked in it, helps the worshipper to keep his mind fixed on the Being to whom he prays. The Hindu knows that the image is not God but is only a means of communicating with the divine. *As Swami Vivekananda[14] has aptly put it, "the whole religion of the Hindu is centred in realization. Man is to become divine by realizing the divine. Idols or temples or churches or books are only the supports, the helps, of his spiritual childhood: but on and on he must progress. 'External worship', say the scriptures, 'is the lowest stage; struggling to rise high, mental prayer is the next stage; but the highest stage is when the Lord has been realized'."*

**Q: Why didn't Hinduism settle on a monotheistic path? It appears to have the largest pantheon of gods and goddesses.**

**A:** Monotheism is not the only path to religious experience, although the concept of the one Reality, the one Supreme Being, is there in Hinduism. The multiple god forms that Hindus worship doesn't make the religion polytheistic; the Vedas state clearly that beyond the gods and goddesses, there is also the formless and attributeless Brahman.

**Q: Who is this Brahman?**

**A:** To quote Bansi Pandit[15] again: "Actually, there is only one Reality or Truth, but there are two dimensions to this Reality. One is the transcendental (impersonal) side without form and attributeless, representing absolute knowledge, absolute bliss which we call *Nirguna Brahman*. The other is the immanent (personal) side of Reality which is the merciful creator, preserver and controller of the universe, which we call the *Saguna Brahman* or *Ishwar*."

Brahma is that reality in its role as the creator of the universe; Vishnu portrays its role as the preserver and upholder of the universe, while Shiva is the same reality that will one day destroy the universe. These three principal

---

[14]  Swami Vivekananda, "Hinduism – a universal religion," a paper read at the Parliament of Religions at Chicago in 1893, in *Hinduism* (Chennai: Sri Ramakrishna Math).

[15]  Pandit, *The Hindu Mind*.

gods of Hinduism, constituting the *Trimurti*, represent three different ways of looking at *Saguna Brahman*. Hindus also worship other divinities, each endowed with special powers and areas of responsibility. For example, Lord Ganesha is the "remover of obstacles" and Saraswati, the female energy (consort) of Brahma, is the goddess of knowledge. All gods and goddesses endowed with different looks, powers, and attributes that Hindus worship actually symbolize the various aspects and manifestations of the *Saguna Brahman*; none exhausts God's actual nature.

**Q: Personal realization of the Divine is what Hinduism seeks of its followers. How is this possible?"**

**A:** Personal experiential realization of the Divine can be through the practice of devotion (bhakti yoga) or the path of intense contemplation (raja yoga). The literal meaning of the word *yoga* is "union with the Supreme Soul." Raja yoga requires us to train our minds to control the outgoing senses and then meditate upon the pure consciousness (akin to a state of no-mind) as distinct from the ordinary consciousness of the intellect where the mind still clings to thoughts, memories, etc. For both types of yoga, there is a need to observe moral discipline, dharma (righteousness), non-violence (ahimsa) in word, deed, and thought, and reverence for all forms of life and the law of karma (executed work, deed, or action). Strictly, only when we have worked out our karma can we hope to be in a position to sense and experience the inner divine light and achieve God realization.

**Q: Is this really possible for ordinary mortals?**

**A:** Our Vedic seers have said that it is in our grasp at all times. But it requires a tremendous amount of effort and patience to rewire one's brain from its default mode of sticking to habits and conditioning stemming from one's materialistic leanings. Only when one can move away from all this, shed one's ego-personality, and be free of all attachments and aversions can one reach the stage where the expanded self-awareness finally breaks free of all confines to revolve around pure consciousness. This is the state of the Supreme Being (Brahman) that is in all of us. This independent journey towards enlightenment which lets you connect with your Higher Self is an enriching experience, a self-discovery. We may call it true spirituality.

**Q: How do Hindus view the concept of the soul?**

**A:** Most Hindus accept the ontological concept of the soul; they call it *Atma or Atman*. It exists unperishable in each one of us but is beyond the grasp of the mind and the senses. It is distinct from both the mind and the external body. We regard the individual soul and the universal soul to be the two sides of the same reality. More succinctly, we can say that our soul is nothing but pure consciousness. When one dies, this consciousness leaves the physical body, untainted by the mind, to merge with the infinite ocean of pure consciousness or *Brahman*. As with the cycle of creation and destruction of the universe, the atman also undergoes its own version of cycle called *samsara*, the cycle of rebirth in which individual souls are repeatedly reincarnated. *Atman* can be viewed as the divine spark of *Brahman* within us and within all things. To become aware of this we must overcome *Maya*.

**Q: What is *maya*?**

**A:** Essentially, the word means "illusion", but not in the normal sense of the word as a figment of imagination. According to the Upanishads, the world in an absolute sense is an illusion in that what we perceive as things and forms are temporarily phenomenal, a virtual reality created by our brains. That is to say, the universe is not what it seems to be but is something constantly changing. Pure consciousness or Brahman is the only reality. *Every human experience is an illusion. Seeing things as disparate and not as One (Brahman) is a result of Maya.*

"*The world is an illusion not because it does not exist, but because it is not what it appears to be all the time. It is never the same, it is an aggregation of matter and mental construct, just like in a dream…*"[16]

---

[16]   V. Jayaram, *www.hinduwebsite.com/hinduism/essays/maya.asp*. Interestingly, our illusion of reality (perceived reality) has been likened to a holographic image. The concept regards the universe as a giant hologram containing both matter and consciousness as a single field. The holographic model of reality offers

## Q: What does *dharma* actually mean?

**A:** Dharma means "that which upholds". It is a cardinal principle in Hinduism and includes righteousness, truth, ethics, morality, justice, responsibility and duty to your family, your community, your vocation, etc. So, basically Hinduism lays down a framework to lead a clean and honest life as a good human being and to do right things. But what you actually end up doing, that is, your actions and the effects of your actions, constitute your karma.

## Q: Is the Bhagavad Gita our equivalent of the Bible or Koran?

**A:** As has already been mentioned, Hinduism is not a religion that owes its origin to any one person, institution, or dogma. We have many sages, many scriptures, and many ways to know God. The Bhagavad Gita is one of the most popular Hindu texts and is known as a *smriti* text (the remembered tradition). This is considered by some to be of less importance than *shruti* (the heard text, such as the Vedas). It has, nevertheless, an important place within the Hindu tradition. The Bhagavad Gita, or "Song of the Lord", is part of the sixth book of the Mahabharata, the world's longest poem. The Bhagavad Gita takes the form of a dialogue between Prince Arjuna and Lord Krishna, his charioteer at the Kurukshetra battlefield.

Arjuna had gone to war to regain the kingdom stolen from his family, the Pandavas, fourteen years ago by his ruthless cousins, the Kauravas, but he falters before the war starts. He doesn't want to go to war, but Lord Krishna prevails upon him to take up arms.

Arjuna had argued that if he and Krishna were to fight the war, they would be killing their kith and kin and destroying the family dharma, and thus incurring sin. Lord Krishna addresses the incorrectness of this view by explaining first the eternal nature of the soul and then telling Arjuna that he would be neglecting his personal dharma as a warrior by refusing to

---

some thought-provoking explanations of the puzzle of entanglement or non-locality in particle physics, and also of many out-of-body, paranormal, and mystical experiences. [Ref: M. Talbot, *The Holographic Universe* (New York: HarperCollins, 1991.]

fight, by wrongly renunciating action instead of renunciating attachment to action. Righteous acts, however difficult, carry no karmic debt. Knowing all beings to be eternal souls does not mean that their hurtful actions can be absolved. Lord Krishna wants Ajuna to fight the cruel Kauravas, but to do so with a strong and compassionate hand.

An insight we get from the Bhagavad Gita is that life is not meant entirely to practice dharma, but rather it is the purpose of dharma to assist the real goal of life, which is to understand the eternal soul and its relationship with the Supreme Soul, Krishna. In other words, *the Gita is not about fighting evil; it is about lifting our souls to levels we never thought possible.*[17]

---

[17]   J. M. Greene, *Gita Wisdom: Insights into Sacred Teachings,* (Mumbai: Jaico Publishing House, 2008).

# APPENDIX 2

ഓം

## JAYA JAGADEESHWARI STOTRAM
### (penned by Gowri in her diary)

*Jaya jagadeeshwari nathajana paalin*
*Bhava bhaya mochini shailasudhe*
*Shangara bhaamini sangada haarini*
*Pankaja dalanibha nayanayudhe*
*Manimaya mouthika haara samujwala*
*Manditha shobhitha gaathri ume*


*Jaya jaya maadhava sodari shankari*
*Janani bhagavathi paalayamaam*


*Thapana samaprabha vasana parishtidha*
*Tharuni manohari sindhusudhe*
*Suratharu moolanivaasini mohini*

*Guruguha poojitha padayugale*
*Naarada thumcheru sevini bhaamini*

*Kaaruna krithi jagajjanani*
*Jaya jaya madhava sodari shankari*
*Janani bhagavathi paalayamaam*

| | |
|---|---|
| *[Malayalam handwritten text]* | *Shooli kapaali thamoguna shaalini*<br>*Kaali kapadini kalpalathe*<br>*Thaandava bhairavi chandda virodhini*<br>*Kundala shobhitha gandhayudhe*<br>*Brahmasurendra marudgana sevini*<br>*Janmaja dukha vinaashakari*<br>*Jaya jaya madhava sodari shankari*<br>*Janani bhagavathi paalayamaam* |
| *[Malayalam handwritten text]* | *Paalana naashana kaarana kaarini*<br>*Baalasudhaakara khandadhari*<br>*Neela manohara gaathri sureshwari*<br>*Leela naadaga soothradhari*<br>*Palana kulamani mouli jaganmayi*<br>*Angaje girije gajagamane*<br>*Jaya jaya madhava sodari shankari*<br>*Janani bhagavathi paalayamaam* |
| *[Malayalam handwritten text]* | *Paahi kurumbe paramadayaakari*<br>*Pranatha janaathi vinaashakari*<br>*Aganitha gunagana shaalini shoolini*<br>*Animaadhyashtaka sidheekari*<br>*Kwanitha mahaamani noopura raajitha*<br>*Suravara sevitha padayugale*<br>*Jaya jaya maadhava sodari shankari*<br>*Janani bhagavathi paalayamaam* |

# APPENDIX 3

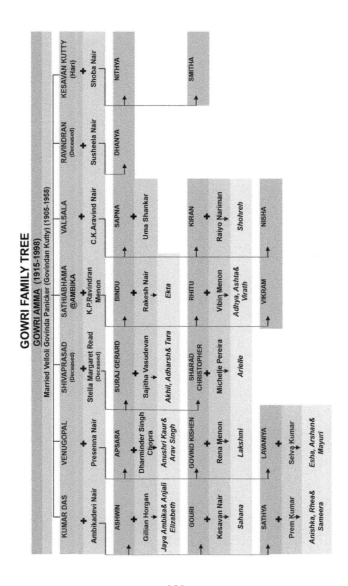

**GOWRI FAMILY TREE**

GOWRI AMMA (1915-1998)
Married Velloli Govinda Panicker (Govindan Kutty) (1905-1958)

Lightning Source UK Ltd.
Milton Keynes UK
UKHW012309290721
388013UK00001B/87